Mission Impossible

Mission Impossible

The Unreached Nosu on China's Frontier

Ralph Covell

Hope Publishing House
Pasadena, California
1990

Mission Impossible © 1990 Ralph R. Covell.

All rights reserved.

For information address Hope Publishing House
P.O.Box 60008, Pasadena, CA 91116

Printed in the United States of America.

First edition

Manuscript Editor: Faith Annette Sand

Cover Design: Michael McClary / The Workshop

Library of Congress Cataloging-in-Publication Data

Covell, Ralph R.
 Mission impossible : the unreached Nosu on China's frontier / by
 Ralph R. Covell.
  p. cm.
  Includes bibliographical references.
  ISBN 0-932727-35-2 : $8.95
  1. Nu (Chinese people) — Missions. 2. Missions — China.
 3. Baptists — Missions — China. 4. Missions, American — China.
 5. Covell, Ralph R. 6. Missionaries — China — Biography.
 7. Missionaries — United States — Biography. I. Title.
 BV3423.N82 1990
 266'.61516 — dc20   89-19918
                                             CIP

Dedication

Our China team members dedicate this book to all of our children who often ask us, "What were you and Mom (Dad) doing in China?"

Table of Contents

Preface		viii
Chapter 1	Westward Lies the Course of Empire	1
Chapter 2	Thunder Out of China	18
Chapter 3	Destination Chengdu	34
Chapter 4	Learning Chinese—A Tunnel With No Lights	50
Chapter 5	The Independent Nosu—A Hidden People	84
Chapter 6	A Foundation of Living Stones	103
Chapter 7	You Can't Hurry the East—The Uncertainty Deepens	122
	Pictures	144
Chapter 8	Keeping On Keeping On—A Long 1949	151
Chapter 9	Liberation at Last	179
Chapter 10	An Uneasy Interlude—From Liberation to Chinese Volunteers in Korea	206
Chapter 11	Left With No Choice	234
Chapter 12	A Painful Exit: Death, Dentention and Deportation	257
Chapter 13	A New China—God's People Alive in a Bitter Sea	285
	Pinyin Alphabet Pronunciation Guide	309

Preface

Newspaper headlines in late 1946 chronicled the intriguing story that American airmen, bailing out of their crippled B-29 on its flight between India and Chengdu, China had been captured by the Nosu people, enslaved in their mountain homes, and married off to their daughters.

At the very time this story was in the American press, a group of young Conservative Baptist missionaries went to China's Tibetan border to work among these Nosu people. Their story is worth telling for several reasons. First, they were seeking to bring the Christian message to the Nosu minority nationality, long-neglected and overlooked in the Daliangshan, the Great Cool Mountains of Xikang Province. While missionary efforts in China had crisscrossed this huge nation, reaching to most crooks and corners, the Nosu, often arrogantly referred to by the Chinese as "savages," remained a "hidden people." Evangelicals are concentrating today on the unevangelized peoples of the world. So it was in 1946 with our missionary team. We were not satisfied, as many young people today, merely to be a home-based support team. We had a commitment that took us into danger at the edges of the Middle Kingdom in what was and is a "mission impossible."

Second, this missionary experience in chaotic China in the 1946-51 civil-war period adds one more bit of information about the last gasp of the Western missionary saga in China. The attitudes of these missionaries and the methods they used enable us to see both the positive and negative dimensions of the work of Christian missions in China. As we engaged in the thrilling and rewarding task of pioneer evangelism and discipling we experienced all the drama of frontier missions—war lords, head-taking, opium, revolution, Communists, imprisonment, romance, spies, house-arrest, deportation, death—and the unavoidable humdrum of daily living, language study, inter-personal squabbling, committee meetings, and bureaucratic decisions. This account focuses on the humdrum, as well as on the exciting adventures, because without these "warts," cross-cultural mission is only a romantic, illusory dream.

Some mission enthusiasts may be disturbed to see warts on the "mission body." They may protest that this can only be true of "unspiritual missionaries." Sadly to say, this is false. The warts were found everywhere, whether with denominational, interdenominational, "faith," spiritual, or unspiritual missionaries! We all made our dumb mistakes, and, even when we were at our best, people all too often perceived our commitment and faith as arrogance and presumption.

Finally, the lessons these missionaries learned may be of help in the ongoing task of world mission. Missiology, the science of missions, was a very young discipline at that time, at least on the American scene. Our group did not have many books to read, only a few solid works on missionary strategy from which to profit. Today, the assessment of past missionary failure in China continues. Could anything have been done differently? Were we really imperialists? Why, without the presence and help of the missionary, deemed so necessary in those days, has the Chinese church grown so remarkably? Was the very missionary presence a hindrance? These and other related questions beg for answers.

I wish we could report a massive turning to Christ among the Independent Nosu. If only they had accepted the Christian message as did the Sediq, a sub-group of the minority Gao Shan people in Taiwan, for whom I would later translate the New Testament and portions of the Old Testament. In God's providence, this did not happen. Perhaps telling this story will stir God's people to pray, not only for these Nosu, but for others of China's unreached minority nationality peoples.

We are telling this story in the first person. This does not mean, however, that it is my personal account. We want it to be a group story—told by one of the members but trying to reflect the stories of us all. We are mainly using primary sources—prayer letters sent to personal supporters, correspondence with mission headquarters in Chicago, intimate exchanges with family and friends, and personal reminiscences after the fact. Occasionally, we have resorted to secondary sources to integrate our personal accounts with the broad context of China. What happened when the Communists liberated that part of China where we lived? How did we intersect with all that was going on in China during these hectic days? Did we seek in any way to interpret these events for our stateside supporters or for the mission board?

Our story during these five years after the end of World War II and the advent of the People's Republic of China is but one small slice of China's long history. In retrospect, 1951, the year when all but two of us left China, seems like an eternity past. We do not wish to leave you there. Nostalgic return trips to the Great Cool Mountains, now a part of Sichuan Province, in June 1986 and 1987 helped us to see the revolutionary changes that have taken place in the countryside and in the churches and it is fitting to end with this new China, even though it does not satisfy all our expectations.

A word about the title, "mission impossible." This frontier area of China was on the outer edge of the government's control—an arena of conflict among several warlords, the setting for intrigue and retaliatory raids to take heads between the Chinese and the "raw savages" in the high mountains. Even more serious, it was the "golden triangle" of China with opium pervading and dominating every facet of society. Our Chinese partners in the missionary task, from other provinces in the country, could not believe that such an area was in their beloved China. For them and for us, as it had been in generations past for missionary pioneers in China, it was a "mission impossible."

Today we have a new China. The Chinese church is growing rapidly, and it is our prayer that its members and Christians from other minority nationalities may write the final chapter of "mission accomplished" among the Independent Nosu.

All of our team members and some staff of the Conservative Baptist Foreign Mission Society have examined the draft copy of this manuscript and given valued suggestions. I am particularly indebted to Alice Mathews and Alyce Van Til for valuable editorial advice. For all remaining errors I accept full responsibility.

Apart from a few secondary sources, we will not weary you with footnotes. And, in keeping with most recent writing on China, except for well-known names we are using *pinyin*, the current system of romanization used in China, to indicate Chinese names and expressions.

1

Westward Lies the Course of Empire

Hong Kong looked like heaven to us. My wife and I had just exited from the far-western interior of China and had every reason to be ecstatic. We were alive, free and ready to put ourselves back together for a new future. But it was not a happy day. I had been deported from China, one of our missionaries had been in jail for eighteen months, one young mother of four small tots was dead and ten members of our China group were still trying to leave the country.

The goal which had brought us ten thousand miles westward from our American homes to do God's will in China's huge empire was unachieved. The unreached Nosu, a hidden people near the frontier regions of Tibet, were still unreached with the gospel. It had been a "mission impossible." What had happened to our China dream? Had we been wrong to have such a vision, to attempt such a mission? Or had we come to China at the wrong time? Maybe the fault was with us? To understand it all, we have to go back to the beginning.

An Unexpected Delay

Our mission commenced in the fall of 1946 on the west coast of the United States. We had been told that the East could not be hurried, but we did not expect that the "slow-down" in life would begin before we arrived in China. Early plans had us sailing from San Francisco to Shanghai on about October 1, 1946. A prolonged shipping strike upset this estimate; so we sat and cooled our heels for over two months on the West coast. As we impatiently fretted about our delay, someone wisely suggested that our early plans did not allow us to have any time as a group speaking to our large supporting churches. And so, beginning with Portland, Oregon and ending in San Diego, California with stops in San Francisco and Huntington Beach, we had four large farewell services. Each of us was introduced and asked to give a short testimony. We talked about our conversion to Christ, our call to missionary service and why among many possible boards we had chosen the Conservative Baptist Foreign Mission Society. The evening always concluded with a stirring missionary message by Dr. Vincent Brushwyler, the General Director of the Conservative Baptist Foreign Mission Society (CBFMS).

The atmosphere was electric in each meeting! Each of the host churches was accustomed to missionary meetings, but this was something new. Twelve missionaries representing a new board were setting out on a challenging spiritual venture to China's exotic frontiers. The congregations were excited and their fervor added further fuel to our own expectations of what God was going to do through us in China. These meetings almost created a revival atmosphere.

With the extra time we had in San Francisco, we organized a tentative field conference and met once for a "business meeting" to discuss future strategies in China. We tried, probably in vain, to anticipate many bridges before we reached them, but even this helped us to think more concretely about the future. We had many questions. How would we get through customs without paying an arm and a leg? Who would accompany the baggage on the long trip up the Yangtze River? Where would Dottie and Bennie Benson, whose ultimate destination was south China, study the language? How wise would it be for Ruth Mayo to stay alone at the orphanage in south China while waiting for the Bensons to complete their language study? As usual, money was most on our minds: would our new board have enough money? how would we receive our salary in inland China? how much could be received in personal gifts? would the money allotted for field expenses be enough?

Getting Acquainted

A by-product of the church and business meetings was that all of us got to know one other. For many of our team, this was the first time we had seen each other. Although with the same mission agency and heading for the same destination, we were from many different places, each with varied experiences and backgrounds. Could we work together as a team or would our differing personalities split us apart once we got to China?

Fortunately, what we mutually shared bound us together and outweighed our differences. Most of us were from small communities, either rural or bordering on larger cities. With the exception of Jim and Virginia Garrison, who sailed for China about six weeks after our first party, we came from homes that were at least nominally Christian. For those who had been converted in their pre-teen years, our church homes had kept before us early the idea that being a missionary was God's "best calling" in life.

As would be expected for a group of evangelical missionaries, we all had had a specific conversion experience. For John and Irene Simpson who had grown up in homes where parents were actively involved in a Christian ministry, this experience was natural, with no dramatic break with a past, sinful life. Bennie Benson, by contrast, did not begin to follow Jesus until his mid-college years and the change was more abrupt. But with all of us, reared in the revival tradition, a personal commitment to Jesus Christ, often made in an evening evangelistic service, was that basic bond which drew us together as a band of Jesus' disciples.

In contrast with many missionaries going to the field with a minimal training in this euphoric post-World War II period, all of the men, with the exception of Lee Lovegren, who had received his Ph. D. in psychology, were seminary graduates. The wives and single women, in addition to having an equivalent of a college education, were required to have some formal Bible training. In many instances some had further professional training, as in nursing or Christian education. We were hardly naive enough to think that education—ours or anyone else's—would save China. Neither, however, did we believe that cross-cultural Christian service demanded anything less than the very best of our minds or hearts. Before the advent of the many faith mission societies, a college and seminary education was normative for missionary service. In making this demand of us and its appointees to other fields, CBFMS was doing no more than returning to the roots of the missionary movement.

Missionary Call and Motivation

To go to a Christian college or seminary was to be confronted with the challenge to consider foreign missions. Lucy Carr recalled that during her college days at Maryville College in Maryville, Tennessee one of the biggest vocational impacts on her life came from a strong Student Volunteer Union. This was but one chapter of hundreds affiliated with the Student Volunteer Movement, founded by Dwight L. Moody, Robert Wilder and John Forman at Mount Hermon in 1886. Over the years thousands of students had signed the mission declaration statement and affirmed that they wished to go to foreign lands to join in "evangelizing the world in this generation."

In the late 1930s and early 1940s, the SVM lost its original vision and vigor and as a result had been replaced on many of the campuses where the members of our group had studied by the Inter-Varsity Christian Fellowship. Operating largely on secular campuses and with a low-profile emphasis on apologetics and evangelism, Inter-Varsity did not have a strong missions program. Most of the mission ferment took place on Christian and Bible college campuses through still another student organization, the Student Foreign Missions Fellowship.

SFMF was structured to be a national organization. In practice, however, most of its chapters were on campuses along the Atlantic seaboard. Frequent city-wide rallies and conferences were held in Philadelphia and New York. Speakers at these events included leading missionary figures of the time: T.J. Bach, Robert Glover and Samuel Zwemer. I helped to organize many of these and ultimately in 1945, I was elected student president of the national SFMF. This was largely an honorary position. Most of the hard work was done by a New Jersey pastor, Herb Anderson, in later years to become for a short time the General Director of CBFMS.

In early 1945, the leaders of IVCF and SFMF felt that it was to the advantage of both to merge. SFMF would become the missionary arm of IVCF, enabling it to have an impact on many secular campuses where, up to this time, it had been slow to penetrate. Many SFMF chapters on Christian campuses feared that this merger would be the death knell to their own missionary emphasis. In an effort to allay this legitimate fear, I took off two weeks from seminary classes in the spring of 1946 to visit many of these schools in the southeastern United States to explain the details of the merger and to encourage them to support it.

The first fruit of the marriage between IVCF and SFMF came even as our party of missionaries was in the middle of the Pacific ocean on its way to Shanghai. From December 27, 1946 until January 2, 1947 a large student missionary convention was held in Toronto at the University of Toronto. Hailed as the most significant student gathering since the first SVM meeting at Mt. Hermon in 1886, this convention drew 571 students from 151 colleges, universities, Bible colleges and seminaries in the United States and Canada. Truly ecumenical, its participants came from 52 different denominations. With a focus totally on missions, this convention was the first of many similar student gatherings, later to be held triennially in the post-Christmas holiday period at the University of Illinois at Champaign-Urbana.

As we studied at Moody Bible Institute, Wheaton College, Eastern Baptist Seminary, Northern Baptist Seminary and Asbury Seminary, this was the kind of mission-centered environment in which we found ourselves. Spiritual euphoria surrounded us—we were concerned not merely about local evangelism, but about a world far from us. As World War II came to its dramatic close and the Western allies emerged victoriously, so we thought nothing could defeat the Christian church as it sought to wage spiritual warfare worldwide. Rather naively, we wrote papers and preached missionary sermons on the demise of Buddhism, Islam, Hinduism and other world religions. Even as the West had proved its superiority over Japan, so would Christianity fulfill the needs and aspirations of other religions and thus deal them a death blow. We were Americans and American Christians had the obligation to enlighten the world spiritually. In a half-joking fashion, Dan Carr used to tell us that he wanted to establish the First Baptist Church in Lhasa, Tibet. These dreams and other like fantasies were a part of the era and we could hardly escape them.

In our better moments, however, our missionary vision went beyond American dreams and personal fantasies. With some of us, the driving force was to obey the last command of Jesus Christ: "All authority is given to me in heaven and on earth; go therefore and make disciples of all nations (Matt. 28:18,19).

This was my own principal motivation. I made my first serious commitment to Christ in my high school years. Instrumental in this decision was a fresh understanding of the Bible. I could not conceive how non-Christians could be reached for Christ without having the Bible in their own language. Very quickly I became concerned to be a Bible translator and to put God's Word into another language. My appointment to CBFMS was not to China, but to the work of Bible translation. China was the first field where this need surfaced.

Others were more impressed with the multiple needs of China. The turning point for George and Hannah Cole, who would join us two years after our first group sailed, was Duncan Roberts' book, *While China Bleeds*. Melodramatic and telling the tragic story of China's war with Japan, with all its accompanying death and misery, this volume portrayed a China in desperate need. For the Coles and many others like them, this need, with seemingly so few to meet it, constituted a clear missionary call. What further mystic visions were needed? Was not the love of Christ which impelled us to meet human need sufficient?

Dan Carr's inspiration to missionary service was capped by reading *The Splendor of God*, an exciting biography about Adoniram Judson, early Baptist missionary to Burma. Judson's pilgrimage from New England to Burma was a model Dan wanted to follow in heading toward China and Tibet.

Intertwined with the call to obedience and the concern to meet human need was the conviction that Chinese could enter the kingdom of God only through hearing about and accepting God's revelation in Christ. Hannah Cole testified that "the realization that millions have NO HOPE for eternity because they have never heard the name of Jesus, constantly bothers my soul." We had heard all the arguments that might have persuaded us that this was a silly belief, particularly for enlightened people in the twentieth century. But we found it difficult to explain away the many Bible passages that presented an exclusive message. Theoretically, we were able to argue that there might be hope in God's infinite mercy for those who had never heard of Jesus, but we were not about to base our obedience on this kind of ambiguity. The early church took the missionary mandate of God's decisive action in Jesus seriously and we saw no reason to do otherwise.

Personal contact with missionaries were very significant for our missionary vocations. My pastor's parents had been missionaries with the China Inland Mission (CIM) and his sister, Dorothy Foucar, continued to serve with the CIM. His Biblical sermons were sprinkled with illustrations from China.

Dottie Benson came from a Syrian family and her father spoke Arabic. A missionary couple with the CIM, Mr. and Mrs. Arthur Saunders, on furlough from China, wished to retool for possible ministry among Chinese Muslims and came weekly to the home for Arabic lessons. This constant contact with the Saunders gave Dottie an early interest in the Middle Kingdom (the term the Chinese use for China when speaking in Chinese is *zhong guo*—middle kingdom).

Several of our group already had had cross-cultural experience. This only added rigor to their missionary commitment. Irene Simpson had been born in India of missionary parents and her earliest memories were of helping her physician father meet desperate human needs. Her husband, John, whom she had met at Asbury College, had spent one term with the CIM in Yunnan Province, ministering both to the Chinese and to the Lisu people. Ruth Mayo, who accompanied us to Shanghai but then went on to East China to serve as nurse in an orphanage, had already worked in China for many years with Bethel Mission of China.

Lee and Ida Lovegren, the leaders of our group, had been affiliated for eighteen years in China with the American Baptist Foreign Mission Society. During World War II he was an interpreter in China with the United States Army air corps, working with the Office of Strategic Services. We were fortunate to have someone with the Lovegrens' experience as our senior missionaries. Lee spoke good Chinese and although he was more of an educator and administrator than he was a pastor or preacher, he had a heart for evangelism. With a mind of steel, he knew how to ride with the punches when the going got rough. Ida's references claimed her to be an "outstanding Bible woman," and one of her former colleagues with the ABFMS asserted that she "led more women to Christ than any other full-time missionary."

Dan Carr had been in the Navy chaplaincy, serving for a period of time in the Philippines. Bill Simons, who with his wife Flossie, joined us in 1948 in West China, also had a similar experience in the Philippines in the Navy chaplaincy. Of our initial party of ten, only four of us had not yet put our missionary motivation to the test. This gave us a sense of maturity and perseverance in our commitment to China.

None of us had been smitten by the "blinding light" that propelled David Treadup, John Hersey's mythical missionary,[1] but there was a quiet, determined, decisive readiness to be agents of God's will and kingdom in China. Although far less dramatic, this type of call stood the test of time much better.

Why A New Mission Agency?

With the exception of John and Irene Simpson, whose background was Methodist, we had all grown up in Northern Baptist churches, our education had been in Northern Baptist seminaries and our ordinations, except for Dan Carr who had been affiliated with the Southern Baptists, were with the Northern Baptist Convention. Why, then, were we heading to China with this neophyte, upstart organization, the Conservative Baptist Foreign Mission Society?

As is usually the case with any ecclesiastical disputes, the strife in the Northern Baptist Convention came partially from strong personalities, men and women in places of power and responsibility, who could not work out their differences amicably. A seeming lack of missionary vision on the part of the American Baptist Foreign Mission Society also entered into the picture. One of the first of many American mission agencies, ABFMS had an illustrious history. Confining its activities largely to Asia and the then Belgian Congo, it had been able to establish many large national churches which were now assuming more and more responsibility for evangelization and nurture in their own lands. Missionaries were no longer needed, ABFMS leaders said, in the same number as in the past. But many of us in Northern Baptist seminaries and churches felt there were other fields that ABFMS could have entered to begin new ministries. To reach out farther and open new areas for work did not fit with the "intensive policy" that governed ABFMS. Its leaders reasoned that it was better to concentrate intensively on a few areas and not dilute energy and resources by using an "extensive" approach. A fine policy possibly, but to prospective candidates and interested churches it did not communicate vision and excitement.

Far more basic than personality conflicts and an apparent lack of vision were theological issues. Although doctrinal rumbles had reverberated through the convention for many years, these did not crystallize sharply until 1919 with the formation within the Northern Baptist Convention of the Fundamentalist Fellowship. Meeting as a caucus a day or two before the annual convention meetings, this group of pastors and concerned lay persons tried, usually unsuccessfully, to give more doctrinal direction and coherence to the convention.

The critical watershed was the doctrine of Scripture. Was the Bible trustworthy and authoritative, particularly in the birth narratives of Jesus Christ as recorded in Matthew and Luke? Whenever conservative-minded pastors brought these issues to the convention floor, a counter motion was proposed affirming what came to be called the "evangelical policy." On the surface this statement was very sound, affirming cardinal tenets of the faith: the authority of Scripture, the trinity, the deity of Christ, salvation through faith alone, the forgiveness of sins and the sanctifying work of the Holy Spirit. However, when anyone wanted more specifics on the disputed sections of Scripture, another policy came into play. Termed the "inclusive policy," it recognized the obvious fact that Northern Baptist churches and institutions were pluralistic. Some oft-quoted excerpts include:

> ... it has not been our Baptist custom to limit too explicitly the form in which these doctrines must be held and expressed. The Board, composed like our churches, of men and women of diverse opinions, has heretofore included and

should include among its officers and missionaries representatives of various elements among our people.[2]

This conflict over the authority of Scripture created tension for many years and in 1943 a number of conservative leaders formed the Conservative Baptist Foreign Mission Society. To them and to us, it seemed difficult to work closely together in Christian ministry when there were those who could believe and proclaim Jesus Christ as virgin-born and those who would deny it. For church work at home in America, the conflict might not be too serious—Baptists are able to work rather independently and need not associate closely with those who differ from them. But how would this work in pioneer cross-cultural evangelism among people hearing the gospel for the first time? Would these people understand different trumpet sounds from a closely-knit band of missionaries representing the same missionary agency?

We had hoped that the conflict would not result in this seeming impasse. While Dan Carr was still a student at Eastern Baptist Seminary, he visited Northern Baptist headquarters in New York city to have a personal interview with Elmer Fridell, newly-appointed foreign secretary of ABFMS. Dan would have been satisfied with any statement by Fridell that he believed the Lucan and Matthean accounts of Jesus' birth to be factual. After two hours of discussion, Dan felt he was no closer to an answer to his question than at the beginning. For him and many others of us at Eastern Baptist Seminary, such calculated ambiguity was the last straw.

One hope yet remained. Was it possible that CBFMS, as its leaders professed to hope, might remain an alternative Baptist mission agency within the Northern Baptist Convention? Its function would be to have fields of its own and to be a conduit for money and young people coming from the large majority of conservative Baptist churches within the NBC. What would be the harm in this— these churches were not going to give their money to ABFMS or send their young people to serve with this agency?

Both the mood of most of the churches and many of the institutions within the NBC seemed to favor this. And certainly there was precedent with other ecclesiastical groups and within American

Baptist history. First, a look at another pluralistic denomination—the Church of England. Operating under the aegis of the Overseas Council of the Church Assembly are twelve societies. Two of these, the Church Mission Society and the Society for Promoting Christian Knowledge, represent respectively the low and high communions within the Church of England. If rather highly organized Anglicans can provide structurally for differences within their ranks, should there really be any problems for free-wheeling Baptists, historically known for their flexibility?

In fact, Baptists in America had once acted in this fashion. Nineteen hundred forty-three was the centennial of the founding of the American and Foreign Free Baptist Board of Foreign Missions. The issue then was slavery and whether it was right for missionaries to be appointed who were slave-holders, or whether a mission board should receive monies tainted by slavery. Many members within Baptist churches felt strongly that any mission agency must be strongly anti-slavery—hence a new society. Once the struggle between north and south had subsided, the two mission societies were reunited. Might not this have been a good pattern for ABFMS and CBFMS?

At many levels within the Northern Baptist Convention, a "one denomination-two societies" approach was very feasible. My ordination to ministry in 1945 was by the Harbor Baptist Association of the Southern California Baptist Convention of the NBC. Both in questioning by the association and before the messengers at the First Baptist Church in Redondo Beach, no one made an issue of the fact that I was about to be appointed by CBFMS. At this point in history such an alternative ministry was a viable option for a young person loyal to the NBC.

The same mood prevailed at seminaries, such as Eastern and Northern, at least in the 1943-47 period. While faculty members had their own personal opinions, none of them felt there was any reason why CBFMS should leave the convention. I remember chapel services when one day the speaker was Ray Buker, Sr., the first foreign secretary of CBFMS and the next day the service was led by a representative of ABFMS. Students were free to choose. Representatives of both groups were provided with rooms where they could interview prospective candidates among the students.

Despite historical precedent, models available within other denominations and a general mood of cooperation at convention institutions, local churches and church associations, the pattern of "one denomination-two systems" was not to be. Actions by a small appointed committee of nine leaders in May 1945 and by the annual convention at Grand Rapids a year later effectively excluded CBFMS from the Northern Baptist Convention. Whether we young people liked it or not, we had to carry out our missionary service in a new ecclesiastical context.

Without this new Baptist mission agency, most of us would have sought to go to China with the China Inland Mission. Once CBFMS was formed, it was as if a flood gate were opened and the candidates rushed in. Nearly 75% of my own graduating class from Eastern Baptist Seminary went to the mission field, most with CBFMS.

We were not disappointed in CBFMS. Quickly the board processed us through a rigorous, formal appointment process, matched each missionary with nine or ten churches, anxious to find someone to channel their money to and worked through our China leader, Lee Lovegren, to locate a field of service in China.

How Do You Find a New Mission Field?

We were all committed to go to China, but where? The country is vast and although there were few Christians, most of the nation had been divided up by hundreds of mission agencies, a time-honored process called "comity." One missionary friend had told Lovegren of "the one unreached area remaining in China," the Jianchang Valley in Xikang Province, along the border of Tibet. This province, popularly called Eastern Tibet, had been carved out of Sichuan in 1939.

Lovegren already knew about this area. The ABFMS, his first mission board, had worked there from 1905-17 and off and on in subsequent years until the early 1930s. ABFMS missionaries hoped that this Xikang field would be one more stepping stone on a trail of mission stations taking the gospel from Chengdu, through Yunnan and on to the borders of Burma. Unfortunately, when we reached Xichang in 1947, only a few Chinese families were left from the

Baptist True Doctrine Hall which the early Baptists had established there.

The Border Service Department of the Church of Christ in China had a few workers in Xichang, the principal city. Their work, although focused on the "Lolo tribes people," was largely social in nature with minimal evangelistic outreach. The CIM planned to commence work in Xikang, but its missionaries would be located four days west of Xichang in the heart of the Great Cool Mountains.

We were not the only group eyeing this field in 1946. The Nazarenes and the National Holiness mission agencies were also considering it. Because Lovegren was in China in 1945 and 1946 fulfilling his military duties, he was able to make CBFMS intentions clear both to Chinese and Western friends. No rigid, formal comity agreements were in force for that isolated part of China. In effect, this meant "squatters' rights." If we could place our large group of missionaries there quickly and act in a cooperative spirit with both the CIM and the Border Service Department, there should be no conflicts. With this informal assurance, almost the only thing possible, CBFMS proceeded with its plans for work in China.

Not Alone in Going to China

Our group of CBFMS missionaries did not go to China alone. Sailing with us on December 15, 1946 were 670 missionaries, representing nearly every Christian denomination. Three hundred other passengers were returning to business and diplomatic posts not only in China, but in other parts of Asia. An earlier sailing of the same ship, the *Marine Lynx*, in October 1946 had taken four hundred missionaries to China.

Such a large number of American missionaries going to China was not that unusual. From the early 1800s, China had been the favorite mission field for American churches. Christianity had come to China in successive waves in the seventh, thirteenth and sixteenth centuries, but the Protestant effort did not commence until about 1800. Propelled by the national sentiment of "westward lies the course of empire" and a baptized version of "manifest destiny," thousands of American young people gave themselves for missionary work in China. The height of this advance came early in 1927, when at least eight thousand American missionaries were serving in China. Results were never proportionate to the number of missionaries. If measured by numbers of church buildings, schools, hospitals, workers, institutions of mercy and money expended, the mission in China was successful. The missionary presence seemed to reach everywhere. But in number of converts—the bottom line—nothing much happened. The Christian message was always viewed as foreign by the non-Christian Chinese. As a result, when we went to China in 1946, the Protestant community numbered about 750,000 and the Roman Catholics approximated two million. What were these among a population of 400,000,000?

Rather than be a deterrent for missionary activity, the very paltry nature of the results impelled to greater activity. From the time of internal disturbances in China in 1927 until 1946, missionaries had alternately come and gone—advanced and retreated. Now it was a time for advance and from October 1946 until June 1947 several large sailings from San Francisco once again swelled the missionary population in China.

The Marine Lynx

Our long-awaited sailing time was Sunday, December 15. The ship was the *Marine Lynx*, a fairly new Liberty Ship of twelve thousand tons used to transport troops during World War II. Its crew said it had been "converted" for our use, but the huge dormitories with hammocks stacked four deep in bunk style did not convince us. Getting the nearly one thousand people aboard was a gala occasion. We began the process about ten in the morning and were on our way shortly after four in the afternoon. As the sailing time drew near, a navy chaplain on the pier organized a choir to sing "O Zion Haste," a song that symbolized our vision and aspirations on this new spiritual adventure.

A sad note amid the joy of these varied festivities was that two of our party, Ed and Phyllis Larson, were not given final medical clearance at the last moment and could not board the ship with us.

They had to dispose of their luggage, most of it already aboard ship, as best they could.

Sailing under the Golden Gate Bridge and out into the wide ocean beyond, I reflected on how much speedier our two-week voyage was than that of early pioneers to China, whose trips could easily take three or four months. Our passage was not only much faster, but more convenient. It was easy for me as a single person to say this because my time was my own and I could do a lot of study—Latourette's *The Chinese Their History and Culture*, review of my Greek and some beginning study on Chinese radicals, that part of a Chinese character that gives a clue to its meaning.

For married couples, particularly those with small children, the trip was a nightmare. Irene Simpson and Lucille Carr were placed in a separate dormitory with their two small children and had to take care of them for most of the day on their own. No husbands were allowed into this area and the wives could not come into the men's bunking area. This forced separation hardly made for the best communication. Nobody really complained—all were just happy to be on their way.

We were not very good sailors. The seas were rough and nearly everyone got seasick. With such close sleeping quarters four deep, we only hoped that those with the most upset stomachs were on the bottom bunks! A bucket was placed at the foot of each set of bunks for the more unfortunate. Happily, it did not take most of us long to get our sea legs—it would have been tragic not to be able to use this spare time to good advantage. And then who wanted to miss the super meals always associated with ocean travel? But if the meals were good, the way they got to us was not. Food was served cafeteria style and put directly on metal trays (not on plates!) to be eaten with oversized spoons, knives and forks. It was military style the whole way.

The spirit of rapport and camaraderie among the seven hundred missionaries was electric! We talked endlessly with each other about our specific destinations in China, about the vision we had, about mission theory, strategy and methods and about the worsening political situation in China. Each evening vesper services were held and on Sunday, to accommodate the large number who wished to attend, three worship services were held. Our own party met each day for Bible study, prayer and discussion as to how we would proceed inland once we reached Shanghai.

Most of us knew little about the Chinese language, but we did study when we felt like it. What a privilege it was for us all that Henry Fenn, Director of the Yale Chinese Language Institute, was one of the passengers. One afternoon he gave a lecture on new techniques for learning and teaching Chinese. Whenever possible, Lee Lovegren held a daily language lesson to help us learn basic rudiments of Chinese, as well as a few common phrases that would stand us in good stead in our early days in China.

Being a single person among couples had both its advantages and disadvantages. Even though we crossed the international date line at just the right time to miss my twenty-fourth birthday on December 23, the group presented me with a luscious fruit cake and candles. At other times they were not so kind. Among the several hundred missionaries aboard were many eligible, attractive, young, single women. My friends egged me on to invite one of these to join us in a Christmas Eve party. Rather than allow the two of us to have a pleasant, friendly evening, they used every contrivance to put us in embarrassing situations. Little did they appreciate some of the tragedies, documented in missionary records, arising from "shipboard romances." Particularly did I feel vulnerable because of a broken relationship only a few months earlier with a young woman from Philadelphia.

Christmas was not too different from what it would have been at home. The crew put up a large Christmas tree in the emergency dining room and decorated it with all the proper trimmings. Christmas parties were held all day long on the 25th. The U.S.A. Presbyterian Board in San Francisco found out ahead of time from the shipping line how many children (195 plus 22 infants) would be on board and arranged to buy Christmas presents for all of them.

A daily news bulletin kept us informed on what was happening each day aboard ship. We were more agitated about news from China. The big item was from the capital at Nanking, where the National Assembly was debating the draft of the new Constitution. The Communists were laughing at what they deemed to be another nationalist trick. American politicians were encouraged. President Chiang Kai-shek had killed proposed amendments that would have perpetuated the one-party rule by the Nationalist Party (Kuomintang). This followed the advice of George Marshall, the presidential envoy to China and Leighton Stuart, the American Ambassador, who had long urged on Chiang the need for non-Nationalist parties, such as the New Democrats and the Young China party, to play a more active role in Chinese politics.

We noted these events and they concerned us. Yet somehow they dimmed in importance as day by day we drew nearer to the land of our destination. December 30 was the most exciting day of the trip. Japan was in sight! At first it was just a small speck on the distant horizon, but, by early evening, we were in the Van Diemen straits off the southern tip of Kyushu. We soon left Japan behind and about midnight we reached the mouth of the Yangtze River ("long river" in Chinese). On December 31 we sailed up the Huangpu River for the remaining nine miles of our trip.

What a relief finally to arrive! The long days of reading, learning, conversing and relaxing had been a good preparation for the task ahead. But many of the children were sick with colds, mumps and other ailments and families were anxious to move on to their final destinations. The westward course of our travel had brought us to an ancient empire that was to be our home for the next few turbulent years.

Endnotes

1. Hersey, John *The Call*. New York: Alfred A. Knopf, 1985, pp. 61-70
2. Shelley, Bruce *Conservative Baptists: A Story of Twentieth Century Dissent*. Denver: CBTS, 1962, p. 24.

2

Thunder out of China

Where to Now?

Immigration procedures in any country are unbelievably difficult. China was no exception. With so many passengers to be processed, custom agents in Shanghai boarded the *Marine Lynx* shortly after the ship began its journey from the mouth of the Yangtze up the Huangpu (Whangpoo) River toward the dock. For this inspection we had spread our carry-on baggage all over the deck. No place was left to stand or walk.

Everyone was debtor to Chinese customs. I had brought too much Ivory soap—it would last for one year. Bennie Benson complained that he had been assessed for having two typewriters, when really he had only one. To verify this, the custom agent checked all of his baggage again. He removed the non-existent extra typewriter from his working sheet, but he turned up several other dutiable items that raised his custom fees even more. Bennie remarked grimly, "the trouble with us is that we think too much." Often in the coming years as we struggled through language learning and many other adjustment problems, we repeated Bennie's observations to one another as an ongoing motto.

We had become tired of life on the *Marine Lynx*, but at least we had a place to lay our heads. In crowded Shanghai that was a problem. Over a year previous, Lovegren had made arrangements for us to stay in the large compound that was headquarters for the China Inland Mission. But with fifty-eight of its own missionaries arriving on the same sailing, the CIM home was already desperately overcrowded. And so it was with other facilities. Many mission agencies had their headquarters in Shanghai, but who was able to absorb seven hundred missionaries all at once? The October sailing of the *Marine Lynx* had brought four hundred missionaries two months earlier, and many of these missionaries were still stuck in the city by a transportation bottleneck.

Fortunately, the National Christian Council had been working on beds for all those groups that had no mission headquarters in Shanghai. It sent a tentative placement list aboard the *Marine Lynx*, and each of our group was named there, except Simpsons, Bensons, and me. Fred Jarvis, a missionary friend with the Scandinavian Alliance Mission (now The Evangelical Alliance Mission), had already learned of these omissions and found three more places for us.

We waited in groups as chartered busses and trucks took us and other missionaries to various places. I was assigned to the Blackstone Apartment on Rue Lafayette in what formerly had been the French Concession of Shanghai. Run by the Methodists as a kind of boarding house, it was arranged in dormitory style with eleven cots in each of several large rooms. The Carrs were boarded in a spare room in the home of Ralph Mortenson of the China Bible Society; Lee and Ida Lovegren were put in a downtown room of the Army-Navy YMCA; the Bensons stayed in a hostel for the children of German missionaries, and the Simpsons were placed at the China Bible Seminary in Jiangwan on the outskirts of the city. Ruth Mayo had lived in Shanghai previously and stayed with friends.

Our initial euphoria at having a place to lay our heads was dampened when we learned the differing prices we were paying. My "bed" cost more than the rooms either the Simpsons or Bensons had. As Dan, our first mission treasurer, paid the amounts from our never-too-fat field budget, he complained of gouging, "If that's practical Christianity, I'm two steps higher than a saint." We were all settled, but hardly comfortable. Shanghai's weather, typical for this time of year, was rainy, windy, and cold. Often the rain was mixed with snow and sleet. The homes where we were staying had little heat. Hot water for bathing and shaving was at a premium. The only time I really felt warm was in bed at night, and on cold nights even this was uncertain. The Carrs bought a locally-made kerosene stove that smelled up their room but took away some of the chill. Little charcoal burners, something like California "smudge pots," kept public buildings tolerably warm.

Out on the streets of Shanghai, riding in rickshas, we just about froze. We had not prepared well for this kind of cold weather, and heavier winter wear was still in our freight. The Carrs and Simpsons ordered padded gowns for Danny and Linn Ann, and others of us bought long cotton underwear. I took to wearing two pair of pants; when outside I put the nicer pair underneath, and when I came inside I reversed them with the better pair on the outside. A locally-bought raincoat helped a bit, but in the muggy cold it sweat on the inside. The dreary days multiplied one after another throughout most of January. I made up my mind early that this port city was not for me. Inland China, I reflected, had to be better than this.

Too Many Holidays

Our woes would have been settled if only we could have gotten at our freight. The procedures were complicated, as they can be in the Orient. Our basic problem, however, was too few working days down at the customs *godown* (warehouse). Our first day in Shanghai was the foreign New Year which extended two or three days beyond January 1. This was followed shortly by Russian New Year, which, because of the many Russians in Shanghai, meant that another day or two was lost in these celebrations. If this were not enough, these two holidays were followed shortly by the real "biggie"—Chinese New Year. The formal holiday period was only two or three days, but the effect upon Chinese Customs lasted at least a week.

Whenever it was not a holiday, we all went to the *godown* and sorted the luggage into piles to prepare for the customs examination. I was the only one with procedural problems. Somehow my shipping agent in San Francisco had not listed my belongings as luggage, but as freight. This was super *ma fan* (trouble). I finally gave up doing it by myself and turned it over to a custom broker. Even he did not find it easy, and it looked as if I might not receive my belongings until after we had gone inland. Eventually, I did receive my "freight" and was able to get at my rubbers and winter clothes. Not, however, before I had gotten a nasty cold and bronchitis which plagued me for the rest of the time in Shanghai.

A Transportation Bottleneck

Our arrival on the *Marine Lynx* had swelled the missionary population in Shanghai severalfold. This crowded situation was compounded by the arrival of the *Marine Falcon*, a sister ship of the *Lynx*, on January 18. Everyone wanted to leave to go to their permanent posts in China, a situation lending itself to bribery and corruption. Profiteers, or even members of the shipping companies, bought blocks of tickets on busses and trains and would not sell them except for a great profit. We got no help when we went directly to the bus or train companies. The refrain was always the same—we are already sold out!

The bottleneck became even more critical in late January with the tragic air crash near Hankow which took the lives of thirty passengers, including eleven missionaries who had been with us on the *Marine Lynx*. Best known to all of us were Dr. and Mrs. Schuyler Garth, a Methodist Bishop and his wife, who were making a brief survey visit to China. He had been spokesman for the missionary community during our ocean voyage and had helped all of us in innumerable ways. Another family, R.D. Vick, his wife and small baby, had been living at the Blackstone apartment with others of us who were part of the *Marine Lynx* missionary group. Their small baby was the only survivor of the wreck. Also killed were Mrs. Miller and her three small children. Later, after our arrival in Chengdu, we were to meet her husband, a missionary with the China Inland Mission.

This air crash was only the last in a series of six accidents during a five week period, claiming a total of 140 killed, 19 missing and 21 injured. The upshot was that all passenger planes were grounded, tightening the bottleneck. Problems in getting our freight, the cold wintry weather, the transportation snafu, and the usual problems of adjusting to a new and strange culture cast a dismal pall over us. This first month of our "missionary" experience was not encouraging.

Pocket Your Shock

I do not know what we expected Shanghai to be like, but none of us was prepared for what we found! Nothing stood out like the contrasts—modern cars competing with rickshas, sampans dodging ocean-going steamers on the Huangpu River, large, multi-storied Western-style buildings along the famed Bund casting their shadows on traditional, poorly-built Chinese structures.

We were appalled by beggars everywhere, usually hideous in appearance with diseases and deformities. Some, we learned, were professionals, often going to the extremes of deforming themselves or their children to elicit more pity. We never got used to them and always struggled with what we should do—salve our conscience by contributing something or learning to ignore them.

Intermingled with the glitter and glamour of street life, the opulence of the Wing On and Sincere department stores, and the affluence of the banking establishments was the crunching poverty, symbolized best by Chinese coolies sweating profusely as they labored painfully with all the heaviest work. The ricksha pullers were twentieth-century slaves. Even small boys pulled heavy ricksha loads. Dressed usually in rags, these poor coolies made only enough each month barely to keep alive.

When we rode in rickshas, we would gladly have paid the opening price that was quoted. So what if we were overcharged several times? That was a pittance for even our meager missionary budgets. Very quickly though we got caught up in the local culture—bargain the price down to the going rate and perpetuate the cycle of poverty. How did one sort out what was right, just or even loving? We resisted the label of "sucker," and yet we wanted to remember we were missionaries—we had come to help people, not to take advantage of them, even if that were customary.

The streets were filled with a cacophony of sound. What a blare of car and truck horns, shouts of ricksha pullers, the calls of street hawkers cluttered along the sidewalks selling their wares, and the general hubbub of street traffic!

In all of this hustle and bustle we were easy suckers for ever-present pickpockets. We tried to be careful. I never went out with any significant sum of money, without putting on my money belt, tied tightly about my waist, right next to my skin. This was safe, but clumsy. How did I get at my money when I wanted to make a big purchase? Usually by finding a men's room where I partially undressed!

Money belts were inconvenient, but they prevented serious loss. Dan Carr lost his wallet with over one hundred dollars as he tried to board the always-crowded trolley cars that travelled up and down Nanking Road and other busy downtown streets. Working in twos or threes, pickpockets knew exactly what to do when naive foreigners were trying too hard to force their way aboard. At times they were very bold. Riding on a trolley one day, I felt a slight pressure on my chest and instinctively dropped my hand to my shirt pocket. Voila, I had another person's hand with my fountain pen in it! He hastily apologized for the inconvenience and moved quickly to another part of the trolley.

Unfortunately for those who should have known better, we often acted like bulls in the proverbial China closet! Each day one or another of our group suffered an embarrassing incident. Once it was a misunderstanding with a ricksha puller—failure to bargain a price clearly at the beginning. A traffic policeman eventually solved this one in favor of the coolie. Another time it was wrong communication with a small exchange shop, one of seemingly myriads along almost any street. On another occasion Dan Carr overreacted when someone accidentally bumped into his wife. As he rushed toward the scene, the offender fell to the ground as if hurt, pleading for sympathy from the quickly gathering crowd. Familiar with these types of tricks by sidewalk beggars, a nearby policeman intervened, this time on Dan's behalf.

The ever-fluctuating exchange rate confused us. We were used to a stable currency. Here, every day we had to make decisions. Did we exchange our money at the "official" bank rate of $3370 yuan for one American dollar? Or did we tacitly break the law and opt for the much more attractive "open" or "black" market rate of $6700 yuan per dollar? It made a difference in how much you could buy!

Professing to oppose the black market, but rarely enforcing the law, the government, with its "inside" information, was the big profiteer in these market shenanigans. One day private exchange shops operated everywhere; the next day they were all banished to be replaced by government-run shops; and within a few days the private shops were in business again. Even old-timers in Shanghai were puzzled, to say nothing of us newcomers.

Money exchange was often done by hawkers who followed us around and offered the "best possible price." Once Dan Carr confused one of these men with ever-present panderers and followed him down a back alley and up three flights of rickety stairs into a house of ill fame! He beat a hasty retreat.

The visible Shanghai was enough of a shock. Unseen to most of us visitors were the opium dens, pirates, smugglers, gamblers, and the cabarets filled with Russian, Chinese, and Japanese women with their seductive wiles. Shanghai was a metropolis filled with intrigue of every type, a city whose name was both a noun and a verb. We were there only as a transit point to somewhere else, but we never adjusted to its haunting mystery and adventure.

The Shanghai That Was

From the beginning of its modern history, Shanghai had been this kind of city. Young in age compared with many Chinese cities, Shanghai was founded in the Tang dynasty (650 AD), but never attained any commercial importance until the development of silk production in the seventeenth and eighteenth centuries. At this time it may have had as many as fifty thousand people.

The city's real growth did not occur until it became one of the five open ports, created in 1842 by the unequal treaties with the western nations. These nations turned it into China's major port and trading center, a gateway to China's vast internal markets.

Located on what has been called a "muddy flat" area along the Huangpu River, Shanghai had its old Chinese city. This was soon augmented by the foreign presence on the Bund stretching along the river. Over the years, Shanghai was partitioned into areas of foreign influence: the French Concession and the International Settlement. Although allowed to live and conduct business in these foreign-controlled areas, the Chinese had no rights nor privileges and were second-class citizens in every sense. Signs could be found at the entrance point to these concessions prohibiting "dogs and Chinese."

For foreigners with their exclusive clubs and private domains, life in Shanghai was one party after another, spiced with teas, dances, cocktails, dinners, races, and gambling. The "Shanghai mind" excluded Chinese, like unwanted animals, from all of these social activities.

Over the years, between its modern founding in 1842 until our arrival in 1946, many epochal events in China's history transpired in this port city. During the vicious Taiping civil war in the 1850s and 1860s, millions of poor Chinese peasants fled from their ravaged homes in the Yangtze Valley and found refuge in Shanghai.

Although many of these returned to their homes when the Taiping rebels were defeated, the Chinese population in the city began to increase rapidly. By now the foreign presence, including many nationalities, not a few of whom were missionaries, had increased to five thousand, up dramatically from the very few who dared to make their homes there in 1842.

On May 4, 1919, Shanghai students, along with their brothers and sisters all over China, marched to protest the decision made at the Paris Peace Conference not to return Shantung to China. Workers in Shanghai supported the students' demands by numerous strikes directed against Japanese businesses. Here the Chinese Communist Party had been formed in 1921. A continued anti-foreign animus came to a head in 1925 with strikes by thirty thousand Chinese workers employed in Japanese mills in Shanghai. In the ensuing confusion, white policemen fired on Chinese crowds, killing several, in what was subsequently called the "Shanghai massacre." This served only to exacerbate what had been a growing division between the white and Chinese population.

In the mid-1920s China was still struggling to find her political identity. The Manchu dynasty was overthrown in 1911, but in subsequent years the country was ravaged by continuous conflict between warlords. Hope for stability and national unity was instilled again by the union of Communist and Kuomintang leaders. Unfortunately, this was never achieved. Shanghai was the turning point. While engaged in 1927 on an expedition to the north to eliminate warlords, Chiang Kai-shek turned his forces suddenly on Shanghai and, with the help of traders, businessmen, and the secret societies, liquidated all Communists and leftists. This commenced the intense hatred between the Kuomintang and the Communists which dominated Chinese politics until 1949.

Shanghai's structure came tumbling down in 1937 when Chinese soldiers evacuated the city in the face of an attack by ninety thousand Japanese troops. This conflict with Japan, started earlier that year at the Marco Polo bridge near Beijing, was the beginning of the "war of resistance" that tore China apart over the next eight years. The aftermath was both good and bad. The good was that in the midst of this war, the western powers finally relinquished the "unequal treaties" with their humiliating provisions and restored a measure of sovereignty to China. The bad was the war itself, with its tremendous loss of life, and the opportunity it provided for Communist forces to put themselves in a position ultimately to take control of China.

A Century Past of Missionary Work

Missionaries came to Shanghai at the very time when the unequal treaties opened that city to the Western traders. At least one Chinese leader never forgot this connection. Prince Kung, the younger brother of the Xian Feng emperor, once remarked to Sir Rutherford Alcock, then British consul in Shanghai, "Take away your opium and your missionaries and you will be welcome."[1]

Even as Shanghai was the center for traders doing business with all China, so this large coastal city became the staging base for missionaries penetrating every province. Many of the major mission boards set up headquarters here. Shanghai was the usual port of entry and departure for missionaries. Here were the banking facilities that enabled mission boards to receive monies from abroad and despatch them to their scattered missionaries. Over the years as crises came and went, Shanghai became the city of refuge where missionaries fled for safety.

Although Shanghai was hardly representative of all China, one could take the pulse of the missionary movement from this strategic center. Here, for example, were held the large national missionary conferences of 1870, 1890, 1907, and 1913. And when the National Christian Conference, the successor of these past missionary-oriented conferences, was held in 1922, Shanghai was the logical place for the gathering. The National Christian Council had its headquarters here, and the first General Assembly of the Church of Christ in China met here in 1927.

Shanghai was the headquarters of the Christian Literature Society whose publications were distributed all over China. Here was located St. John's University, which Kenneth Scott Latourette called "the most efficient of the mission colleges of the time."[2] From this bustling hub of the empire, the *Chinese Recorder*, the best-known of many missionary publications, was edited and distributed.

Roman Catholics also used Shanghai as the center of their work in China. Within Shanghai, Xu Jiawei (Zikawei), tracing its heritage to Xu Guangqi, the famous Jesuit convert of the early seventeenth century, was undoubtedly the hub. Schools, a hospital, works of mercy, a library, a publishing house, and much more were headquartered in this sizeable tract of land on the outskirts of the city.

The best known of the Catholic endeavors at Xu Jiawei was the famous Jesuit meteorological observatory. Three times each day it issued weather reports and typhoon warnings to ships sailing in nearby seas. The International Settlement and the French Concession, as well as steamship and insurance companies, paid the Jesuits generously for their services.

Since missionaries had been in China for one hundred years before our arrival in 1946, most Shanghai residents understood who a missionary was. That did not mean missionaries were accepted; they were only tolerated. We inherited both the good and the bad will. Most people appreciated the "good deeds," always lauded by the Chinese as the quintessence of their own Confucian ethic. Schools, hospitals, and homes of mercy for the handicapped of society were usually welcome, although some people wondered why they were not completely free as befitting works of charity.

On the negative side, the Chinese of Shanghai had several complaints: missionaries "have disturbed the roots of an ancient faith" without really giving them a solid dose of the Christian faith; they treated the Chinese as "uncivilized barbarians," without taking time to learn their culture; missionaries exploited the ignorant who could not really answer their assertions; they lived above the people rather than becoming one with them.[3]

The Past in The Present

Some of the problems of Shanghai's past were only an interesting interlude of history. The unequal treaties had been abrogated by the United States in 1943. The French Concession and International Settlement were no more, but street names and styles of houses, buildings and churches reflected this unpleasant past. Opium dens were very much in evidence, but did not have their past legal status.

Unrest over the foreign presence still sparked student riots and demonstrations. Even as the *Marine Lynx* sailed up the Huangpu River on December 31, students at Qinghua and Yanjing Universities in Beijing marched to protest the presence of United States Marines in that city. Particularly were they incensed over one Marine who had allegedly raped a Chinese girl on Christmas Eve. This disturbance quickly spread to Shanghai by January 2, 1947. A U.S. Army officer was beaten with canes by a student crowd as he strolled with his Chinese girlfriend along Ave. Joffre in the old French Concession. Another student demonstration snarled traffic near Nanking Road and the Bund, the waterfront road.

We were reminded of the significant role of students in China's revolutionary past as we saw them marching with their placards. One read "China is not an American colony." Other students shouted that even as they had resisted Great Britain in 1925 and Japan in 1931, so now must they resist American aggression. We could not follow all their arguments, but we got the message: students wanted to help China be its own country, to stand on its own feet, to make its own decisions, to determine its own destiny.

Despite these student demonstrations, 1946 was an advance over the past. At least Chinese authorities could try the Marine accused of rape within their own legal system. This had been the most galling feature of the unequal treaties—the provision called extraterritoriality, which simply meant that a citizen of another country could not be arrested by Chinese authorities and could not be brought to trial by a Chinese court.

Thunder Out of China

If many of China's past problems had been solved, the weight of the present and of the near future seemed almost unbearable. At almost exactly the same time as we reached Shanghai, the noted book *Thunder Out of China* hit the public market. Written by two reporters with *Time* magazine, Theodore White and Annalee Jacoby, this hard-hitting book gave a coherent and consistent account, although some felt prejudiced, of China's recent, painful history.

In the authors' opinions, the recently concluded war of resistance against Japan only served to reveal more starkly the on-going problems within Chinese society—problems that would be the focal point in the escalating civil war between the Kuomintang and the Communists. The book clearly talked about these open sores: war lords seeking their separate kingdoms to the detriment of national unity; corrupt officials such as Kung Xiangxi who preferred to justify inflation rather than deal with it; landlords and loan sharks oppressing the peasants.

In this corrupt context, White and Jacoby pointed out, the Chinese army was no asset. They described it as a "pulp, a tired, dispirited, unorganized mass, despised by the enemy, alien to its own people, neglected by its government, ridiculed by its allies."[4]

The situation was not helped, in the authors' view, by China's allies either on the diplomatic or military front. By the ill-famed Yalta Treaty, Russia had gained partial control of Port Arthur and Dairen. The treaty enabled Russia to establish itself in Manchuria where she was able to plunder Japanese industry.

America had a military presence in China, but this may have been more of a hindrance than a help. White and Jacoby commented:

> The uneducated American attitude was a major tragedy in a land of many tragedies. No one attempted to explain the war to the American soldier, to teach him how and why the Chinese people were as they were. High diplomacy made it impossible to tell the American soldier that the Chinese people loathed corruption even more intensely, because it affected them more bitterly. No one, finally, tried to

distinguish between the Chinese people, who were profoundly good, and the Chinese government, which was profoundly bad.[5]

I often wondered if we American missionaries were any better. We may have read a bit more and had a few more orientation sessions. Nevertheless, we found it only too easy to make quick judgments and to assume, somewhat naively, that our religious answers would solve all of China's ills.

Was White and Jacoby's book all unrelieved pessimism, with no hope that the approaching storm would go away? The only hope they offered was that America should push for a multi-party government that would really represent all of the Chinese people. No longer could America give unconditional support to Chiang. They concluded that "we ourselves must become the sponsors of revolution. Our policy must offer the masses of Asia the same things that the Russian revolution promises them—bread and equality in their daily life."[6]

When we arrived in Shanghai, there were things both to encourage and discourage. An encouraging bit of news was that for the first time since the Kuomintang had come to power, there was a transition, multi-party government. A new constitution was to go into effect by December, 1947. Despite the fact that the Communists themselves would not be represented, the National Assembly's 1,744 delegates would be 48% independents, 42% Kuomintang and 10% representatives of minor parties. This was progress!

This encouraging news was offset by another clap of thunder. General Marshall in mid-January 1947 threw up his hands in despair at mediating the Kuomintang-Communist struggle and returned to Washington. In his view China's dilemma had no solution.

A Time for Missionary Work?

Often we asked ourselves—was this a time to begin a new mission work in a China racked by a struggle-to-the-death? The events were sobering, but we reminded ourselves that missions had always been in this dilemma. When Luther Rice, Adoniram Judson, and others sailed for British-occupied India precisely at the outbreak of the war of 1812 with Great Britain, it hardly seemed to be a propitious time. But they did it, and somehow God overruled their naivete and mistakes.

During our voyage on the *Marine Lynx* we had been well aware of China's problems, but we were convinced that God would somehow overrule. Surely, we thought, God would not abandon unevangelized China to a godless ideology. This conviction was only slightly different from its more secular version embraced by most of the American people: Chiang and his nationalist forces might not win over all of China, but neither would the Communists gain a victory.

And so as the thunder reverberated in China, we continued in our preparations to go inland. I finally got my freight freed from customs, but then immediately faced the need for re-export papers to get it out of Shanghai. This paperwork with its constant pressure was frustrating, but necessary.

Just to get about Shanghai was maddening. The Chinese had invented new ways to strike. One was a "go slow" strike, when all busses and trolleys went as slowly as possible; over the course of one day companies lost a lot of money. Then there was the "ride free" strike; everything operated at normal speed, but passengers were not charged for their rides.

When we could get about with any ease, we visited the China Inland Mission headquarters. Because of my seminary experience in InterVarsity Christian Fellowship, I wanted to meet David Adeney, who was responsible for much Chinese student work. Old friends of mine, Anne and Eber Hazelton, were in Shanghai at the time, and I spent time visiting with them and their teenage daughter, Wanda, in their apartment on the CIM compound.

As a group, we joined occasionally in evening worship times with our CIM friends. These Anglican-type worship services attracted missionaries from many countries. For me it was the first time to sing from the CIM hymnals that had no music notations. Most of the tunes were new, but this forced me to pay more attention than usual to the words. Whether in the CIM home or in a local church—I think particularly of the Shanghai Community Church—it was cold!

Never before had I sat through a church service without taking off either my hat or overcoat.

The cold weather took its toll. Most of us had the sniffles, and my sinus infection periodically became more inflamed. Linn Ann suffered through a bout with measles, as did many of the other missionary children staying in Shanghai. Dan Carr had a severe attack of appendicitis, leading to an appendectomy. This kept him out of action for a couple of weeks, but time seemed to mean less and less as we found no way to leave Shanghai and go on our way to Chengdu. We had heard through CIM missionaries in Chengdu that they had provisionally rented a home for us, but how were we to get there?

Our spare time gave me the chance to do some research on the Nosu (this term as well as Yi or Lolo will be used to designate these people) at the Royal Asiatic Society library. How grateful I was for the courteous attitude of the librarians. Since the freezing weather made their unheated reading room impossible for serious study, they graciously allowed me to take one book at a time back to the Blackstone Apartment. I did not do any writing on the Nosu until I got to Chengdu, but this material, along with that available at West China Union University, helped fill in many gaps in my knowledge about this fascinating people.

Before we left Shanghai, Lovegren asked the Lutheran World Federation if it would serve as our financial agent in China. For a minimal charge the Lutherans did many necessary things for us: exchanged U.S. money into Chinese currency, maintained a Chinese bank account for us, transmitted money inland as we needed it, met new missionaries, found local housing, and arranged for air or river passage to west China.

At one time we had hoped to proceed as a group to Chengdu. With the transportation bottleneck threatening to get even worse, it seemed best to get a few of us on our way. Lovegren, with the help of some friends, got space on a small, unpretentious river steamer heading for Chungking. We decided that Bennie and Dottie Benson and I would be the ones to go first. It was not an ideal way to travel, but anything was better than Shanghai. And so, on February 1, we embarked on the next stage of our China adventure on the *Min Tsu*, a small, dirty, overcrowded river steamer.

Endnotes

1. Hauser, Ernest *Shanghai: City for Sale*. New York: Harcourt, Brace and Company, 1940, p. 72.
2. Latourette, K.S. *A History of Christian Missions in China*. London: Society for Promoting Christian Knowledge, 1929, p. 628.
3. Miller, G.E. (pseudonym for a diplomat) *Shanghai: The Paradise of Adventurers*. New York: Orsay Publishing House Inc., 1937, pp. 164-83.
4. White, Theodore H. and Annalee Jacoby *Thunder out of China*. New York: William Sloane Associates, Inc., 1946, p. 132.
5. *Ibid.*, p. 165.
6. *Ibid.*, p. 324.

3

Destination Chengdu

Up The River

The luck of the draw meant that Bennie and Dorothy Benson and I were the fortunate ones to go up the Yangtze River to Chungking and then Chengdu. We were really the only ones available. Dan Carr was still recovering from his appendectomy, John Simpson had to wait for his freight to clear customs, and Lee Lovegren was needed to help in a myriad of details. We did not object. We had not come to China to sit in Shanghai.

The Bensons had first-class space on the *Min Tsu*, which provided a small room with two beds. My ticket was for third class, but this was no problem, since I could buy a first-class meal ticket and sleep on a cot and air mattress in the Bensons' room. We thought we were a bit crowded, but we had seen nothing yet. Much worse off were the five CIM adults and two children who were in a below-the-deck small, dark, dismal dormitory room sleeping thirty-six people. Fourth class was even worse. People in this class slept wherever there was open space—on the deck, on tables, in parlor rooms, anywhere—rolling up their large, padded sleeping quilts, together with their sundry toilet articles during the daytime hours.

We soon learned that the *Min Tsu* was not a passenger ship, but a freighter with a few passenger accommodations. We had one of the two first-class cabins. The main cargo was 620 crates of banknotes for the Bank of China in Hankow, and hundreds of large pipes.

Sailing up the "long river" (the meaning of the Chinese term for *Yangtze*) in winter, we were even colder than we had been in Shanghai. Rooms were not heated, and our only salvation was the thermos bottles we had brought with us. Hot water is never a commodity in short supply in China. Our thick, warm Chinese quilts served us well for getting warm during the night. We wanted to see each day's new scenery, but the chilly winds blowing along the river often forced us inside.

Our cabin was near the bow of the ship on the starboard side. Just a room away was the dining nook for first-class passengers. The three of us took our meals each day with three Chinese passengers. This was our first real introduction to Chinese food and chopsticks.

For the first few meals, eating was a chore. Chinese eat fast, and we could not keep pace. First of all, we always had a moment of grace. And then there was the matter of the chopsticks. The spirit was willing, but the hands were slow! But if we had our problems, our Chinese friends did not. The food disappeared before we could really get into action. And so we compromised. We brought spoons along to buy time, while we gained more proficiency with the chopsticks. The trip aboard the *Min Tsu* has had its lasting effect on me. To this day, I eat Chinese food much faster than I do our western cuisine. The habit of survival has persisted.

We feared that we might not subsist well on a totally Chinese diet, and so we had prepared a few "goodies"—army K rations bought in Shanghai, tangerines and bananas, bread and jam, and canned meat. We replenished this stock as we went along from the hawkers who poled their little boats alongside our steamer and sold us anything we might want. UNRRA (United Nations Relief and Rehabilitation Agency) relief products were plentiful in China, and everyone got into the act of selling the food products that were on the black market.

We boarded the *Min Tsu* on Saturday night, but did not leave port until Sunday. The sing-song cadence of the Chinese coolies as they loaded the ship kept us awake all night. A further delay came when a sudden snow squall reduced visibility so much that the ship was not able to proceed out the Woosung River to the entrance of the Yangtze.

This four-week steamer trip introduced us to much more than Chinese eating—here was the beginning of the real China to which Shanghai was a very superficial—often unreal—introduction. We learned quickly how friendly the Chinese people are and how gracious they were to these "dumb foreigners," who never did anything right. I had learned just enough Chinese to be dangerous. One day when I inadvertently stepped on a man's foot on the crowded deck, I blurted out, *"xie, xie"* (thank you), even though my mind told me I should have said *"dui bu qi"* (pardon me). At least I had tried to say something, and he seemed to be forgiving.

We learned quickly that the Chinese sense of modesty was different from ours. Parents encouraged their babies, and even older children, to relieve themselves where they were, whenever the urge came. For the babies, slit pants were better than diapers. Bathing was done semi-publicly, and many passengers, including the women, lounged about in their underwear. From the Chinese standpoint this was all very normal. But for us, though it was traumatic, it helped us to see that modesty is cultural. What you are not used to bothers you.

It was a thrill to be on the great Yangtze River. I did not pretend to know much about China, but from the time I was a small boy, the very name "Yangtze" had an aura of mystery, even intrigue. One author has commented that the Yangtze is "China's Main Street."[1] Along its waterways travel as much commerce as is carried by some even longer and larger rivers, such as the Mississippi, Nile, Amazon, and Congo. Originating in the Tibetan highlands to the far West, the Yangtze meanders for about 3200 miles through varied scenes in China before reaching the ocean near Shanghai. Within the Yangtze Plain, extending inland nearly six hundred miles to the Sichuan Basin, live 650,000,000 of China's population.

As we began our trip, the river's width stretched to two or three miles. Fortunately, for the sightseeing we wished to do, we sailed close to one bank or the other. The countryside was barren and brown, since it was planted with winter wheat, not nearly as green as a field of rice paddies. Small mountains, really more of the foothill variety, jutted up everywhere, and, occasionally, we saw snow-covered mountain ranges in the distance.

Destination Chengdu

We passed the large cities of Nanking, Wuhu, Anjing, and Jiujiang, but the scenery was made up largely of hundreds of little hamlets. Some houses were constructed of wood, but the majority were made of thatched straw. The river bustled with activity. Junks passed us constantly, and we saw many fishermen in their smaller boats along the shore. Most interesting were boats being pulled upstream by people tugging a tow line as they tracked along the bank of the river. It seemed quaint at the time, but by the time we had gone farther upstream, we joined the boats being pulled.

We usually did not sail at night. One reason for this was that the river was low—the cubic feet of flow was about 60% lower in February than in July—and it was dangerous to continue in the darkness. This factor was compounded by the ever-present danger from pirates and robbers. Anchoring close by some city port every evening gave us a good opportunity to observe the water merchants as they came up to the boat, using long bamboo poles with a hook on one end to cling to the ship's side, while they tried to sell their wares.

The first stop of any importance was on February 6 at Hankow, one of the three cities making up the complex of Wuhan. We disembarked here and visited with friends of the *Marine Lynx* days at the Lutheran home. We hoped that we might get some Western food to break the long string of Chinese meals, but this was not to be! We caught up on world news, as well as on the continued deteriorating situation in China. Most alarming was the ongoing skyrocketing of prices and an escalating exchange rate that had now reached $10,100 Chinese dollars to the American dollar—and that was week-old news. We saw that the damage done by Japanese bombing in Hankow was much more evident than anything we had seen in Shanghai.

What little extra time I could find, I used to catch up on correspondence that had fallen behind badly during the trip up from Shanghai. The trip from Hankow to Yichang took five days. The more we proceeded west, the narrower the river became and the more rugged the scenery on both banks. The countryside was greener with more trees and foliage. Here and there along the bank we saw signs "Travel at Your Own Risk." This gave us food for thought, particularly when we scraped bottom and realized that the water depth was only seven feet. But to live and travel anywhere in China at this time was not a "no risk" situation, and we were not about to stop now. God, we knew, was faithful, and, whatever the real or supposed dangers, our lives were in his care.

We arrived in Yichang after dark on a Thursday evening and decided to stay on board. We were going to change to a smaller boat here, and to take all of our belongings off by sampan without any light was precarious. The next day we hauled everything up to the old compound of the China Inland Mission, now being used by the Yangtze Gorge Project. The pastor of the CIM church in Yichang helped us for the next few days. His poor English was much better than our poor Chinese, and, with heavy dependence on sign language, we did just fine!

We felt secure and reasonably comfortable, but it was still very cold. The small charcoal heaters in the house were not much help. The rooms where we stayed were not well insulated, and the blustering wind, along with the steadily falling snow, chilled us to the bone. As usual, however, we lacked no hot water, only the will to take a bath.

Servants at the home provided delicious meals for us. Eating by ourselves increased our skill with chopsticks. Once we were not sure what we were eating. The cook announced it as chicken, but both the skin and bones were all black. No choice here! We assumed it was spoiled, and, at first, declined to eat. Finally, the cook helped us to understand that this was an *wugu ji*, a special delicacy called "black-boned" chicken. It was indeed delicious, and in our next few years in China, we never again refused it.

During the war of resistance against Japan, Yichang was a strategic city, with the result that it had been bombed very heavily. About 90% of the city had been razed, and the horrible destruction was everywhere apparent. These few days in this city along the Yangtze helped us to feel a bit more poignantly some of the suffering through which the Chinese people had gone.

After three days in Yichang, we proceeded up the Yangtze gorges, the most anticipated section of our trip. Our new river steamer, the *Ming Xie*, was even smaller than the previous ship, for the river was very low. We were fortunate even to be able to go, for this was the last boat carrying passengers to make the gorge trip until spring, when the river would be higher. We were even more crowded than before. In one small cube of a cabin that measured no more than six feet in any direction there were now five of us. The Bensons and I were joined by two single women: a medical doctor and a nurse from Australia. Our concepts of privacy changed in a hurry! Bennie and I allowed the women to prepare for the night's sleep first, and, then, when the lights were out, we stumbled our way in and bedded down. The two new arrivals slept on the upper bunks, Dorothy had one of the lower bunks, and I the other. Bennie, last of all, moved a cot into place between the two lower bunks. This fully occupied all the remaining space in the cabin. In the morning we reversed the process, with Bennie and me vacating the cabin first.

This crowded cabin produced one of the more memorable China jokes. Dottie dashed off a hurried letter on one of our stops to her mother, in which she casually commented that "Ralph and I sleep on the lower bunks." She neglected to say that Bennie was on the cot between us! Only later, when she saw her letter, reproduced by her mother without any editing and sent out near and far to many friends, did she realize what she had said.

The gorge area extends some 125 miles above Yichang toward Chungking. Altogether there are twelve well-known gorges, one of them extending about twenty-five miles in length. The scenery could not have been more different from the lower Yangtze. The river narrowed dramatically—at times it seemed not much wider than the width of our boat. Probably it never narrowed to less than 150 yards. Sheer cliffs, ranging from 500 to 2,000 feet, rose precipitously on both sides of the river. We saw snow-covered mountains in the distance poking their majestic peaks above beautiful valleys. I had spent considerable time as a boy in Colorado, and the scenery, surely as incredible as could be found along any of the world's rivers, reminded me of the Royal Gorge.

Along this stretch of river were seventy-two turbulent rapids, most of them prominent and dangerous, during the low-river season. Twice we had to disembark by rope ladders into small sampans which took us to the river bank to walk, while the steamer was pulled gently by cable over the jutting rocks. Clambering aboard and then disembarking was a clumsy activity. It was made even more challenging when the sampan rowers waited until they had us in the middle of the river, and then demanded more money for the trip than what we had originally bargained for. We were, in fact, between a rock and a hard place, and usually had to give in.

Along both banks of the river, Chinese families carried on their daily chores—women washing the family clothes in the river and spreading them out to dry on the rocks, people making offerings to the river gods for safety, worshippers burning incense at joss houses, farmers plowing their hard fields with crude implements, and men fishing with cormorants.

We were fascinated by the many junks, large and small, that were being pulled upstream by "trackers" against the strong current. Several men, or even several dozen, were involved in this backbreaking task. Since the cliffs came down so directly into the river, this tracking could be done only along narrow paths that were gouged right out of the bank.

Beyond the natural beauty were many evidences of human artistry. Temples and pagodas clung precariously to the higher peaks, and along the cliffs were drawings and hieroglyphic-type writings going back to China's ancient past.

Because of the many danger spots on the river, we did not travel at night. This allowed many sampans to nuzzle up to the ship and hawkers to sell us fruit. In a way, we did not feel the need for extra things now, since our food on board ship had improved dramatically. The steamer's cook had once worked on the Dollar Lines in the United States, and he had gained the knack of preparing hamburgers, french fries, and potato chips. These, always served with boiled rice, helped to break the steady monotony of a Chinese diet.

Through Chungking to Chengdu

It took us five days to reach Chungking, the largest city in Sichuan province. We arrived early in the morning, but we did not reach the China Inland Mission home until 3 p.m. A little more adjustment to the culture would have saved us time, energy, and mental anguish. Like most new arrivals in the Middle Kingdom, we thought the wharf coolies in Chungking were trying to gouge us by charging too much to move our belongings off the ship and to the

CIM home. And so, rather stupidly, we worked out all of the arrangements by ourselves. We managed it, and may have saved a few shekels, but we only added to the evidence that we were "ugly" Americans. It would take a while for us to learn how to fit in with China's way of doing things.

Chungking had been the wartime capital of nationalist China. Located on a series of hills, which have been likened to the superstructure of a huge ship, it is wedged between two rivers, the Jialing and the Yangtze. Noted in the summer time as one of the three "furnaces of the Yangtze," it was now more like an ice box. What a relief, after the long trip along the Yangtze River, to find some warmth and comfort in the CIM home located on one of these hills. Robertson and Betty Small, in charge of the home at that time, went out of their way to make us comfortable. Dottie found most delight in the luxury of having a new bar of Ivory soap, freshly placed in her room. We were finding out how even small things seemed to "make our days."

We left early the next morning for the final stage of our journey to Chengdu. We had a choice in our bus travel. We could pay a higher fare and be guaranteed arrival in two days or we could give the regular amount, in which case it could take us as long as two weeks! We paid the higher price! The bus was far from comfortable. The seats were hard and small, there was no space for our long, American legs, and it was wall-to-wall people, chickens, grain, and anything else a Chinese traveller might bring along. The only familiar faces were those of the Australian doctor and nurse, who had accompanied us from Yichang.

The roads were rough, and the bus springs were broken. The balance of the bus was also suspect, because all of the really big luggage was in a large rack on top. This weight was increased by the presence of many "yellow fish," non-ticketed passengers picked up and left off outside the cities through which we were travelling. Their fares went directly into the pockets of the driver and his mechanic.

The presence of a mechanic was the only guarantee of our two-day passage. He usually sat on the front hood of the bus and often fixed the engine while the bus coasted down a long mountain side in neutral. It did not help us to know that the brakes were also in poor condition!

The countryside was vintage Sichuan. Everywhere were low, green rolling hills, interspersed with lovely mountains. The plains and these hills and mountains were completely cultivated, predominantly with rice, but also with peas, beans, mustard seed, and orange trees. Whenever we stopped, we bought delicious fruit—pomelos, oranges, and tangerines. The latter we felt were a bargain by our standards, selling for sixteen for one American dollar.

On our one overnight stop, we stayed at the hostel of the China Travel Service in the city of Neijiang. We got to the city in the early evening, but after eating, we still had some time to look around. The long day's travel over hill and dale had worn us out, and the night's rest was welcome. Rooms were small and unclean, and, as usual in a Chinese inn, the chatter of people drinking tea and gambling went on well into the night. We could afford a poor night's rest—our twenty-six day trip was nearly over, and nothing really bothered us.

We were met at the bus station on February 26 by the very hospitable Sam Jeffrey, who was in charge of the China Inland Mission home. Like other CIM homes in which we had visited or stayed for short periods, this one was sparse, clean, and comfortable, and we were made to feel very welcome. Each bedroom was small but had a small table, a wash stand, a bureau, a bed with rope springs, and a thin mattress. Each morning *amahs*—Chinese household help—brought us a jug of hot water for washing and did our sewing and laundry as needed. Once a week we got hot water for a bath.

The bedrooms were not heated, but we were encouraged to go to the warm living room for our reading and writing. This was the place to receive Chinese or missionary guests. The courtyard was small, but had a nice garden where it was pleasant to walk. It was bordered, in customary fashion, by a high compound wall that went along a very crowded alley leading on to one of Chengdu's major thoroughfares.

At this time, Chengdu's reputation rested more on its ancient history than on its modern development. Two thousand years previous, during the Zhou Dynasty, the kingdom of Shu moved its capital to this site. Later, during the Han Dynasty (206 BC-220 AD), the brocade trade brought so much prosperity that the city became known as *Jincheng* (Brocade Town) and earned the nickname "storehouse of heaven." It became the "city of hibiscus" during the Five Dynasties period (907-960), when a local feudal lord had those colorful flowers planted atop the town wall.[2]

Although situated on the level Sichuan plain, Chengdu had an elevation of fifteen hundred feet. Located at the same latitude as New Orleans, it was cold in the winter and muggy hot in the summer. Not as huge a city as Shanghai, it had a population of 800,000—hardly a small hamlet. Far more typical of China than the large coastal cities, its streets were narrow, and largely unpaved, with most of the shops opening directly on the street. The people were much poorer than in Shanghai. Automobiles were more the exception than the rule, and the few on the streets were old and battered. No pedicabs were to be found, and the rickshas were on their last wheels. We were glad to find out that prices were much cheaper than those we had seen in Shanghai or Hankow.

Although much of Sichuan is rugged and mountainous, Chengdu is surrounded by a plain of four thousand square miles. The density of the population in the post-World War II period was eighteen hundred to two thousand inhabitants per square mile. Blessed with an amazing ancient irrigation system and rich natural resources, this area has always been the most productive in all China and scarcely ever had to face the periodic famines seen frequently in north China.

At this time, the missionary community numbered between 80 and 120, one-third British or Canadian. Seven religious groups were represented: Friends, Canadian Methodists, Northern Baptists, American Methodists, Church of England (Church Mission Society), China Inland Mission, and Seventh Day Adventists. Despite the missionary work carried on by these many groups beginning as early as the 1890s, there were only about 1200 churchgoers in Chengdu. Numerous Christian schools had been established, and students studying in these numbered about 50,000.

Getting Settled in Chengdu

We arrived running! Even though still weary from our long, arduous journey, we commenced language study the following Monday. It was held on the campus of the West China Union University on the opposite side of town from the CIM home.

After our initial visit to the campus, the Bensons and I were not sure that we would be allowed to study at the school. The temporary director of the institute, Douglas Sargent of the Church Mission Society, informed us rather curtly that we were not a "cooperating mission" and, furthermore, that we had not applied for study at the school. His attitude softened when we told him that Jesse Moncrief, director of the institute, had given permission to Lovegren for us to enroll. All animosity disappeared when we told him that CBFMS had contributed five hundred dollars for the purchase of sound-scribers and other equipment. Our costs of fifteen dollars per student per month plus a monthly three-dollar equipment fee were slightly higher than that charged to students with cooperating missions. Even this, however, was a bargain for a well-run language school.

At this juncture, our only means of transportation was the slow ricksha, and it took forty-five minutes each way. Classes went on all day, so we did not get back to the home much before 4:30. We knew only a few phrases of the language, and we exhausted them quickly in bargaining for a right price with the ricksha pullers. Gradually some of the men recognized us because of our predictable daily trips, and we did not need to go through the bargaining ritual.

Even though we had started our language study, our minds were on many other things related to getting settled. We needed a better system of transportation. The romance with rickshas lasted for only a few days. They were slow and sitting in the often blustery wind was cold. China is the world's biggest producers of bicycles, and that was good enough for us—we decided to invest in bikes. At an equivalent of $41.75 I got a locally produced hand-brake variety that served me well for this year in Chengdu. Bicycle travel reduced our travel time to campus to a reasonable twenty to twenty-five minutes and provided some badly needed daily exercise.

We all needed more skill in handling our bikes. I had never owned one in America, and spent some time practicing on side roads before venturing on to more busy thoroughfares. I needed to use my bell constantly, shout out that I was coming, and, when it was really crowded, I just got off and walked for a distance.

For Jim Garrison, who arrived in Chengdu about a month after our initial group, his first bike ride was downright embarrassing. He had an eye problem, and people could not be sure where he was heading. A ricksha puller with a passenger was coming down one side of the street, a good distance from Jim. But Jim didn't have his bike under control, and the longer he rode, the more apparent it became that his radar was fixed right on this poor man. Try as both he and the puller did to avoid one another, their fate was as if predetermined. Finally, Jim ran right into him, driving him back between the two poles of the ricksha and into the seat, almost on top of the passenger he was pulling. No harm was done, fortunately, and after trying profusely with insufficient Chinese to apologize to the confused puller, Jim went on his way down the street.

We noticed traffic officers at nearly every intersection, even where there was virtually no traffic. They left no doubt they were in control. Even if a push cart lumbered toward the intersection at a very slow speed, the man pushing it clapped two pieces of bamboo together and held his hand up to indicate he wanted to make a right-hand turn. With great precision, the officer wheeled about to face him, checked in both directions, held up his hand to stop the non-existent traffic, and then tooted shrilly on his whistle to give the cart the right of way.

Chengdu's electric power was unpredictable. The plan was that certain sections of the city would have electricity on three or four different nights of the week. We planned accordingly, but this system was so irregular that we resigned ourselves to nights when we could get nothing done, except by the poor light of an Aladdin lamp.

It did not take us long to become very British. Tea, at each meal plus morning and afternoon "breaks," was soon an absolute necessity. We often drank ten to twelve cups in one day. However, if we wanted to drink anything at all, there were few alternatives. All drinking water must be boiled, and there wasn't much in the way of safe soft drinks, except an insipid carbonated drink called *qi xue*.

The Bensons and I could not settle down in Chengdu while we had only temporary lodging at the CIM home. Any decision about where we might find more permanent housing must await the arrival of our entire group. We were compulsively democratic, and everyone had to be involved in every decision! Planes of the China National Air Corporation (CNAC) were still grounded because of the numerous air accidents, the river was too low for river travel for another month, and our "gang" were still fuming (really freezing) in Shanghai.

Finally, through a connection that Dan Carr developed with the U.S. Army, it was possible on March 10 and 11 for Dan and then the entire group to get space on American military C-54s for the twelve hundred mile flight from Shanghai to Chengdu. These planes, as well as those operated by CNAC, had nothing but bucket seats, arranged along both sides of the plane. If passengers wanted to get a bit more rest, army blankets were spread out for them along the floors. The recent wrecks had made air flight personnel nervous, and so all adults had parachutes buckled on them during the takeoff and for the first few moments of the flight.

The Bensons and I received word of Dan's arrival through American army headquarters in Chengdu and quickly rented vehicles to go to the airport and pick him up, along with a half-plane load of everyone's belongings. The following day we went with Dan to welcome the others. Only Lee remained behind in Shanghai to meet the Garrisons and accompany them up the river. What a joyous reunion at the airport as we excitedly shared all that had happened since we had last been together.

In later years, we questioned the wisdom of depending in this way on the U.S. Army. As evidenced by many student protests in China, the American military was not in good favor with many Chinese people. When the People's Republic of China came to power in 1949, it had good evidence that the relationship between Americans in China, including missionaries, and the U.S. armed forces was far too cozy. From its perspective, this was American imperialism. Could we have done any differently? Would our one small "sin" really add that much to the evidence? Our group might have waited in Shanghai for CNAC to fly again, but, no, our very presence in China during these chaotic years would be sufficient incrimination for the new government. Despite this, our move was still an unwise one.

We learned a few months later of a more serious problem. The American air force personnel who had sold Dan space for the two flights were engaged in unauthorized profiteering. In the subsequent investigation, high-ranking officers visited Dan in Chengdu to get a deposition on the nature of the transaction. Our entire group might easily have gotten in hot water for wrong doing.

Moving to a New Home on the Campus of the University

The first order of business was to find better housing. The CIM home was comfortable and everyone was friendly and gracious, but we had taken up every inch of the space there. More important, the CIM had more missionaries coming. And even the shorter ride by bicycle to campus was too long. If only we could find a home on the beautiful campus! The unexpected happened when fellow language-school students, Ed and Jean Knettler of the American Methodist mission, told us of an empty home on some of its campus property. The house had not been lived in for some time, and we had to hire workers to replace windows, patch floors, walls and ceiling, put in screens, and clean up. What little we put out on this was more than compensated for by a monthly rental fee of only $50.

This home had been available all along, but, possibly with good reason, members of the governing board of the university were not certain what a group of separatist, fundamentalist missionaries looked like! These initial weeks had dispelled a few fears, and, recommended largely by the Methodists and the principal of the language school, Jesse Moncrief of the ABFMS, we squeaked by with just enough votes to permit us to occupy this campus housing. Eventually all resistance was broken down, and we were welcomed with open arms and hearts. During our stay in Chengdu we developed cordial relations, even with those whose theological positions differed markedly from ours.

By late March, we made our move to house #51 Huaxiba (abbreviated Chinese name for West China Union University). What a spacious home compared to our cramped facilities with the CIM! Even our gang of five couples and me could fit comfortably into the large rooms of this two-story home. And since it was right on the campus, a few moments' walk brought us to the language school.

This was particularly convenient for the Carrs and Simpsons with their small babies, since the mothers found it easier both to attend classes and keep some touch with the *amahs* caring for Danny and Linn Ann.

No sooner had we moved into this new home than our freight arrived from Shanghai, via boat up the river and by truck from Chungking. Altogether there were three large truck loads, each having sixty to sixty-five pieces. Some individual items weighed as much as five to six hundred pounds. A day or two earlier, and we would have not known where to put it, and much later would have forced us to buy locally the various things necessary to set up housekeeping on a full scale. We spent the better part of two days hauling it all out, surveying the damage caused by the long transit from America, and then packing away in the large basement the things we could save for our final destination in Xichang. I was hurting for lack of exercise and gave first attention to my tennis racket and an American football.

What was this West China Union University where we were living? As early as 1899, missionaries in Sichuan saw the need for a Christian university in West China that would meet the educational needs of this vast area, even as had Christian schools in east China. After much preliminary planning on the part of representatives of the Methodist Episcopal, American Baptist, and Canadian Methodist missions, the West China Union University was formally opened on March 11, 1910.[3] The turmoil of the 1911 revolution quickly shut down the school, until it was reopened in 1913 with 139 students, most of dubious university calibre.

Located on a spacious campus outside Chengdu, not a city with high military significance, the university was a safe haven during the war with Japan for many prestigious universities in east and north China. For a period of four or five years, Chengdu became the educational center for China. Although committed to a full range of liberal arts subjects, West China Union University had a high sense of its Christian mission. YMCA and Student Volunteer Association groups were formed on campus, and regular meetings were held of "Jesus Study Groups."[4] A Student Center on campus, along with a Religious Study Center, served as gathering places for various Christian groups. During the years when we were studying language on this campus, a University Church, completed in 1949, was being constructed.[5]

With all of us now comfortably settled in this pleasant inland city, we anticipated, with some fear and trembling, the year ahead of us. It was to be a time of rigorous spiritual, cultural, and mental preparation that would set the tone for our ministry in Xikang.

Endnotes

1. Cressey, George B. *Land of the 500 Million: A Geography of China.* New York: McGraw-Hill Book Company, Inc. 1955, p. 173.
2. Kaplan, Fredric M. and Arne J. deKeijer (eds.) *The China Guidebook.* 1984 Edition. New York: Eurasia Press, p. 299.
3. Walmsley, Lewis C. *West China Union University.* United Board for Christian Higher Education in Asia, p. 28.
4. *Ibid.*, pp. 100-101.
5. *Ibid.*, pp. 102-103.

4

The Chinese Language— A Tunnel With No Lights

Living Out the Grace of God

Setting up our household was one thing; running it smoothly with so many disparate people under one roof was another. Our classmates at language school laughingly referred to our community life as the best evidence of the grace of God. How do eleven people live together for one year sharing a common bath, common kitchen, and common living room and dining room? We soon saw that none of us could go it alone—we must operate as one large family.

But this was hard to pull off. We had a wealth of common spiritual experience, and we belonged to one mission society. But among us were staid Easterners, blunt mid-westerners, and wild westerners. One person felt bitter about what he called "the Eastern Baptist clique." Now that Jim and Virginia Garrison had arrived as a part of our group, there were at least eight adult opinions. For some of the time Lee Lovegren and John Simpson were away travelling in Xikang, and Ida Lovegren had the unenviable role of senior missionary. This was a major trial for her, trying to knock some sense into us and our cocky, petty notions.

We had many domestic differences. Some wanted meat at every meal; others thought once a day was sufficient. Some wanted pie five times a week; others thought this was far too often. Some thought we should burn coal, while others favored wood and charcoal. Some wanted Chinese food at every meal but breakfast, and others wanted to mix it equally with Western food. Some thought we should fire the cook, while others wished to "extend his contract" and give him a bonus as well.

When Ida left on an evangelistic mission for Xikang, we had no referee to monitor our squabbling. So we decided to put one unit in charge for each week. This unit—a couple or me—was responsible for planning the menu, arranging for the cook to buy each day what was needed, working with the cook where necessary in actually preparing the food, and turning expenses over to me who had been designated as treasurer. As was the case with most foreigners living on the campus, we had an experienced cook who needed little supervision and could prepare many goodies beyond our fondest imagination. Of course, we had to have ground rules: how much meat a day, how many desserts a week, how much money did we want to spend on eating? Once these details were cared for, we settled into a routine.

Much to my parents' relief, I reported that we ate about as we would have at home. Despite our heavy study load, my weight increased to 162 pounds, more than I had ever weighed. Not too much was available in fresh vegetables, but we got fresh boiled milk daily and meat twice daily, which was far better than I had ever eaten in my life. Desserts came at least every other day. Breakfast was usually a cooked or uncooked cereal—as puffed rice—and two eggs cooked in some form. As we moved further into spring, the fruit increased. We particularly enjoyed the cherries. Evening meals were a bit more formal and always began with soup.

Depending on who was in charge in a given week, we had small crises with the cook, the table boy, the wash woman or one of the delivery persons. Buying the coal needed for cooking and heating was difficult, for its weight had to be checked carefully. Once Jim Garrison suspected that the milk was more water than milk. When he confronted the boy who made the deliveries daily, he emphatically denied that something like this could ever happen. Jim insisted that there was a problem, and finally the milkman brought the cow to our front yard and milked it right in front of Jim. Voila, the little gauge now showed we had pure milk. We had no more problems of this nature.

The house was large, and there was space for everyone. I was on the ground floor of this two-story home and had three very small rooms with a washroom, bedroom, toilet, and screened in porch. I slept on a cot with a thin mattress. Furniture stores abounded in Chengdu, and I bought a fine desk for the equivalent of about three dollars. Unlike other sleeping areas, my room had no fireplace, and it was harder to get warm at night. Fortunately, by this time, winter was yielding reluctantly to spring, and I had no problem keeping warm. In fact, as the weather got warmer—by early summer the mercury was up to 90-95—I slept out on the porch. The breezes were lovely, but neither the wind or the screen kept away the mosquitoes. We were very glad to be able to get coarse, locally-made mosquito nets to protect us.

In terms of our own living standards, daily living was cheap. Eating came to seventy-five cents a day per person, and we did not need to add much for the help given by the three servants, whose monthly wages were never more than five dollars each. The cost for furniture, bikes, extra clothing, or odds and ends required for language study was a pittance. Eventually, we saw that to evaluate our costs in terms of the American dollar was very misleading, both to ourselves and to those who worked with us as co-laborers. As a household, we were spending eight million Chinese dollars a month, an amount that would have lasted an equal number of Chinese an entire year.

Our house was one of four very large dwellings located on this spacious Methodist compound. Each one had a very large yard, and some of this we used to plant a few vegetables. An athletic field was right across from us, and about fifty yards behind us was a small river. Down the road a short distance was the university library, which I used later in my continued research on the Yi people. We had enough open space near the house to build a clay tennis court—not too fancy, but it served our purposes.

We found that we had problems with mice, but a good cat solved this difficulty quickly. We bought a small dog, Hebo, meaning "lively," to help guard our property. Unfortunately, somebody poisoned him, and for the next several days, following the advice of our friends, we had a special alert for burglars.

Having domestic servants meant that we did not need to go out ourselves to buy food daily. Missionary tradition dictated that we "reckon" food money daily with the servants to keep them from skimming off some of it for their own pockets. We arranged for a barber and shoe repair person to come to the house whenever needed.

We had no problem getting medical attention. A fine hospital and medical school were right on the campus. Far more personal was the fact that we had Dr. Fritz Fisher as our own mission doctor in Chengdu. A Jew educated in Austria, he fled from Hitler into Italy, and then continued on to Shanghai. After a short period in Shanghai, he accepted a job in the Methodist hospital in Nanchang. When the Japanese were about ready to occupy that city, Fritz and his wife Emmie left and eventually got to Chungking and Chengdu. During this period of fleeing from one place to another, the Fishers had become Christians, largely as a result of the warm welcome given to them by loving Christian people.[1]

While we were in Chengdu, inflation never caught up with the escalating value of the American dollar, and we always had money left over from our salary. What to do with it? At one point I had $1,300,000 Chinese currency in a local Chengdu bank earning five to six percent a month. This was a losing game since its total value depreciated by fifty percent in one month. Eventually we had to ask that less money be sent to the field for our use.

We worked hard to keep up with world and national news. We were far too early in our language study to be able to read a Chinese newspaper. Jim Garrison had a good short wave set, and when we had electricity—never predictable—we picked up news broadcasts from New York. Eventually we subscribed by airmail to an American-published newspaper from Shanghai which had the advantage of keeping us informed on China as well as on the world.

We found time for a variety of social events. Sometimes it was being invited out by wealthy Chinese friends who liked to practice their English. They regaled us with feasts that might go on for fifteen exotic dishes. We learned slowly how to pace ourselves—how not to shoot our appetites on the first three or four items. Sichuan food is hot and spicy, but if this were not enough, a relaxing game at the end of some of these meals was for the diners to compete to see who could eat the hottest raw spices without a change of facial expression or demeanor. My stomach was never strong enough to compete!

We were often invited out as a group to the homes of other missionaries on campus. The American Baptist folk—the Dryden Phelps, Jesse Moncriefs and Daniel Dyes—were very gracious to us. They were impressed that there was still as large a group of Baptist missionaries as ourselves interested in foreign missions. Wistfully they expressed the hope that the American Baptist Foreign Mission Society would send out more to strengthen their hands in the work. The theological issues separating us from these American Baptist friends were profound, but we enjoyed a good social relationship.

We spent no little time discussing our attitude toward the ABFMS, the agency from which we were "come-outers." Lovegren, of course, had spent many years in its West China conference and was chummy with many of his former colleagues. He asked their advice on a Chinese name for our group, he sought their help in house-hunting in Chengdu, and here we were in a language school directed by an ABFMS missionary on a campus where ABFMS was one of the founding partners! As young missionaries who had staked our careers, as it were, on a fledgling mission society, we wanted a higher sense of our identity. The board in Chicago had no word of wisdom for us—"do what seems best," it advised.

"What seemed best" meant to stay where we were and win our way by friendship. We argued about new missionaries studying the language either at Hankow in central China or on our field in Xichang, both far from the American Baptists in Chengdu, but neither plan proved to be feasible.

We tried to be sensitive in responding to complaints that students on the Huaxiba campus brought to us about Dryden Phelps. They mentioned that in the classroom he denied the bodily resurrection of Jesus and that he seemed to value Confucius above Jesus. We did not hear him make such statements, and we did not wish to be embroiled in controversy. Dryden personally was not a controversialist, and we were not in any position to raise theological issues on a campus where we were guests.

Dryden, like many missionaries past and present, tended to make broad, all-inclusive statements that were not theologically precise. When challenged by others on these matters, he became more specific, but still utilized ambivalent language. This had caused him to be a center of controversy between fundamentalists and others within the Northern Baptist Convention over a ten-year period. In a memo issued July 10, 1947 by Jesse Wilson, Home Secretary of the ABFMS, Dryden stated his agreement with the Christology of the Gospel of John's prologue, Hebrews 1:1-4 and Colossians 1:15-20.[2]

We could have wished for a more definitive statement on the Matthean and Lucan birth accounts of Jesus, as well as on the doctrine of the virgin birth. We understood how many of Phelps' statements were geared to the Chinese context and that not every statement was meant to carry all of his doctrinal convictions. However, when we saw the turmoil which his beliefs created on the West China Union University campus, we were glad not to be associated with him directly and have to deal with the serious doubts which students were bringing.

Opportunities abounded in Chengdu for us to make many new friends. We had the good fortune during these days to make the acquaintance of Geoffrey Bull and George Patterson, British missionaries residing at the CIM home and preparing for work in Tibet. Geoffrey later wrote a very informative book, *When Iron Gates Yield*, about his experiences in the "top of the world." George wrote a total of nine books and many articles and served as TV consultant to the British Broadcasting Company on Asian affairs.

In our early days in China we lived for mail deliveries. Once air travel was restored, we could count on a twenty-eight day turn-around for our letters, fourteen days in each direction. Our loved ones worried about our being in China in these turbulent days and got very nervous if we did not write regularly. We all had supporting churches to keep in touch with, and, within the limits of wisdom, we tried to interpret China to them.

Once every three or four weeks, a letter came from Anne, the young woman from Philadelphia, to whom I had once been engaged. We had resigned ourselves to a "no-go" relationship, but we still kept up a spasmodic correspondence, and I occasionally sent her a small gift. Frank Harris and I frequently talked about our need for mates, but it would be some time before either of us were married. Many attractive Chinese Christian girls were to be found in the numerous student fellowship groups to whom we spoke, but their lack of suitable educational background and the wide cultural differences would not have made them an asset in our ministries. I dated a young Methodist missionary, but her vision and concerns were different from mine.

First Order of the Day—Language Study

Our only reason to be in Chengdu was to study Chinese. We might have gone directly to Xichang and tried to pick up the language on our own with tutors. This was not a recommended method. We felt that qualified tutors would be much harder to come by for a large group in a small population center like Xichang. Furthermore, in our group I was the only one who had studied at the Summer Institute of Linguistics (Wycliffe Bible Translators) and had specialized training to work with tutors. We knew that studying the language in the area where we intended to work would bring too many interruptions. We also believed that the initial study of Chinese is done better in a more formal setting.

The language school which we attended daily had been started in 1912 by the Canadian Methodist Mission for the training of its new missionaries. Even though within a few years it was turned over to the university proper, the facilities continued to be those of the Canadian mission's children school. Rooms were well built and comfortable, and, apart from being cold and damp, were ideal for a school.

We followed a rigorous schedule of study: four periods in the morning, with the predictable half-hour tea break, an hour for lunch, followed by three periods in the afternoon. Seldom did any class have more than two or three students, and occasionally a class was made up of one student and one teacher. With this high teacher-student ratio, we received much individual attention. I, at least, needed it. My ears constantly played tricks on me, whether for individual sounds or the complex tonal system. When tones went up, I heard them coming down, and vice-versa.

During our first weeks of study, we concentrated on learning how to pronounce Chinese words and then how to organize them into simple phrases and sentences of most use in everyday conversation. If we wished to write anything down, we did it with the use of a simple, romanized alphabet. This had been done by Protestant missionaries from their first entrance into China early in the nineteenth century. We dispensed with the normal Chinese writing system which uses complex picture-like characters, until we had an elementary foundation in spoken Chinese. This meant that we had hardly any homework. The best way to learn correct pronunciation was to do it with teachers, and we could not take them home with us!

Our language teachers went out of their way not to use English when explaining a new sound or word to us. They were great actors, opening their mouths wide to point to correct vocal organs and urging us to use mirrors in order to mimic them in producing sounds correctly. I still remember the head teacher, old Mr. Pan, who had taught missionaries for many decades, climbing up on tables and chairs and acting out the meaning of some sentence. Then he would point at us gleefully with a big smile and head slightly cocked when we finally caught on. This monolingual approach was slow and clumsy initially, but progress accelerated down the line when English was not the "escape" language to rescue us from a difficult situation.

As we made more progress in the language, we spent some of our school hours with a sound-scriber, a small voice-recording machine that helped us in going through pronunciation and phrase drills. I had learned the theory of the oral approach to language learning, but I was anxious to study the Chinese Bible. So I made special arrangements to have Pastor Chen, who shepherded the China Inland Mission church, to give me individual lessons every Thursday evening in reading and understanding the Chinese Bible. This was a highlight each week, not only to begin to develop some Biblical vocabulary in Chinese, but also to get to know personally this fine man of God. I treasured the friendship over the years.

The director of the language school was Jesse Moncrief, an American Baptist missionary, who, in addition to his task of teaching at the university, was given the task of directing the training program. He ran a tight ship. Before we recessed for the summer holidays, we had ten tests. Most of these were oral, requiring us to recite the Lord's prayer by memory, to sight read new material, and to read nonsense syllables. Each test successfully passed brought great satisfaction, but, as with almost any other subject, the more we learned, the less we knew. We were in a tunnel with no lights, and the darkness deepened the farther we went in.

In earlier years when China was not going through such turmoil, students in language study had frequent lectures on a variety of subjects. The school was just being reestablished in 1947, and it was difficult to find the people equipped to present special programs. We had a few lectures about minority groups and about Buddhism.

Language school was not all work. Every Tuesday afternoon we went to various homes, most of them on the campus, for afternoon tea and cookies. We played volleyball together, and some of us joined together to form basketball teams to play against make-up groups of Chinese students. A tennis court was in front of the language school building, and John Simpson and I had many fiercely-fought tennis matches. I never seemed to win, but John graciously put up with me as his partner in doubles matches with Chinese friends. These various activities helped us to develop a deep camaraderie with fellow language students, and a sense of "belonging" with Chinese students on the Huaxiba campus.

As we got more deeply into language study, Chinese and missionary friends gave us Chinese names. These were usually transliterations of our first or last names, or maybe a combination of both. My name, for example, was Ke Jaofu. The "Ke" was the sound of the first syllable of Covell, and Jaofu sounded very much like Ralph. The "Jaofu" characters did more than match the sound of my first name; they also had a good meaning—"abundant blessing."

Beginning our Ministries

We did not wait until we went inland to Xichang to begin our ministries. Very shortly, all of us, except the mothers with babies, were involved in speaking here and there in English, a very valuable commodity then (and now) in Chinese society. Within two weeks of our arrival in Chengdu, I had a very busy weekend. Friday evening I spoke to a student group on campus. The students were more interested in English than they were in the Christian faith, but I enjoyed the opportunity to meet them.

One Sunday evening I gave a message to a Christian fellowship group at Sichuan University, a government-run institution. A missionary with the China Inland Mission, Frank Harris from New Zealand, was my interpreter. He corrected my theology here and there in the course of his interpretation, but we had a fine time working together. This marked the beginning of a long friendship with Frank and, eventually, with his family. We were both single and shared much in common. This was my first exposure to a British-type evangelicalism—fully as committed as its American counterpart, but less hung up on many matters. A common way he had of pulling my leg was to ask periodically, "Are you still pre-millennial today?" It was another step in helping me become more of a "world Christian," a term not in use in those days.

One Saturday evening in early summer, I spoke to an Anglican boys' service at their large church facility. This was not the informal service I had counted on, and I found myself wearing a black robe with white trimming. The evening was hot and humid, and very shortly I was soaking wet. I never did find out how to get my handkerchief out of my inside pants pocket without some contorted moves. Despite problems with these unaccustomed church vestments, I appreciated deeply the worshipful solemnity of the entire service.

Many of our group had regular English Bible classes, and they established close relationships with those who attended, not only students on campus, but professional people like bankers and medical doctors. Several of these made commitments to follow Christ. Dan Carr was adept with the accordion and used it in services at the leprosarium, the tuberculosis hospital, in Bible classes, and church services, and in street evangelistic services, working with local missionaries who had good command of Chinese.

Ruth Laube, later to be my wife, who arrived in Chengdu in late 1948, had regular Friday evening Bible classes at Sichuan University. She preferred to spend more time with individual women students who had shown a particular interest in following Christ. She helped Sophia, a Christian student nurse, plan weekly children's meetings for the pediatric ward of the campus hospital. Margaret Sen, a graduate of Huaxiba, had been teaching on campus for over two years and was in need of nurture to grow in her Christian life.

Our group, with all its differences, was a mission team, and we were determined to develop close spiritual relationships with one another. Each night we had a short mission prayer meeting, and on Friday evenings we took turns in leading a Bible study. If language lessons were under control, we frequently went to the campus-wide English prayer meeting on Wednesday evening. We attended the campus church services every Sunday afternoon as a group, and each of us, along with the rest of the missionaries, took our turns in speaking at these gatherings. We often were fed up with some speakers who spent more time on psychology and sociology, while only tipping their hats to the "stories of Jesus."

As our grasp of Chinese improved, we attended Chinese church services. Most frequently I went to the CIM church across town. For a long time it was frustrating, the only intelligible phrase being "Amen." Gradually certain repetitive phrases, like "in Jesus name" and "God's glory" became more familiar. What a thrill eventually to be able to understand half a sermon. It would have been easy, particularly after a heavy week of language study, to settle for "bedside Baptist" church, but this was not the path to effective language learning.

Decisions, Decisions

Being a missionary is a bureaucratic business. Decisions, big and little, take up an immense amount of time. Hardly a letter came from Chicago headquarters that did not raise an issue, usually financial, about the churches supporting us. "First Baptist has dropped some of your support. What other church might take up some of this slack?" "Your personal gift money has been exceeded. How do you wish this money to be used in your work?" "The Maranatha class wants to take on the field project. Please send them a fuller description of your plans."

From our end we created headaches for the wonderful staff in Chicago with our nickel and dime requests. "What happened to the magazine I ordered six months ago?" "Tell my supporters not to send out any more packages of rice." "Pay my tithe to the following ten people." "Send five dollars as Christmas gifts to the thirteen people listed below."

Each of us had a network of friends, relatives, and churches with whom we exchanged a steady flow of letters. We had matters for them to care for, and they had requests for us—pictures, a letter for a special occasion, a testimony for a young people's group, a soundscriber recording to play to the Jane Adams missionary group. We did not mind this—beneath all of the hoopla was a volume of prayer support. Living in the midst of China's chaos, we knew this was indispensable.

Decisions faced some of us individually. In the spring of 1947 Ray Buker wrote that Calvin Zhao and David Adeney of China's InterVarsity had contacted him. Since I had worked during my last year of seminary as a part-time staff worker with IVCF in Philadelphia, they wanted me to help in student work in China. Because my heart was set on Nosu work, it did not take me long to decline. For the next six months Ray kept probing to see if I did not really think that China's colleges were of more strategic importance than illiterate minority peoples in China's mountains. I never yielded to him on this point, even as I recognized the weight of his logic.

Fred Jarvis of the Scandinavian Alliance Mission (SAM) was beating a loud drum for the SAM, CIM, and CBFMS to be the founding board of a "Wheaton in China," to be located in Xian, one of China's ancient capitals. This, he claimed, would offset the liberalism of other Christian institutions, such as the one where we were studying the language. We discussed this proposal in a business meeting or two, authorized Dan Carr to sit in on a meeting in Lanzhou when he went to the Tibetan butter festival, and decided, even as our board did, that we "might be interested." We were not, however, about to divert into this work any of our people who were headed to Nosuland. Any teachers would have to come out with a sense of calling to teach. Ultimately, the project was abandoned as a good dream for the wrong time. China was coming apart at the seams, and one of the first places abandoned by the missionary force was Xian.

We spent too much time haggling over matters related to personality clashes and role differences. Lee Lovegren felt this most strongly. As senior missionary in our group, he was not tied down to language study. He travelled here and there and was faced with making decisions on many matters. Often he had no time to go through our Baptist democratic procedures to make decisions. He understood the people and culture better than we did.

For our part we felt that his decisions were too personal and not straight-forward enough—too much like the way the Chinese did it! He had had a rigid Christian upbringing, and his "sense of rightness" rubbed some of us in the wrong way. Dan, trying to get the language and keep up with the complicated treasurer's books, had to finish some accounts on Sunday. This, in Lee's views, was breaking the sabbath. As a senior missionary, he was tempted to think his experience had taught him the best way to do things.

Money was at the center of many disputes. Lovegren and the Moncriefs had travelled up the Yangtze River together by steamer. As was the usual custom, Lee paid for some things and Jesse Moncrief for others. Eventually, when accounts had to be settled, there were conflicting claims: the money used represented widely different exchange rates. What was really owed in U.S. currency? As a mission, we tried, with only partial success, to keep out of this financial tangle, but we wasted a lot of ink, paper, and breath trying to mediate it.

Lee was generous to a fault. We feared this was about to lead him to offer half of our proposed field to the Swedish Baptists, rather than to invite any of their missionaries to work cooperatively with us. The board squelched this idea quickly, if indeed it had ever been an option.

If Lee had been as impetuous as we young missionaries, our field conference might have disintegrated. Fortunately, he took our guff in good style, changed when we seemed to have a point (or the votes), and never complained about us in letters to Chicago. He assumed, probably correctly, that we would mature with more experience. He was always the gentleman. He wondered in one letter to Buker how he might fulfill his legitimate and necessary role as senior missionary and keep peace in the family.

We were all helped to resolve disputes by a wise, mature foreign secretary. He was closer to some of the missionaries than to others, but he had no favorites. Some of our folk wrote to him as Dr.

Buker, others as Ray, and others as "ol' boy." He wrote to us frankly, calling one person "sassy," but he was fair and impartial. He wrote constantly to us, even when needing to travel to Africa, Europe, or Latin America. His letters always carried a personal touch, a sign that he cared for us. He was disciplined, a person of high principle. We knew he would challenge us on every issue, but that he would stand behind us on reasonable decisions. He kidded us constantly on our radical "Baptist individualism," which was at the root of most of our differences.

Life in Chengdu taught us to hate the institutionalism that went hand-in-glove with missionary bureaucracy. Chengdu was crowded with missionaries, far more than we would have expected for a "mission field," but most of these were bogged down in running institutions—schools, hospitals, homes of mercy. We never doubted the need for any of these—we only feared that they had lost their original, vibrant Christian witness and that they siphoned people away from evangelism and church planting. The Christian population of Chengdu was disproportionately small when compared to the number of missionaries, and a strong evangelistic impact was lacking.

The Storm Clouds Deepen

The civil war stalemated during the middle years of 1947 while we were in Chengdu, but the sense of crisis was everywhere apparent. In April and May, many missionaries of the Scandinavian Alliance Mission (now TEAM) and some from the English Baptist Missionary Society and the Mennonites beat a hasty retreat from Shensi, fleeing Communist forces. If we had given much thought to this, we would have been frustrated. Even as we beat our heads day and night to learn Chinese and go farther inland, here were many missionaries of our own age preparing to return home and give China up as a lost cause.

Theoretically, there was no need to flee from the Communists. Chou En-lai, a leading Communist spokesman, stated that missionaries were welcome in Communist controlled areas. He affirmed that the Communists were not offended by missionary beliefs, but if they had used feudalistic exploitation to acquire land illegally, they must return it.[3]

The situation was not helped by unwise statements made by so-called Christian politicians in America. In a mid-summer address at Buffalo to the Third World Convention of Churches of Christ, Walter Judd, formerly a medical missionary to China who later served as Republican Congressman from Minnesota, blamed the United States for abandoning China and urged Christian churches to embark on a "world missionary conquest." His apparent rationale was that missionaries, by befriending people and helping them raise their standard of living, would enable Americans to "maintain (their) standard of living."[4]

Chengdu was not as much a transportation hub as Chungking and some other cities, and we did not feel the national crisis in the same intense way as these other centers. But the national scene impacted us very directly in causing price spirals. In May the price of rice rose overnight from fourteen Chinese dollars to thirty-three thousand for one *dow*. Within a short time, it escalated to seventy thousand and then eighty thousand. Unable to buy at this price, people tried to steal the rice or take it by force. This led to violent riots with the police out in force trying to quell the disturbance. We were told not to travel on the streets after dark. Some sources alleged that the riots were directly caused by Communist provocation. No one could prove this, but there was further suppression of all liberally-minded political agitators, and martial law was imposed. Few, however, questioned that such wild price fluctuations in this most basic commodity came from the financial instability created by corruption in the nationalist government and by the civil war. Student riots continued in Shanghai, Nanking and Beijing over many sensitive issues, including the precipitous rise of prices for basic commodities.

Interpreters of China

Writing home to friends and relatives, none of us said much in substance about the national and local crises that swirled about us. This was deliberate. We had been warned about mail censorship, or at least the threat of it and, rightly or wrongly, we were careful. We understood the neurotic attitude of the Kuomintang-run government and saw no reason to jeopardize our stay in China. This hardly meant that we did not know what was going on, or that we did not have some strong opinions about it. We were on site in China, and even astute observers at home could not fathom what was happening. I once remarked to Buker about "the corrupt carrying on of the civil war," to which he replied, "What shall we do—allow Russia to take over?" That was hardly the question.

Even though we did not comment on sensitive political matters, we did not hesitate to give our opinions on religious, cultural, or social issues. Many of us had the opportunity to visit the Dujiang Yan Dam, some twenty-five miles northwest of the city, and to marvel at this 2,000-year old engineering feat which provided for the irrigation of millions of acres of land in the Sichuan basin. For us and many who read our letters at home, it was a new idea that China had this kind of scientific expertise so early in its history.

We loved Chinese food, admired the Chinese sense of beauty, and wished that our often-fragmented American families might emulate some of the qualities found in Chinese families. The Chinese sense of history was awe-inspiring—almost any subject under discussion seemed to have its roots five thousand years earlier. The friendliness and generosity of the Chinese endeared them to us. We found it hard to outdo them in politeness and grace. Their sense of filial piety, while subject to misuse in the ancestral rites, was something we wished that we Americans possessed.

Where we had difficulty in sorting out our own attitudes or in interpreting them to others was with the religious life of the Chinese. The Old Testament particularly, but also the New Testament, condemned the worship of false gods, and Chinese life seemed to be filled with false gods and many superstitious practices. Our knee-jerk reaction was revulsion. Like Paul in Athens our spirits were stirred within us, but, unlike Paul, we had a hard time to see anything positive.

In homes we saw the kitchen gods and the god of wealth. In temples, among other supernatural beings, we saw the god of thunder, *Guan Yin* (the goddess of mercy), the god of hell, numerous bodhisattvas or saviours, and innumerable images of the Buddha. China quickly became "the land of graven images." (Jeremiah 50:38)

Our minds told us that this ought not to be in modern China. We had learned from other missionaries that the intellectual revolt in the 1920s and 1930s in China had caused a great reduction in traditional religious life. Whereas several years previous, there had been over two hundred temples in Chengdu, now the number had been drastically reduced: fifty had disappeared completely, seventy had ceased all religious rites, seventy more were used only occasionally and only ten or fifteen had much worship. But despite this decline and the tendency of students and intellectuals to doubt and be skeptical, the pervading religiosity hung over China like a heavy cloud.

All of us wrote about one tragic event on campus. The two-year old daughter of one of the university professors fell into a swift flowing compound stream, and, rather than rescue her, the onlookers, convinced that the accident was the work of an evil spirit, did absolutely nothing. They feared that the spirit would be angry at being deprived of its victim, and would then seek another victim from the rescuer's household. Some had another explanation: to rescue the girl would produce an imbalance between the *yang* (positive) and the *yin* (negative) in that specific environment.

Sickness was usually blamed on evil spirits, and we often saw family members try to exorcise these by using charms, burning paper money, clanging cymbals, and beating drums. More stringent measures might be needed. We knew of one young girl, whose father pinched her severely on the arm and throat until she bled. This, the family believed, would cause the evil spirit to leave.

Equally important were measures to protect against attack by evil spirits. Parents often put round metal bands around the necks and ankles of their children to keep malignant spirits away. Another effective measure was to shave the heads of children, leaving only a tuft of hair braided with a red ribbon. If the child were in danger, a good spirit would be able to grab hold of the child and whisk it away.

Chinese life and beliefs were so different from ours that everything was new and strange. We often allowed our theological convictions to turn into a spirit of condemnation. We did not really empathize, that process where we tried to understand why people did certain things. We found it difficult to believe that the Chinese really had these convictions—somehow it was all a trick of the devil to mislead them. George Cole, who arrived with a later group of our missionaries, spoke for all of us when he commented in a prayer letter: "Christians at home have no vision of the sin and degradation of China."

Over the years we have not doubted our basic convictions—that there is one God and that we may know Him only through Jesus Christ. We need great skill, wisdom, and the help of God's spirit, however, to keep this theological verity from being heard by the Chinese as one more statement of Western superiority. "Everything you say and do implies that you are better than we—so also must it be as you preach about God and Jesus Christ."

We were adept in quoting Acts 4:12. Seldom did we ponder, however, that those early missionaries were never in the position of prestige, power, and wealth that we enjoyed in China. They spoke from a position of weakness and knew God's power. Their statements had far more impact than our bold, often aggressive, assertions of Jesus' superiority.

As a part of our cultural immersion, we went to a huge temple to view the ordination of Buddhist acolytes. The press of the crowd of viewers was so great that the chief priest arranged personally to lead us into the inner sanctuary. As he did so, we men formed a line to hold the crowd back, while the women went in first. In the confusion, I was shut out. Someone told me to go to another small door, and eventually I made it, not without nearly precipitating a riot from others who wanted to get a better view.

The ceremony was a reflection of severe Buddhist discipline. About sixty acolytes, dressed in yellow and blue gowns, were led in and made to kneel on pillows. They clasped their hands over their hearts and repeated the prayer formula, *O mani pad mi hum*. Other priests participating in the ceremony took nine pieces of burning incense and placed them in three rows on the shaven heads of the initiates. A priest ministered to the needs of each one, rubbing his temple and giving him oranges to eat to keep his mind off the excruciating pain. The faces of the initiates were immobile, not showing any outward signs of pain, but they could not keep tears from falling.

Ray Buker questioned us closely on what we reported of our observations. Did the Buddhist priests use a Sanskrit-related Indian language in the service? Did they circumambulate (walk around) the altar as the ceremony was in progress? His ever-active probing forced us to observe and interpret, not merely watch.

Some of the things that had shocked us initially in Shanghai were still not settled. What to do with beggars? We knew that many were professional—that children were deliberately sent out in rags to beg; that some poured red ink on imaginary wounds to elicit pity. But how do you distinguish these from the many who really were desperately needy and barely surviving on China's economic roller coaster?

The "beggar" problem was of one piece with the poverty we saw everywhere. We were not accustomed to the many filthy, squatter-type homes, the ragged clothes, the back-breaking labor of coolies, and the malnourished children. It did not help to contrast all of this with our easy, opulent lives and the fine homes in which we lived. This tension wrenched at our consciences for all of our China years, and we never resolved it satisfactorily. What would Jesus have done?

Dottie Benson ran into this problem in a particularly poignant way. When she was waiting in a ricksha outside a Chengdu city gate, a poor man approached her carrying his small baby daughter, very poorly clad and covered with sores. He held the baby out to Dottie and asked her, *Yao bu yao*? (Do you want her?) Thinking that he meant "Do you want to hold her,"? Dorothy replied *Yao*. Immediately the man ran back into the house, dressed her in the best clothes he could find, quickly returned, and thrust her at Dorothy. Only then did she realize that this father, already burdened with the care of many older children, was *giving* the baby to her with the hope that this would guarantee her future with the rich foreigner.

If we ourselves had come recently from poor homes in America, we would not have noticed things like the variety of varmints that were a part of daily life in our homes—the rats, bedbugs, cockroaches, tarantulas, lice, fleas, lizards, bats, snakes, and many others. When real news became scarce in the grinding humdrum of language study, we filled our prayer letters with such tales.

We all had problems with local customs. One evening we went to an elaborate banquet given in our honor by several important local officials. Dan was hungry and sat down immediately at one of the tables, not noticing that he did so right by two of the dignitaries who were shoving and pushing one another gently. Later he learned, much to his embarrassment, that while they were going through the traditional custom of determining who was to sit in the seat of honor, he had himself accidentally sat in it.

Our senior missionaries, Lee and Ida Lovegren, and a host of other friends, Chinese and American, tried to help us in our adjustments, our attitudes, and the ways we interpreted China to others. During these early days in Chengdu, we met Gladys Aylward, an independent single English missionary, whose very life epitomized what we were not. Defying all bureaucratic odds, she had come to China from England when no mission board would accept her, had led a simple, sacrificing life of love and compassion in war-torn north China, and was now helping as best she could in some of the Methodist work in Chengdu. Later to be enshrined in the book, *The Small Woman*, and the movie, "Inn of Sixth Happiness," Gladys identified very closely with the Chinese in attitude and living style and had learned to empathize, even where she did not understand or agree with them. This was a hard lesson for us impatient, young American missionaries to learn.

Plans Proceed for Xichang

While we were hard at language study, plans were being firmed up for our later ministry in Nosuland. I continued to work on the booklet I was writing for the mission society by occasional periods of intense research at the library right down the street. Once Dr. James Broomhall, who was to head up the CIM party going into Xikang, came through Chengdu and we had extensive conversations with him. An official in Chengdu was a Nosu, and this gave us some limited opportunity to learn a few things about the country and the people.

Of most importance was the trip that Lee Lovegren and John Simpson took into the Jianchang Valley of Xikang. Gone from May 18 until early July 1947, they travelled through the countryside where we would go and tried to line up housing, as well as make personal contacts to facilitate all we hoped to do. Lovegren had been vacationing at the family cabin on Mt. Emei, and Simpson took a "fast" (guaranteed to make it in one day) bus to Leshan to meet him. Like most of these back-country vehicles, this bus used gasoline mixed with alcohol and tied its gas tank up high for a gravity feed directly into the carburetor.

Travel in this part of China made their hair stand on end. The trip to Fulin was no exception with roads out, bridges down, a badly overloaded truck with no brakes going in neutral down precipitous roads, and an army escort to protect from Nosu tribespeople who lived on robbing travellers. Delayed in Fulin for two weeks by washed out roads, they were finally able to continue on to Xichang by walking and by ricksha. After some time in Xichang where they lived with friends at the Border Service Department of the Church of Christ in China, they walked five more days to Huili, later to be the southernmost station for our mission work.

Ida Lovegren, meanwhile, was organizing an evangelistic trek through the same territory. She was teamed up with a seminary student named Niu and Hu Kaixiang, a woman evangelist with whom she had worked previously when she and her husband lived for eight years (1925-33) in Leshan. They proceeded at a leisurely pace toward Xichang, taking the first day by ricksha, the next ten by sedan chair and the final two by ricksha. This was a cold trip with two passes above ten thousand feet and most of the cities well over a mile high.

The purpose of this trip was to preach the Gospel. Basically the team of three did some street preaching, handed out tracts, studied the Bible with small groups, and visited in homes. Unfortunately, most of the tracts we used in these days had been translated from American tracts and were hardly suited to the Chinese environment. But it was the Gospel, we rather naively thought, and God will surely not allow it "to return void" (Isaiah 55:11). However, merely to give out the Gospel is hardly to communicate it, a hard lesson that all of us learned better as the years passed. Fortunately, the Chinese considered it almost a crime to destroy any paper with something written on it, so these tracts lasted longer than they would have in America and probably accomplished more than we thought.

Escaping the Heat at White Deer Summit

To have a mission doctor put us at one disadvantage. If he recommended anything, we had to listen. We did not really think that the daily heat, averaging about ninety to ninety-five, was going to bother us through the summer months. We would just stay in Chengdu and "carry on as usual." To which Dr. Fisher said a very firm "No!" The Lovegrens had already decided that they would spend the summer at Mt. Emei. The rest of us arranged for space in two large cabins at Behludin (White Deer Summit), a six thousand-foot high vacation site frequented by expatriates wanting to *bi shu*, escape the heat. We had no idea what an adventure it would be!

Under ordinary conditions this was a two day trip, about normal for forty-five miles. An unusual series of hard rains made it a nightmare. Unpaved roads and paths became quagmires, rivers overflowed their banks, and bridges were scattered along the riverside like tinker toy sets. We would have done better to wait, for the two days stretched into nine.

Our patience was stretched to the breaking point. The summer cabins we were to occupy were barren, and we had to take everything with us—some furniture, kitchen utensils, bedding, and food staples. We and our *dongxi* (convenient Chinese word for "things") travelled on bikes, larger, more substantial country rickshas, and sedans or *huagan*, borne by two men, that carried one person. The latter were reserved for women or children, and the men and Chinese helpers alternated in biking and being carried in the rickshas. The Garrisons, Bensons, Dan Carr, and I comprised the first group. Lucy Carr, still ill with typhus, came later with Irene Simpson and her husband John, only recently returned from the trip to Xikang.

We made the usual first day's portion of the trip, arriving at the Canadian mission compound at Penxian at 10 p.m., thoroughly soaked from the driving rain. Continued rain delayed us here the next day, and we bought what we could to eat on the street. This was largely fruit and *mian*, a type of noodle—the word *mein* in our English phrase chow mein. Unbelievable for the Sichuan "rice basin," we could not get rice because of the recent riots.

The next day brought us to the small city of Haiozi, where, along with other groups of missionaries heading to the hills, we were put up in the Canadian church. We were only two or three miles from our destination, but a swollen river separated us from it. We were to be here for a long five days, with nothing to do but read and hope the rain would stop and the river would go down. We survived on canned UNRRA supplies that we were carrying with us. Eating on the street was fine, but our gang of foreigners attracted crowds like flies, never the most pleasant experience. We held a make-shift Sunday worship service and were challenged by a solid, Biblical message by one of our fellow travellers, a young Anglican missionary.

One night was particularly miserable, since a sudden squall forced the rain right through the roof above where we had placed our beds. We finally were able to travel on Monday, although not without difficulty. Many local Chinese thought the river god was angry, and they did not wish to help us until the bridge was fully repaired. We finally got some coolies to help us ford the river. I regretted many times that I had brought along my dog from Chengdu and had to care for him as well.

We men led the way over the rock-covered river bottom with water up to our waist, and with baggage either on our shoulders or backs. The women were carried across the stream by several men assigned to each *huagan*, and, in some instances, on the back of the coolies. I dropped my heavy briefcase in the river, and barely managed to retrieve it before it floated away. One coolie with a particularly clumsy load fell and nearly drowned. Dan Carr fell under his heavy trunk, ruining all of its contents and hurting his bad knee so much that he had to stay off it for the rest of the summer. At one point we had to cross in single file high above the river on logs that had been roped together to make a temporary bridge.

Dan had had his troubles—a severe case of dysentery at Haiozi, a fall off the porch at Penxian to hurt his knee, the tumble in the river, and the soaking of the contents of his trunk. Despite it all, he was out in front of us all singing in his booming voice:

> Got any rivers you think are uncrossable?
> Got any mountains you can't tunnel through?

God specializes in things thought impossible
And He can do what no other power can do!

Once across the river, we found the remainder of the trip relatively easy. The incline was steep, particularly the last stretch called the Devil's Staircase, when we went straight up about eight hundred feet. Because Dan was having trouble with his leg, he and his carriers stopped halfway up this last hill. That night he slept in a Buddhist temple where religious activities seldom cease. Sleep was interrupted constantly by priests moving here and there among thirty or forty idols, burning incense, chanting prayers, ringing bells, and pounding gongs.

Once we were here, we agreed that the hard trip was worth it. The climate was cool and pleasant—no toss-and-turn nights such as we felt on the hot Chengdu plain. The view was spectacular with the plain on one side, and range after range of peaks, stretching up higher and higher in the northwest, until, in the far distance, we saw the famed Tibetan snow mountains. At least three of these towered majestically over twenty thousand feet. We understood how our Chinese friends looked at these and other peaks and called them sacred.

We continued our language study, but at a much more relaxed pace, usually with teachers coming to the cabins and giving individual instruction. We partied on many evenings and experienced much more togetherness than we had down in the city.

The sense of community extended to our times of worship. The Anglicans had a "quiet day" during which they prayed specifically for revival, and members from all the mission groups gladly joined with them. We took turns preaching and found much benefit from our varying insights into Biblical truth. We held a joint communion service on our last evening on the mountain. This was the first time many of us had used a common cup in celebrating the Lord's supper, and it gave us a new sense of what it meant for us to be one in faith as we unitedly confessed Christ as Lord.

In this relaxed mountain atmosphere, we caught up on long-neglected reading. Some of it was light bedtime stuff, but I tried to get through portions of Kenneth Latourette's seven-volume work on the *History of the Expansion of Christianity*. Our foreign secretary required all of us to have Latourette's set and to read from it regularly. I had ordered a spate of magazines, and some of these were already coming in the language study days. Included in these were *World Report, Theology Today, Watchman Examiner, His, Reader's Digest, The International Journal of American Linguistics, Bibliotheca Sacra,* and *Christian Century.*

The only thing to mar these weeks at Behludin was a strike by our servants. A member of another mission struck a servant, because she thought he was cheating her. This servant was head of a small labor union of servants, and so he ordered a work stoppage, while a union meeting was called. All of us were represented at this gathering. Once everything had been aired out, life was restored to normal once again.

Toward the end of the summer, several of our folk visited Tian Tai, a nearby mountain temple area, and were both awed and appalled by the degree of superstition which they found. These were valuable learning experiences, but, unfortunately, did not allow the time necessary for us as visitors to develop any close relationships with those who came to worship. In fact, it was a common missionary practice to pass out Christian tracts when visiting temples. We did not ask how we might feel if Buddhists would visit Christian churches and distribute their own literature. We seemed to feel that our possession of the truth could substitute for politeness, common human dignity, and mutual respect.

Getting back to Chengdu was far easier than our trip up the mountain. Garrison, Simpson, and I biked the forty-five mile trip, and despite the excessively hot day and what seemed to be my chronic problem with poor tires, we reached the outskirts of Chengdu by 2 p.m. I learned a valuable lesson on this trip—hot tea in one of Sichuan's proverbial road-side tea shops quenched my thirst far better than a cold drink could have done.

The big event of the summer in Chengdu during our absence had been "the flood." This had happened, in fact, while Lucille Carr and the Simpsons were still there. The river that was only about fifty yards from our home had risen quickly, and in no time at all five feet of water flooded our basement and floated most of our belongings. Many Chinese folk living in flimsy homes nearby sought refuge from the flood in our home. For many there was no place to flee, and several hundred Chinese lost their lives. Our belongings were not badly damaged, but the labels had been washed off of many canned goods. We were never certain when we opened a can what exactly we would be eating.

Back to the Plain

The fall months after our respite from the summer's heat repeated many activities of the previous spring. Language study continued at a more intensive pace, as did our involvement in ministry, social, and recreational activities. Chengdu was now a familiar city, and we felt very much at home.

Some things were different, particularly the holidays unique to the fall. First, came Halloween when everyone on campus came together for a time of fun. An unexpected treat was a supply of Coca Cola brought through some missionary connections with the US Army post shop. Five American army families were living in Chengdu, and since this area was regarded as a "hardship post," they had special access to whatever they wanted. They lived a "plush" life, and we would have done better to keep our distance. The Chinese have always found it difficult to separate among the different kinds of foreigners—they all "looked alike" to them. A fellow missionary, Olin Stockwell, from whom we had rented our Huaxiba home, was later to be arrested and detained by the new government for his alleged connection with the US Army in Chengdu and with the US consulate in Chungking. To the Communists all expatriates were of one piece with American imperialism. We did it in different ways, but our motives were all the same!

We had too many Europeans and Britishers in our language school for Thanksgiving to have much meaning. And so a few of us Americans had a private meal one evening. It was unthinkable for us to miss this holiday altogether. China does not have many turkeys, so a noticeable difference in the meal was that goose was served as a substitute for the main course.

An important event of the fall months was a week-long series of evangelistic meetings held in Chengdu by Bob Pierce of Youth for Christ. Dan Carr was pressed into service with his accordion to accompany Pierce in his solo numbers. If numbers and apparent decisions indicate "success," then these meetings were successful. Chinese life is very drab and dull, and any colorful event, such as represented by flashy American-type evangelism, is bound to draw. And, as for decisions, the Chinese are never so impolite as to disappoint the expectations of a person who has travelled so far to speak to them. How utterly bad it would be to cause him to lose face in front of so many people, and so, if he wanted a decision, a decision he would get! It took a long time for us as missionaries, particularly in working individually with Chinese in our English Bible classes, to learn this hard fact of reality.

We were disappointed that an American evangelist could come this distance to preach to a Chinese audience and apparently not give any thought to gearing his message to the needs of the local context. Closing your eyes, you could imagine the very same message being preached in Chicago. And the illustrations, usually indicating how God had met some pressing need of the speaker, promoted a "gospel of success" mentality in the hearers. Andrew Gih, a noted Chinese Christian evangelist, was Pierce's interpreter, and we wished that he would take off on his own and preach the message without any interference from Pierce. The results, hopefully, would have been more long lasting.

Dawson Trotman, Director of the Navigators, visited Chengdu in the fall with a low-key ministry to arrange for training Chinese leaders. Dan Carr, while a chaplain at the Naval Air Force base in Jacksonville, Florida, had helped to form a Navigator center there and had a great time relating to Dawson during this week of meetings.

As the time drew nearer for us to go to Xichang, many mission business matters had to be settled. In early October, consequently, we took an entire day for Bible study and prayer in preparation for making some critical decisions. Since our first business meeting right before sailing from San Francisco in December 1946, most of our discussion on future plans had been done informally and in the midst of many other urgent activities.

Top on our agenda was whether or not we should use the "black market." By now we could get $40,000 for one American dollar, but should we? Whatever decision we made would hit us and the mission where it hurt most—in our pocket books. Even more serious, the rampant inflation ruined the people's livelihood. As the government printed more and more money—the best way for corrupt officials to make a quick buck—food prices spiralled out of sight, riots increased, and chaos reigned.

We had discussed this matter endlessly in Chengdu and during our time at Behludin. It became the focal point of our praying. We tried to avoid a firm decision by much rationalizing—government corruption thrives on the black market; the American embassy itself is now using a compromise "open market ($25,000 to 1), not as high as $40,000 but not as hopeless as the official rate of $12,000; the Associated Mission Treasurer's office in Shanghai, responsible for the business affairs of many mission agencies, recommends that we use the high rate; other groups wonder why we are so stupid as not to use the high rate.

Some of the missionaries wondered how anything declared illegal by the government could be ethical for a Christian. Others countered that the illegality was a fiction—the government itself was breaking the law by promoting the black market. If the government used this "illegal" market, why should we be suckers and not use it? When all the dust of our rhetoric settled, the best we could do was to agree to disagree and continue on our ambivalent path.

Ruth Mayo, located in our east China field, wrote to Dan Nelson, who was handling accounts for both of our China fields, and requested that her salary be exchanged at the official rate. Nelson was exchanging everything at the black market rate; so when he complied with Ruth's wish, money was left over in her account. Writing to Lovegren he asked facetiously: "What shall we do with this balance? Shall we throw a feast for the Lutheran World Federation? Shall we send it to you or shall we put it into the west China account?"

Reinforcements Arrive

The *Marine Lynx* was still making regular trips carrying missionaries across the Pacific. Among the new arrivals in Shanghai on October 12, 1947 were George and Hannah Cole, Elwyn and Becky Stafford, and Flora Mae Duncan. Despite all the necessary things for them to do during their transit in Shanghai, George and Elwyn had the unique opportunity to go with Glenn Wagner and Harry Liu of the Pocket Testament League to hold three meetings for Chinese soldiers and to assist in the distribution of Gospel portions to them. Not infrequently, four to seven thousand soldiers attended these gatherings. One of the officers, Colonel Yang of the 25th Division, urged his troops to carry the Bible with them everywhere. He pointed out that "our American friends helped us in the war against Japan and now are coming to give us the good news of salvation in Christ."

Friends at the Lutheran Action Center on Hart Road, where the new group was staying, arranged for their transportation inland on CNAC, and after a "milk plane" route that took them through Nanking and Hankow on their way to an overnight stay with the CIM in Chungking, they arrived in Chengdu on November 16. We were and we were not ready for them. Effective November 1, we had rented a house just outside the west end of the campus and opposite a large radio tower. Located on a nice compound and with more-than-usual room space, it was different from most Chinese homes in that it had hot and cold water, and, most important, a flush toilet.

Still lacking was the furniture needed for each room. This was the first order of business when the new missionaries arrived. Some one had to set up a new household and make all the arrangements necessary for daily buying, cooking, cleaning, and caring for the children. Being single, I was a convenient one to move into the new house and take over its management. Language-wise I was up to this task, and it was pleasant to move in with the two couples, of which the husbands had been my classmates at Eastern Baptist Seminary. Not quite as convenient or appropriate were such close arrangements with a single woman, particularly when the Chinese assumed that we were more than just two single people.

The weather was beginning to get cool—often down to the mid-50s—in our bedrooms, and I was glad that this home was warmer than where I had lived at Huaxiba #51. But I and the others were beginning to agree with the Chinese that it was easier, warmer, and healthier to wear more clothes than it was to try to heat these large, spacious homes. At times this was cumbersome. We often studied in our rooms with gloves on, but when it came to typing, we had to find a fire to get some life into our fingers. The language school was no better than our homes, with only minimal heat in three of the classrooms.

Ida Lovegren had weekly—and sometimes daily—worship with the servants in #51, but who would do this in the home opposite the radio tower? By default, the job was mine. Even though I could not do it right away, I prepared hard and long for a short Christmas worship service in the home. I used slides as a kind of a crutch, commenting on each one as it showed a different aspect of the Christmas story. I was gratified, and even surprised, that I was able to depart from my well-memorized text and ad-lib a bit. All of us joined in a few Christmas songs, and then we offered a short prayer thanking God for His unspeakable gift. We had prepared a simple tree, as well as presents, for all of the servants and their families.

From this time until my departure in February 1948 for Xichang, I held weekly services for the servants in which all the others joined. This meant an extra commitment of seven to eight hours a week to get together very simple lessons on the prodigal son, the call of Matthew to follow Christ, and other stories. I learned quickly that with the Chinese nothing works as well or holds attention better than a good story. Even if my vocabulary was inadequate and my grammar and syntax a bit wretched, the main point got across.

Christmas was a big day for us and for Chinese Christians. The holiday celebration began with a 4:30 p.m. Christmas eve program for all of the foreign community. Our time with the servants began Christmas day, followed by a time of opening presents for those in our home. At noon we all went over to house #51 and opened presents for those at both homes, following which we had a traditional Christmas meal. Late in the afternoon we went over to the Stockwells who had a Christmas program, complete with slides and the Christmas story, for all the servants of the several homes in the large compound. In the evening we held a Christmas party which included a birthday party for me.

As big as Christmas was, it meant only one day's vacation from our grind of language study. Not so with Chinese New Year, when all of China closed down for two weeks. This was our big vacation time, and for most of us it was a welcome rest from the frenzied activities of the fall months. Dan took this opportunity to go to the Tibetan Butter Festival at Kumbum Lamasery, just beyond the northwest China city of Lanzhou. This lamasery, headquarters of the Panchen Lama, had over four thousand priests and was considered second only to the one in Lhasa. The festival gained its name from the fact that all the buddha images, as well as the dragons, flowers, castles, and scenes from hell and paradise were carved from butter.

Dan had wanted me to go along with him on this risky venture which took him over Communist-held territory in north China, but my departure for Xichang was getting near, and I did not want to get stuck in Lanzhou if murky weather should move in and delay our return. Dan returned from this trip enthused with the possibility of reaching Tibetans in the Muli Kingdom, not too far from our proposed area of work among the Nosu in Xikang.

Our lives continued in normal humdrum fashion as we moved into 1948, but China's blood pressure was going up. Communist victories were escalating in the north and in central China. Despite all that Chou En-lai had already said about Communist attitudes toward missionaries, there was little doubt about anti-foreign attitudes in the Communist-controlled areas. We heard that three missionaries had been killed in the area north of Hankow and that others were being evacuated. Some feared that this heavy activity around Hankow presaged new Communist thrusts to the south and west and that Sichuan province would soon be in danger. Rather naively, we felt that Sichuan, the richest agricultural province in China, might be taken, but that the Communist forces would really find nothing of interest to them about Xichang.

Despite it all, we continued to plan for the future. Jeanne Simpson was born to the Simpsons on January 25, 1948, remembered as the first snow-day in Chengdu in over four years. Our CBFMS office in Wheaton arranged for a Swedish Baptist single woman, Esther Nelson, formerly a missionary with the ABFMS in China, to work with us in Xikang. Jim Broomhall came through Chengdu once again and informed me about a Nosu man studying at Huaxiba who might be able to help me with the language and culture.

Even more important, the long-anticipated time for several of us to leave Chengdu had arrived. Ida had not returned to Chengdu after leaving the previous spring for Xichang. She joined Lee in the summer at Mt. Omei, but then returned in mid-September to Xikang on another evangelistic trip. Lee had come to Chengdu in mid-summer, but had returned to Xikang in the fall to continue in preparations for the rest of us. The Bensons had hoped to leave for Ganxian, Jiangxi in early winter, but Dorothy's pregnancy delayed her until late summer 1948. Bennie went down for a period to help Ruth Mayo with some problems in the orphanage and returned in late May, about two weeks before his daughter's birth.

Sunday, February 27, I flew to Chungking as the transit stop for the journey on to Xichang. In typical Chinese fashion, the servants at the home sent me off with firecrackers and hoopla. George Cole and Elwyn Stafford escorted me to the air office, where I caught the loaded truck taking passengers to the airfield. This was my first air flight, and I did not like it. Bucket seats were lined up on both sides of the DC-3, facing center, and were not comfortable. The field in Chungking was like a small postage stamp in the middle of the Yangtze River. I held on for dear life to keep us from landing in the water!

I had a nice room in the China Inland Mission home with a little porch facing out on the Chungking hills. I had hoped to be here at most for only a few days, but my stay dragged on until late March. The reasons for this were many. When I went in on Monday, the 28th, to confirm my flight for the next Friday, I was told that the plane would not fly because of poor weather. This apparently was better than telling me they were overbooked. I learned later that the plane did make the trip.

From that time on, the weather was indeed bad. Day in and day out, the delays mounted. Often I was at the airport at 5 a.m., waited all day with waning hope, only to be told to be back at the same time the next morning. Once we actually took off, flew for nearly two hours, but then could not land because of a dense cloud cover. Radio contact was not so precise that the crew wanted to risk flying into the very high peaks surrounding the city. I soon became a joke at the CIM home. The servants there never changed my bed. Several times the missionaries thought that I had left for sure, only to welcome me back once again for supper in the evening.

In the midst of all this frustration, the chance came for me to give up on the uncertain CNAC flights and go in to Xichang by the chartered Lutheran plane, the *St. Paul*. This Lutheran-sponsored DC-3 was the work horse of the missionary enterprise. Licensed in December 1947 to operate in China, it had flown missionaries of every denomination to every province in China. In addition to its human cargo, it had carried freight, UNRRA relief supplies, hospital equipment, pumps, and jeeps. As the crisis worsened in China, the United States consulate asked the Lutherans to use the *St. Paul* to evacuate missionaries from north China. The price tag of two hundred dollars for each flying hour was not prohibitive in view of its carrying capacity of five thousand pounds. Particularly was this true of the formidable terrain where our group wished to go.

The James Broomhall family had also been waiting in Chungking to go into Xichang. When the St. Paul showed up for them rather unexpectedly one noon, Jim and Janet very graciously invited me to go along with them. Quickly I organized my few belongings, hurried to the airport and climbed aboard. When we taxied to the end of the runway, the tower informed the pilot that, because of an extra fifty gallons of gas, the plane was three hundred pounds too heavy for takeoff. It did not take me long to figure out that the difference was me and my baggage! Nor did I question the need for a properly loaded plane on that mid-river, short airfield with mountains looming up ahead. I really felt disappointed, however, to stand at the end of the runway and watch them leave without me.

I used my month's time—or what was left of it after running back and forth between the home and the airfield—as best I could. Sundays gave me the opportunity to go to a Chinese church and practice my listening ability. I talked with the manager at China Air Transport about flying our freight from Chengdu to Xichang if the *St. Paul* were not able to help us. In the mornings I studied Chinese on my own, and in the afternoon two students from the nearby Chungking Theological Seminary came to teach me.

Patience had its reward. On March 23, just four days after the time when we had not been able to land in Xichang, Chungking was finally left behind for good, and I made my first entrance into the charm and harsh reality of China's badlands, the home of the Independent Nosu.

Endnotes

1. Stockwell, F. Olin *With God in Red China*. New York: Harper, 1953, pp. 23-24.
2. Wilson, Jesse R. "Statement Concerning Dryden L. Phelps, Missionary to West China of the ABFMS."
3. New York Times, February 23, 1947., 29:5.
4. New York Times, August 18, 1947. 15:2.

5

The Independent Nosu–A Hidden People

Recent News

Beginning in mid-1944 and extending into 1946, news stories filtered out of China about American airmen who were lost as they flew supplies over the hump from India to the base of the 20th Air Force in Chengdu. Now and again, planes apparently disappeared in the wild region near the top of the world known as "Lolo-land." Not only were there high mountains, such as 24,900-foot Minya Gonka and 21,900-foot Mount Grosvenor, but also dense jungle and wild tribespeople, who both took slaves and killed people who came into their territory unprotected by guarantors.

In October, 1944, an Air-Ground and Aid Section was organized by the 14th Air Force in Kunming to seek and help any American personnel who might be lost in Independent Nosuland. This expedition, which originated in Lugu, where the Carrs and we later lived, to the north of Xichang and proceeded into the high mountains about Yuehsi, Tianba, and Fulin, found the remains of a B-29, stripped of most of its guns. Further investigation to the southeast was made impossible by broken bridges and dense, impenetrable jungle.

Later in the fall of 1946, similar rumors of slave-held American airmen resulted in another expedition into this remote area. Several weeks of search yielded no results, and the investigative team left the area. Nothing in the few remaining years of the Kuomintang rule over China or in the subsequent period of the Marxist government lent any credence to American personnel being held captive by the Nosu. However, when we returned to Xichang in 1986, we found a film troupe of about fifty people taking scenes for a Hong Kong-sponsored movie in Chinese, entitled *Tian Pusa*, (Heavenly God). Named after an ancient belief of the Nosu people, this film told the story of an American airman lost in a flight over the hump, enslaved by the Nosu who forced him to marry a local girl, and ultimately rescued by the Liberation Army of the Communists. It was a great plot, but probably more fiction than fact.

Interest Over The Years

This was not the first time that the Nosu had been in the news. From early in the rule of ancient Chinese dynasties, the tribespeople living in this area had been a problem. Always fiercely independent, they had resisted any control from various dynasties, and, at times, had forged alliances with other groups more to the south to oppose the government. One notable example had been the involvement of the Lolo-type tribal groups in the Nan Zhao kingdom near Dali in what is now Yunnan Province. This upstart kingdom was defeated by Kublai Khan, the Mongol ruler of China in the thirteenth century. The Nan Zhao White Pagoda, directly opposite our compound in Xichang, was built in memory of this early tribal kingdom.

The Lolo peoples have also attracted the interest of people from outside China, whether adventuresome explorers or missionaries. One of the first of these was Marco Polo who, during the time when he investigated the wonders of China, visited Chengdu and Yaan and travelled down the Jianchang Valley, along the Anning River, to Xichang, then called Ningyuanfu.

The first European to go through this area was E. Colborne Baber, British resident at Chungking, who in 1878 travelled to the Jianchang valley to discover its trading potential. British merchants, with hearts set on profitable trading, had tried to penetrate China's inland markets from the west through Burma and Yunnan. One of their young interpreters, Augustus Margary, helping in this endeavor, was ambushed and killed on February 21, 1875. The Chefoo Convention between Great Britain and China settled this dispute, elevated Chungking to the rank of a treaty port, and opened up all of southwest China to exploration and trade.[1]

Baber's route took him across the Dadu River at Fulin, from where he proceeded through Yuexi to Lugu, Xichang, and Huili. He crossed the Yangtze River to the south, where it is known as the Jinsha Jiang (River of Golden Sand), and then on the east side of the river returned through Yibin to his starting point at Chungking.[2]

In the same year, George Nicoll and Charles Leaman of the China Inland Mission also reached Xichang and Huili, and, crossing the River of Golden Sand, proceeded back to Chungking, where Leaman had the opportunity to compare notes with Baber on the Nosu language and culture. In days of poor transportation and inaccurate maps, these two early journeys were amazing accomplishments.[3]

After these two trail blazers had pioneered the path into this wild country, others began to follow. Alexander Hosie, also stationed in Chungking with the British consular service, made three expeditions through this area in 1882, 1883, and 1884. He noted that Jianchangfu was the best-known local name for the present Xichang, although Ningyuanfu was also used. Vicomte D'Ollone, a major in the French army, engaged in a mission to interior China from 1906-09, and a portion of his trip took him into Independent Nosuland. Like those who went before and after him, he agreed that the Lolos were a "black branch of the Caucasian race" with features that showed their kinship with the Indo-European race.[4] He noted Roman Catholic missionary work in Weilizhu, Dechang, and Xichang, even as he pointed out that the priests in all of these areas were experiencing great difficulty. An almost constant state of tension and strife between the Chinese and Lolos created a disturbed and impoverished society.

Samuel Pollard, a missionary among the Miao in southwest China, was the first European to travel into this country by crossing the River of Golden Sand (Yangtze River) from Yunnan Province in the south. His trip into Babuland, the name given to the territory by local Chinese (the word "babu" may be a corruption of two Chinese words meaning "hill climbers"), was done secretly and lasted for about six weeks. He noted that the Nosu, almost singly among the tribes in southwest China, had "withstood the advance of

Buddhism."[5] In general, this was an uneventful venture, although on one occasion he had to foil the plot of several Nosu leaders to kidnap him and his companion.[6]

When visitors were not careful to arrange for guarantors or protectors (baotou), the usual procedure for outsiders going into the area, the results were tragic. In 1909 Donald Burk, a Britisher, accompanied by about a dozen men, was killed by the Nosu at the small village of Lianchanao. Those with him were taken captive and eventually sold as slaves. This incident led to difficulties between the British and Chinese and sparked escalating hostilities over the next few years between the Chinese and Lolos.[7]

Origins of the Lolo

The Nosu or Lolo are but one of fifty-five minority groups in China. In China there are fifty-six national groups, but the Han—the usual name given to the Chinese majority—are the dominant group. The Han are undoubtedly an amalgamation of many other ethnic groups in China and have constituted the majority since the time of the Qin dynasty (221-207 B.C.)[8] In most cases, each of the larger minority groups includes many sub-groups. Thus the Gaoshan minority of Taiwan is a general name like our "Indian." At least ten sub-groups are subsumed under this general name, such as Atayal, Amis, Bunnun, Sediq, and Paiwan. The same may be said of the term Yizu or Lolo, which include different groups and sub-groups. The specific people we are interested in live in Sichuan Province north of the River of Golden Sand in and on both sides of the Jianchang valley. This area includes both the Great Cool Mountains and the Small Cool Mountains.

The precise origin of the Nosu or Lolo and the route by which they arrived in their present home in the Daliangshan and Xiaoliangshan (The Great and Small Cool Mountains) are unknown. Ethnologically, they belong to the Tibeto-Burman family. Within this very broad classification there is a general Lolo division, under which are the following sub-divisions: Lolo, Moso, Lisu, Woli, Lohei, and Aka. Most of the latter minorities live in Yunnan rather than in Xikang. The Lolo group of tribes may have been known as early as the Zhou Dynasty (1122-221 B.C.) under the name of Lu, but the term Lolo appears first in records of the Yuan or Mongol Dynasty.

By the time of the Ming dynasty, eleven Lolo tribes were listed in the records of the Nan Zhao as being subject to this Shan state located in Dali, the present Yunnan Province.[9] When the Mongols under Genghis Khan defeated this kingdom, many Lolo tribes remained unconquered, and tribal kings were in power as late as 1727, when the Manchus suppressed the tribes with great savagery and put the kings to death. Thousands of Nosu at that time refused to acknowledge defeat and withdrew across the River of Golden Sand to the Daliangshan area. The remainder accepted Chinese rule but have been slow to adopt Chinese culture. One cannot understand the historic hatred between the Chinese and the Nosu without taking this background into account. These people, like the American Indian, feel that possession is ownership and resent the massacres of their ancestors and expulsion from their own land. When they raid Chinese villages to take slaves, livestock, and other provisions, they are only taking their rightful "rent."

Although one traditional explanation has been that the Nosu originated in the Tibetan ranges farther to the west, the view now, as seen in various mainland China publications, is that they migrated from the Yunnan area south of the River of Golden Sand and have gradually occupied the area in southwestern Sichuan known as the Ning District (Ningsu). An interesting alternative to this view adds one extra step: they came from the area in Yunnan around Chuxiong, migrated to the Gansu region in the northeast, and then returned to the approximate site where they now live.[10]

The Nosu as We Found Them (1945-1951)[11]

The Independent Nosu

The Nosu in this area of some 300,000 square kilometers number about 750,000, slightly more than the Chinese population. They are called Independent Nosu, in that by contrast with the "dependent" Nosu south of the Yangtze River, they have stubbornly and militantly refused to be subjugated by Chinese authority or to be assimilated by Chinese culture. This does not mean that they do not speak

Chinese nor have many Chinese customs. The Chinese called them *shen yi* or unripe ones, while the dependent Nosu they referred to by the term *shu yi* or ripe ones.

Even many of the cities of the Jianchang Valley, where the less militant and more sinicized of the Independent Nosu live, were fortified with walls, and individual homes outside of the city walls looked like small fortresses. When we went even into the lower mountains, it was necessary to arrange for guarantors who would assure our safety from one place to the next. The day of kidnapping and selling people as slaves was not a thing of the past.

The simmering hostility, always present between the Chinese in the valley and the Nosu, frequently broke into open warfare. The issues were usually opium, rifles, and slaves. Chinese bands made quick raids into the mountains, often to wreak revenge for some Nosu offence. This usually included the taking of a few heads. Only a few days elapsed before the Nosu made a retaliatory raid on a Chinese village, with the same bloody consequences. During my first few days living in Lugu, I was horrified to see a man casually walking through the streets carrying on his back a basket filled with ten Nosu heads, still dripping blood.

Names

The name Nosu means a "black person" and refers to all the people, although its primary designation may originally have been to members of the pure-blooded ruling class. Frequently, the term Lolo has been used to designate these people. This name probably originated with the Chinese, who thought that the Nosu kept the souls of their parents in miniature baskets or hampers. The Chinese word for this basket is *lo-lo*. However, the connotations of the term were vile—roughly comparable to a derogatory expression like "nigger," "chink," or "wop." Even worse, when the term was written in Chinese, the dog radical was used. Because of these connotations and the smoldering hatred among the two groups of people, the Nosu reacted with resentment whenever the Chinese called them *lolo*.

However, there is a legitimate term *lolo* which is used by the people themselves. Their principal totem animal over the centuries has been the tiger and, in their language, the term lolo means tiger. They can even refer to themselves as the "tiger nationality." The men call themselves *lolo po* or *lopo*, and the women use *lolo ma* or *loma*.[12] The reason the people reject the term *lolo* is that the Chinese tend to use it in a derogatory sense.

Daily Life

The Nosu live in villages, often perched in precarious positions on the mountain sides. Many do not dwell in villages at all, but in dispersed, independent homes. The house of a family is always a unit by itself, but sometimes several houses are built side by side to form a hamlet. The house is built of wood supported by poles, walled with stamped earth and roofed with planks. Stones are placed in rows above the plank roof to prevent the house from being shaken by the wind. Around the house is a square enclosure surrounded by earthen walls, built higher than the house itself. In one corner of the enclosure may stand a watch tower, two or three stories high, in which the people place guns and weapons to protect the house from raids. The houses of the dependent Nosu reflect a semi-Chinese style with thatched or tiled roofs. The poor serfs live mainly in mud huts or hovels. Houses of strictly Nosu architecture have no windows. The lack of windows or anything resembling a chimney means that smoke from the open fires used for cooking is trapped in the house and produces chronic coughs, as well as ever-recurring eye ailments.

The Nosu have little in the way of utensils. They eat squatting around the hearth, using only their hands, or a crude wooden spoon to take the food from a communal dish. In some areas there are brightly-painted serving trays and individual bowls made of wood. Their ordinary food is very crude; the basic dish is a bread cake of buckwheat made of badly kneaded, unleavened dough and containing little or no salt. To this buckwheat cake is added rice, potatoes, boiled or roasted in the ashes, and sometimes meat, which they prefer when only half cooked. Wheat is sometimes used to make gruel. The people seldom eat vegetables, and no use is made of milk or butter, rather strange for a people owning great herds of cattle.

For special occasions the meal is more elaborate, containing much more meat and accompanied by an abundant supply of beer or wine.

The chief occupations of the Nosu are pastoral and agricultural. They have sheep, cattle, ponies, pigs, and various types of poultry. Nosu territory can never be economically independent of its neighbors, since no salt is found in the area. Other necessities, such as cloth, needles, firearms, and ammunition must be obtained by trading wool, wax insects,[13] sugar, coal, and opium. The mountains are rich in minerals and are a fertile source of revenue, much coveted by the Chinese. Corn, buckwheat, and oats are the staple foods for the Nosu. Besides these products, they raise wheat, rice, potatoes, beans, and turnips.

The Nosu men wear trousers, a vest buttoned at the side, and a mantle that is draped over their shoulders. The lower part of the leg is gripped by a narrow band wound around it, but the latter does not confine the wide trousers which always hang loose at the calf. They use the mantle for a blanket at night, either when reclining on the floor in their own homes or when crouching down to sleep on the streets of a Chinese village. Men like to wear a single earring in the left ear. On their heads are the conspicuous "horns," symbol of the unknown god.

Women wear a bodice with a high, close-fitting collar, which comes up to the chin, and a long skirt, pleated and adorned with flounces, which comes to the heels and swings with the rhythm of the wearers as they march along. Their shoulders are covered with a mantle. The head-dress varies for young girls, married women, mothers, nobles, or serfs, and fashions are different from clan to clan. Turbans are apparently reserved for the nobility. Both men and women go barefoot, but in winter they wear sandals of straw or short felt boots. This type of dress is not reserved for special occasions; the women are attired this way even as they weed their rice paddies, do other types of heavy work, and go to market.

Social Culture

The Independent Nosu were divided into two classes—the Black Nosu and White Nosu. The Blacks were the princes, lairds, land owners, and wealthy farmers. Racially, they were the pure blooded descendants of the early Nosu. The Whites were the serfs, the slaves, farm laborers, and freemen tenants, subject to control by the Blacks. Racially, they are an amalgamation of Chinese and many minority peoples, enslaved during the centuries and now freely intermarried. These White Bones lived near Chinese villages, were subject to Chinese authority, often adopted the Chinese style of dress, and frequently chose surnames from the Chinese "Book of Family Names." This class division was not confined to Independent Nosuland. It also existed among the Nosu farther south. And even within Independent Nosuland, notably in the Xichang area, there were both Black Bones and White Bones who had been subjugated by the Chinese.

The complexity of the divisions and ramifications of this caste system make it difficult to generalize. Within the White class there were three degrees of serfdom. The first degree was little removed from slavery, but those who passed into the third degree were practically freemen and could own property and have their own serfs.

This system was rightly called feudal. The lords or Blacks rented the land to the Whites. The Whites had to give a certain proportion of the produce of their land to their overlords. In times of warfare between clans, they had to give military aid. On special occasions of birth, marriage, or death it was obligatory to give tribute. It was not totally one-sided. The Blacks, on their part, pledged their power to protect their serfs or slaves in case of conflict with the serfs and slaves of another lord. The children of the Whites were born to be slaves and were the property of their fathers' overlords. The children of the Blacks did not need to learn any occupations, except hunting for recreation. Their daughters were trained to manage the household affairs and held a high position in the family.

The clan was the most important unit of the social organization. A clan was a group of blood-related families. Property was transmitted and descent reckoned through the male. A woman who married into the clan lived in the husband's locality. These clans occupied several consolidated villages or were interpenetrated by other clans, but clan solidarity was strictly maintained. Within the clan there was no fighting, and all disputes were settled amicably by the mediating efforts of the elders.

However, between clans there was much fighting. Frequently, they organized into parties against one another, usually the clans related by marriage. If there was fighting between these larger groups, the women connected with both by marriage sought to be reconcilers. If verbal means were insufficient, one went to the battlefield and prostrated herself naked on the ground between the warring groups. This resulted in peace, but the woman, ashamed of her conduct, committed suicide.

Apart from such convenient, temporary alliances, there was no over-all organization of these clans into one tribe with one central government. To this extent it is a mistake to refer to the Nosu "tribesmen." The clan was the basic unit, and there really was no tribe or tribes.

Within the clan the family was the fundamental unit. It was bilateral, and both parents were recognized. The nuclear family consisted of the parents and the unmarried children. The household unit also had the slaves of the family, who were considered property to be bought or sold at will.

Social Customs

Marriages were arranged by the parents and middlemen. Marriage between clan members was prohibited, but it was absolutely imperative to marry inside the class, i.e., Black or White, with violation punishable by death. The marriage of parallel cousins was forbidden—that is, marriage between a man and his mother's sister's children or his father's brother's children. Cross-cousin marriage between a man and his mother's brother's children or his father's sister's children was common. When parallel cousins met, they assumed a formal and decorous attitude to each other. Cross-cousins, on the other hand, were privileged to jest and take certain liberties when they met.

The marriage itself was a long process. After the initial payment of the dowry had been made, the friends of the bridegroom went to take the bride. She coyly resisted and caused her suitor's friends to be splashed with water, after which they were given wine to drink. Following this, she was escorted to the bridegroom's home, either by horse or piggy-back fashion.

On the wedding day, the elaborate ceremonies included the exchange of gifts and contests between parties of both families. The day following the ceremony, the bride went back to live for three to five years with her parents. During this period, she could have sexual relations with any of her former lovers, particularly male cross-cousins, or her husband. When she became pregnant, the husband was notified and built a house and welcomed her back to live with him. The first child might not be his, but he had to assume the role of father.

The Nosu were liberal in their divorce practices. If a man wished to leave his wife, he forfeited all claims to the money he had paid at marriage. If the woman desired to break the union, she returned the money plus heavy interest. Children were disposed of by mutual agreement.

Polygyny was practiced, but the husband had to have his wife's permission to take concubines. When the husband died, the wife was given to a brother or nephew. A young man might even marry his maternal grandmother, provided the grandfather was dead and the invitation came from the woman. In Nosu society marriage was thought of as a compact between groups rather than between individuals.

In common with other aboriginal peoples, the Nosu had elaborate ceremonies at the time of death. When a person died, cloth was used to wrap his arms against his sides, and his legs against the front of his body in a doubled-up position. The body was wrapped to two poles, which were used to carry the corpse. After a few days of chanting, lamentation, and feasting by the community, the dead person was taken to the funeral ground, where an animal was killed—a cow by the well-to-do, or a pig by the poor. The corpse was carried over the dead animal, after which it was taken to the cremation site.

The funeral grounds were sacred groves. These trees were not used for any other purpose than the cremation of the dead. An offering of wine was poured out, and then the light was put to the funeral pyre. If the body burned readily, it was taken as evidence that the deceased was a good person. If it was difficult to get the body to burn, this was taken as an evil omen. When the body was finally reduced to ashes, it was covered with dirt. The relatives and friends then returned to the home of the deceased, ate the flesh of the animal that was killed, and drank wine.

At one time it was thought that the choice between cremation and burial depended on whether the family was poor or rich. Yi writers now stress the fact that to cremate fits best with the ancient Nosu tradition. The Nosu, it is believed, are descendants of the tiger, and only by cremation is the soul freed to return to its original tiger state.[14]

Religious Life of the Nosu

The Nosu follow a popular folk religion with some traces of monotheism. The people believe in, worship, and fear spirits, both good and bad—those of their ancestors and others—and demons with unlimited supernatural power. All of life is interpreted in terms of these spirits who control all events, either for weal or woe.

Beneath this frenzy of belief and activity directed toward the spirit world, there is still a lingering belief in a "high god." The Nosu believe in a supreme creator spirit, known as the "sky god" or the "god of heaven." He is invisible and has no image. This high god has a son, who busies himself in the affairs of human beings and is called Gee Nyo.

The people also believe in a controlling evil spirit. Every person has a soul which lives on when the body dies. This soul, during a period of three years when it is becoming accustomed to life beyond the grave, is kept by the relatives in the form of an effigy of the deceased inside a small basket, which the Chinese call *lo-lo*. On certain anniversaries this figure is brought out, and the people recite special prayers. At the end of the third year, they throw the figure out and the soul is judged, after which it is sent to a heaven or hell.

One expression of the continuing belief in a high god is the Nosu concept of the *tian pusa* (Heavenly God). This is expressed by the tuft of hair that remains on the shaven head of many men, both young and old. This hair lock is termed the *tian pusa* and is considered so sacred that even the man's wife is not allowed to touch it. When the man wears a turban, he rolls a portion of it around this forelock of hair, and it projects like the horn of an animal. Often the end of the lock escapes in a little pack. The people recognize that it is the heavenly god who made them and continues to care for them. They profess to know nothing about this god, nor do they worship him in any way. In the Yuexi area, the local clan head, Lin Guangdian reported a specific name, A-pu-gga-sa, for the creator god.[15]

Elements of Daoism, shamanism, and fetishism are found among the Independent Nosu. Nosu sorcerers adore Lao Zi as the founder of their religion and the organizer of their scripture. His image is often found in their homes, and the names of Daoist gods worshipped in their ceremonies. This indigenous Chinese influence is all the more significant, when one recognizes that Buddhism has had no impact at all on the Independent Nosu.

Liu Yaohan, a well known Nosu author, has written an entire book suggesting that the ancient Yi culture is the origin of many basic Daoist beliefs. He argues, for example, that the yin and yang concept, so basic to Chinese thinking, originated with the *ci-xiong* duality found thousands of years ago among the Yi. He analyzes at great length the "ten month solar calendar" of the Yi and shows its influence upon Chinese life.[16]

The influence of shamanism is seen both by the significant position of the sorcerers and also by the emphasis placed on divination. All the sacred ceremonies, ritualistic sacrifices, exorcisms, oracles, divination, and sacramental formulas are in the hands of a sorcerer-priest known as the *bimo*. The name literally means "old man who understands moral and religious doctrines, teachings, and sacred books."[17] He is in charge of the religious life in each clan, and no religious ceremony would be complete without his presence and authority. All he does conforms to the formulas of the sacred books. He is the only master of the literature, and he fills the role of public writer or scribe for the nobles and princes and tutor for the small children. He encourages the nobles to know the national literature, of which the serfs and slaves are totally ignorant.

The most typical activity of the *bimo* is to cast out the demons which cause sickness. Many types of diseases, particularly malignant malaria, typhus, typhoid fever, tuberculosis, and skin ailments, are rife in Nosuland. These diseases are attributed to the evil influence of demons which dwell in people. Traditional herbal medicine is considered impotent to effect a cure.

It is here that the *bimo* is indispensable. First, he has the patient breathe on an egg, after which he seduces the demon to enter the egg where it assumes its proper shape and is recognized by the priest. The *bimo* then cuts open the egg and makes a careful examination. From this he can tell what kind of animal must be killed as an offering to the demon.

The *bimo* then makes a rough effigy of grass and rubs this up and down the body of the patient, repeating his sacred utterances as he does so. In this fashion the demon is compelled to leave the patient and enter into the straw man. Following this, the *bimo* leads in an elaborate ceremony by which the straw man is escorted into the open, and the demon is commanded to be off.

The *bimo* enters into every phase of Nosu life. When the crops are threatened by prolonged drought, he is called to pray for rain. In this ceremony a cow is killed. In the past before the men went into battle the same ritual was performed. The skin was hung up, and the warriors passed under it, after which they drank strong liquor mixed with the blood of the cow.

Another common type of ceremony is more sacrificial in nature and is conducted by the shaman or *suto*, whose chief credentials are that he is possessed by a demon or spirit. He comes to the crossroads near the sick person's dwelling, carrying a live chicken in his hand. Eventually he kills this and then goes into the house. Two images with three legs are placed on the road. One represents the demon of disease, the other represents a friendly spirit. The latter has a stick in his hand which he uses to chase the demon. The feathers of the hen are stuck on the demon to assure him he has attained his end—death has gained a victim.

Other religious figures are the *hsiang si*, almost always women, who act as fortune tellers and palmists. They are experts in giving details of the future.[18]

In common with beliefs of these traditional religionists worldwide, Nosu life was filled with taboos, incantations, black magic, and elevating to the status of gods the forces of nature, such as thunder, lightning, the wind, mountains, sun, and moon. Faced with these hard realities of Nosu life, Jim Broomhall often wrote to us about the difficulties of ministry where the kingdom of the power of darkness reigned.

When an important leader got sick or died, hundreds or even thousands of sheep and cattle were slaughtered to fulfill all the demands of the spirit world. This, along with the ravishing oppression of opium, kept the Nosu people in a never-ending cycle of poverty.

Nosu Writing

The Nosu language is a part of the Tibeto-Burman branch, which, in turn, is a part of the larger Indo-Chinese family. Like Chinese, it is monosyllabic and tonal. Scholars of the Yi language recognize at least six major dialect areas in Sichuan, Guizhou, and Yunnan provinces.

The Nosu writing system was probably both phonetic and ideographic in ancient times—that is, it expressed both a meaning, often in picture form, and a sound value. Similar to the Chinese character, the Nosu symbols represent an entire syllable and not just a single consonant or vowel. As suggested above, the writing was the property of the *bimo*. A priest's reputation rested on the number of written symbols he could read and write. Unfortunately, this led each priest to invent new symbols, the better to confuse a neighboring *bimo*. In the early post-war years, each *bimo* probably had an inventory of five to six thousand symbols.

Modern linguists are puzzled about the origin of this elaborate Yi writing system. "It is generally assumed that the original stimulus for the development of this system was a vague acquaintance with Chinese writing, although there are few recognizably Chinese elements in the system."[19]

Nosu characters are written with a piece of bamboo or wood and a crude type of ink made by mixing soot and water. The signs assume an extremely simple geometrical form—curves, right angles, and intersecting points. One way of writing the words is from top to bottom with the columns going from left to right. Another way of writing is to go horizontally from right to left.

Nosu books are of two sorts. *Bimos* living in the Daliangshan put their manuscripts in the form of a roll, while the dependent

Nosu have books that differ little from Chinese books. For those in the form of a roll, the characters are written on papers sewed at the back and wrapped in a cover of hemp cloth. The books are then rolled around a thin stick. No intervals exist between characters nor are there punctuation marks.

The manuscripts of the Independent Nosu represent Nosu thought. They are filled largely with religious sentiment and many magical incantations. From these manuscripts we may get a picture of the myths and legends of the people.

In common with other minority nationalities of southwest China, the Nosu have elaborate legends on the origin of the universe and of mankind. Some Nosu believe that they came from the calabash, and they give reverence to it as a symbol of fertility. Others of the Independent Nosu and some dependent Nosu near the city of Chuxiong in Yunnan believe that the heavenly god created the people out of the snow which he sent down to the earth. This type of belief, among people who live in areas where it may snow heavily, lends some support to Chinese scholars who assert that the people's religion originated from their tendency to personify the forces of nature.

Nearly all of the minority peoples have a legend of a flood. The usual account is that only one couple, male and female, survived, married, and produced children. The Nosu twist to this tradition is that only one person survived and went to the heavenly kingdom, where he took a female genie (*xiannu*) as his wife.

A prominent Nosu myth describes the way in which people attained independence from the heavenly god and became, as it were, the master of their own destiny.[20]

The manuscripts contain material which reinforces the belief that the major totem animal for the Nosu is the tiger. We have already noted that the name *lolo* means tiger. Pictures may be found in the ancient Nosu manuscripts showing a tiger moving the universe, setting it in motion and sustaining it. The Nosu call Mt. Emei, where some of them once lived, by the name *lomo shan* or "mother tiger mountain." At an earlier time in the history of the Nosu people, their priests wore a tiger skin. In some areas the Nosu put a drawing on the door of their homes which is pronounced *nie loma*. This is a type of ancestral tablet and means the "spirit of mother tiger."

Scholars have also taken this to indicate that early Nosu society was matriarchal.

In some mythical way the mother tiger was involved in the creation of mankind. One interesting Chinese expression tells how "tiger blood became water and gave birth to mankind." One of the reasons the people give for cremating the dead is that this will enable the person to return to his or her original tiger state. Some manuscript material relates how the Nosu believed in a kind of "tiger divination" which enabled them to obtain success in planting good crops, in hunting, in building homes, in marriage, and in warfare.

More recently, some Nosu writers, possibly hoping to cause the Chinese to have a more progressive view of their people, suggest that this primitive "tiger world view" was later conceptualized in a more abstract way by Lao Zi and Zhuang Zi to become the *dao* of Chinese philosophy.[21]

Many attempts have been made to give to the Nosu the message of Jesus Christ. To our knowledge, none of these has been successful. Would it be any different in the post-war years as missionaries from the Conservative Baptists, the Border Service Department of the Church of Christ in China, and the China Inland Mission made yet another attempt to breach this ancient stronghold?

Endnotes

1. Hosie, Alexander *Three Years in Western China. A Narrative of Three Journeys in Ssu-ch'uan, Kuei-chow, and Yunnan* London: George Philip and Son, 1890, xiii-xvii.
2. Broomhall, James *Hudson Taylor and China's Open Century* Book 6. pp. 179-183 (First draft). Also see Special Proceedings of the Royal Geographic Society, vol. 1, 1878.
3. Broomhall, James *Ibid.*, pp. 194-196.
4. D'Ollone, Vicomte *In Forbidden China. The D'ollone Mission 1906-09 China-Tibet-Mongolia* London: T. Fisher Unwin, 1912, p. 12.
5. Kendall, R. Elliott (ed.) *Eyes of the Earth. The Diary of Samuel Pollard* London: The Cargate Press, 1954, pp. 68-69.
6. Pollard, Samuel *Tight Corners in China*. London: Andrew Crombie, pp. 59-70. For further information on the Lolos in the writings of early missionaries working in southwest China see Samuel Pollard *In Unknown China* Philadelphia: J.B.

Lippincott Co., 1921; Clarke, Samuel R. *Among the Tribes in South-West China* London: Morgan and Scott, Ltd.; Grist, W.A. *Samuel Pollard: Pioneer Missionary in China* Reprinted by Ch'eng Wen Publishing Company, Taipei, 1971, and Kendall, R. Elliott *Beyond the Clouds* London: Cargate Press.

7. Lin, Yueh-hua *The Lolo of Liang Shan* (Liangshan Yi Chia). New Haven: Hraf Press, 1961, p. 10.
8. See *Yizu Wenhua Yenjiu Wenji* (A Collection of Research on the Yi Culture) p. 35. Many Chinese writers on this subject quote a saying by Mao that the minority people need to be taken seriously since the Han people came from the minorities.
9. Several works discussing the origin and early history of the Lolo are: de Beauclair Inez *Tribal Cultures of Southwest China* Taipei: The Chinese Association for Folklore, 1972, pp. 3-39; Feng Han-yi and Shryock, J.K. "The Historical Origins of the Lolo," pp. 103-127; *An Introduction to the South-Western Peoples of China*, West China Union University Museum Guidebook Series No. 7, Chengdu, 1945; Selections from the *Weekly Bulletin of the China Information Committee*, Chongqing, China, September 22, 1941; *Yi Zu Wenhua Yenjiu Wenji* (A Collection of Research on the Yi Culture) Chuxiong Yi Minority Cultural Research Center of the Yunnan Academy of Social Sciences. Kunming: Yunnan People's Publishing Company, 1985, and Liu Yaohan *Zhongguo Wenming Yuantou Xintan Dao Jia Yu Yizu Hu Yuzhouguan* (A New Investigation into the Origins of Chinese Civilization, Daoism and the Tiger World View of the Yi Minority) Kunming: People's Publishing Company, 1985.
10. For this and other possibilities see *Yizu Wenhua Yenjiu Wenji* (Collection of Research on the Culture of the Yi Minority), pp. 26-41.
11. All of this material, except where otherwise noted, is taken from Covell, Ralph R. *The Challenge of Independent Nosuland* Chicago: Conservative Baptist Foreign Mission Society, 1947, 11 pp. The data in this material came from research in the libraries of the Royal Geographic Society in Shanghai and the West China Union University in Chengdu. It was supplemented by material from Dr. James Broomhall of the CIM and Dr. Levi Lovegren and John Simpson of CBFMS from their travels in Xikang during 1947.
12. *Yizu Wenhua Yenjiu Wenji*. p. 37.
13. The Jianchang valley, particularly the area around Dechang, is a famous breeding ground for the wax insects which grow on the *chongshu* (insect tree). When transported to the area about Leshan, known as the home of the wax tree (the Chinese term is *bailashu* or "white wax tree") and placed on the wax tree, a pound of insects can produce as much as five pounds of wax. It is used, along with animal and vegetable tallow, to make candles for light in homes. Since the use of kerosene oil in China, the demand for and value of this product has decreased. See Hosie, *Three Years in Western China*, Chapter 11 "Chinese Insect White Wax," pp. 189-201.
14. See material in *Yizu Wen Hua Yenjiu Wen Ji*.
15. Graham, David Crockett *Folk Religion in Southwest China* Washington, DC: Smithsonian Institute, 1961, p. 83.

16. See Liu Yaohan *Zhongguo Wenming Yuantou Xintan* (A New Investigation Into the Origin of Chinese Culture) Kunming: Yunnan People's Publishing House, 1985, preface and pp. 1-25.
17. Graham, *Folk Religion*, p. 78.
18. *Ibid.*, p. 79.
19. Comrie, Bernard (ed.,) *The World's Major Languages*. New York: Oxford University Press, 1987.
20. For more detail on myths and legends of the Yi people and of other minority nationalities see Zhu Yichu and Li Zixian (eds.) *Saosu Minzu Minjian Wenxueh Gailun* (An Outline of People's Culture Among the Minority Nationalities) Kunming: Yunnan People's Publishing Co., 1983. See particularly chapters 3 and 4.
21. This material on the "tiger world view" and its relationship to Daoism and ancient Chinese thought is found in Liu Yaohan *Zhongguo Wenmin Yuantou Xintan Daojia yu Yizu Hu Yuzhouguan* (A New Investigation of the Origins of Chinese Culture, Daoism and the Yi Zu Tiger World View) Kunming: Yunnan People's Publishing Press, 1985.

6

The Foundation of Living Stones

At Long Last

The flight from Chungking, with the billowing clouds dissipated during the last half hour, revealed dramatically the majestic splendor of the Great Cool Mountains. Rugged peaks in every direction towered up to 15,000 feet and seemed to point their sharp peaks right at our small DC-3. To the north, the incomparable Minya Gonka at 25,000 feet stood alone among these small hills!

If my mind were contemplating the beauty of God's world, my heart had a sense both of peace and expectation that I was nearing Xichang, the city that had been in our prayers and even dreams for over two years. Now, at last, we could settle down and get at the task before us.

Xichang in 1948 was a small city of about 35,000 people resting on the side of a sloping hill just above beautiful Qionghai Lake. A local tradition had it that the old city had been destroyed by an earthquake and rested at the bottom of this lake. Across the lake a huge mountain range, some peaks still covered with snow, rose almost out of the water. Slightly to the west the Jianchang Valley, with the Anning River at its center, made its meandering way among the high mountains on both sides. The first impact of this scenic combination of lakes, mountains, rivers, and valleys was to leave me breathless.

The city itself did not match the natural beauty. Most buildings were dirty, adobe structures. A few shops along one or two of the paved streets were built of a poor quality reinforced concrete. Most streets were narrow and dusty. A crumbling city wall remained on two sides of the city, and there was a noble south gate located right in the midst of a busy market area.

Most of the people were not dressed well; in fact they were poor, dirty, and ragged. Far too many (one estimate put the percentage at seventy-five percent of the total population) had huge external goiters which seemed almost to weigh them down.[1] Many were stunted in their growth, and had a dull, tired expression, probably induced by the opium in which as many as sixty percent were involved. On many streets, outnumbering the Han Chinese, were Nosu who had come to the city to buy and sell, and, if their business were done, to return the often-long distances to their mountain homes. If night were too close, they squatted down, pulled their black wool mantles up above their heads, and slept along the streets by the shops.

I learned quickly that Xichang's weather was superb, ranking along with Kunming as one of the best climates in China. As an old-time resident of sunny, Southern California, I rejoiced that for the first two weeks we enjoyed complete sunshine. In the middle of the day it was warm, but the mile-high altitude and low humidity make it easy to bear. Later we learned how the spring and early summer monsoon rains cooled off things quickly, and in the winter it was cold, although with no snow.

While Lovegren was still in China during the war years, he had hoped to obtain the property used by the Northern Baptists during their years in Xichang. Located on a lovely hill overlooking the city, it was now being used by the Chinese military. Therefore, on one of his earlier trips to Xichang, Lee rented a large piece of property just up the street from this old Baptist compound. It was near the top of the hill on which Xichang was located and across from the famous Nanzhao White Temple. The compound—the name usually given to the large living area surrounded by a six-foot wall topped with sharp glass—consisted of a square of houses, placed around a central courtyard. Each of the houses was strictly Chinese in style and built of adobe, with walls about three feet thick. The floors were either dirt or a crude cement. The roofs were made of tile, and there were no ceilings. On the north, west, and south sides of the compound, the houses were arranged in units of three rooms, each with about 150 square feet of living space. The east side, along the street, was more adequate with five such rooms. To the outside of this inner courtyard of homes was an outer section containing similar type homes for the domestic help, and also a large garden, one acre in size.

We had several options in our use of this property. We could tear down the old, decrepit homes and build new ones. This would be more comfortable, but it would be time-consuming, costly, and separate us even further from the people whom we sought to reach. We could repair these buildings, until they were exactly as we wished them. This hardly seemed practical. We steered a middle course, putting in warmer, wood floors where necessary, and thoroughly whitewashing the interior walls.

Eventually, when it seemed wise to buy this property (the proper term was to "lease in perpetuity"), we made other repairs. This included screening to keep varmints out, putting up a matted ceiling to cut down both the air and dust that came through the roof, and putting in translucent oil paper to substitute for glass in the window space. Electricity, running water, and indoor toilets (even the non-flush type) were not available to us. We tried to be careful what we ate at night, for it always was precarious to search in the dark courtyard for one of the outhouses.

Buying the property was not as simple as it sounds—certainly it was far more than finding the needed money. This came to $2500, although the registration and taxes meant adding another twenty-five percent to this amount. The real problem was that in the back of the compound there were several graves belonging to nearby Buddhist temples. To move any grave in China was a serious matter, and the severity of the issue was intensified by the fact that it was sacred temple land, originally selected because it was a propitious site. The owner could get nowhere with the temple officials until he hired a geomancer, an expert in discerning the "wind and water," to select another "favorable" spot. And, even when this new holy site had been found, we had to wait for the right holy day for the removal of the graves.

When I first arrived, I lived in one of the rooms along the west wall of the compound. The Lovegrens had one of the these rooms, and the middle room was shared by us as a living and dining area. These living quarters were hardly more than one star, but they were comfortable, reasonably clean, warm and adequate, even for our large party still studying in Chengdu.

In all of the hustle and bustle of getting settled, we forgot that Good Friday and Easter were right on top of us. This is not difficult in a society where there is no hype for these holidays. For the first service, the Lovegrens and I went to the small church operated by the Border Service Department of the Church of Christ in China. This meeting, as well as the one two days later early Easter morning on the Xichang city wall, were milestone experiences. First, they were both conducted totally in Chinese, and I understood nearly everything! This was very important, since I had been in China for nearly eighteen months and wondered if I would get over being deaf and dumb. Second, when we sat on the city wall and watched the sun's rays begin to lighten the high surrounding mountain peaks where the Nosu lived in their many small villages, it symbolized that the more active phase of our ministry in China was beginning.

The Lovegrens and I were not the only foreigners living in Xichang. Working in cooperation with the Border Service Department were two English Baptist couples, Bill and Win Upchurch and Ernest and Edna Madge. Veterans of many years of missionary service in north China, they were very helpful to me and the other neophytes in our group. Jim and Janet Broomhall and their family, as well as Ruth Dix, Joan Wales, and Floyd Larsen of the China Inland Mission, also had a home in the city, but their main efforts were to establish an outpost at Zhaojue in the heart of Independent Nosu country.

I was not one to waste time and started formal language study the Monday following Easter. My teacher, a local young woman named Liu who had been recommended to me, was a very talkative person, and this made it easy not only to cover what was required in the language material, but also to engage in free conversation and pick up many new expressions.

If only I could spend seven or eight hours daily in this kind of Chinese study, I thought, I would make great progress. Alas, it was not to be, at least in the immediate future. On Tuesday morning, totally unexpected, a telegram arrived that the Lutheran mission plane, the *St. Paul*, was beginning the next day on Wednesday to fly our Chengdu missionaries to Xichang. I immediately stopped my study and rushed to a truck company on one of the small, downtown city streets. Lee Lovegren was not in Xichang at this time, and much of the talking and decision-making rested with me and my poor conversational Chinese. We managed with some help to make a down payment on the rental of a truck for use on Wednesday and started to return to our home. Just at that moment, Mr. Niu, a man helping us in business matters, rushed up to say that another telegram had arrived stating the plane would arrive in fifteen minutes.

By the time we hurried back to the trucking company and headed to the airport, the plane was already circling the city. When we finally reached the airport, it had landed, left its first load of freight, and was poised at the end of the dirt runway for its return trip. Over the next three days, the *St. Paul* made a total of six flights to Xichang, and we made ten trips in our rented truck to carry the freight, baggage, and people. On each of these days I was at the field at about 5:30 a.m. and stayed until late in the evening.

This was not a cheap operation, but in the long run it was less costly than trying to bring in the freight and people over the often washed-out road that ran from Chengdu through Leshan and Mianning to Xichang. On that road the missionaries could easily have lost everything to marauding bands of robbers. We recouped some of our expenses by arranging for fifty-seven local people to fly in the empty plane back to Chengdu or Chungking. Fortunately for us, the local CNAC flights were so irregular that authorities did not object to our competing in this fashion.

Flying in this part of the world is never safe. Normal factors of mountains and weather, plus lack of regular plane maintenance, were compounded by urgency. The *St. Paul*'s pilots saw their priority as evacuating missionaries and other expatriates from Communist-dominated north China. They could snatch time only here and there from their busy schedule to help us. To save time and work in all their flights, they usually came straight in for landings without circling around. We held our breath once on a freight load when the brakes gave way, and the pilot had to turn the plane into a ground loop to keep it from going through a wall at the end of the field. When the day's last flight was into Xichang, the crew, an American and two Germans, stayed with us and enthralled us with thrilling tales of escapades in evacuating people from Communist areas.

Each family brought in with them one or two servants. It was hard enough to find capable help in Chengdu, a rather large metropolitan area. We feared that this kind of domestic help would not be available at all in Xichang, and so arrangements were made for the families to bring in these helpers who had already learned how to handle household responsibilities, as well as to care for their children. This did not mean that the missionary mothers abandoned their child-caring responsibilities. It enabled them to find time for language study and freed them to assist in some phase of the ministry.

With these many flights of the *St. Paul*, all of our original group—Carrs, Garrisons, Lovegrens, and Simpsons—were now in the Jianchang Valley. Dorothy Benson was awaiting the birth of their first baby in Chengdu, while her husband, Bennie, and Ruth Mayo were beginning their work at the orphanage in south China. The Coles and Staffords, along with Flora Mae Duncan, continued language study in Chengdu. Still another party made up of Bill and Flossie Simons and Ruth Laube would arrive in China in the fall of 1948.

Even though living in separate homes on this large compound was better than being packed like sardines in #51 Huaxiba, it was far from ideal. While getting settled, everyone had to eat together the common meals cooked on open, charcoal burners. Tensions arose from many sources: our "fish bowl" existence, children fighting, servants reporting to their respective families what other families were eating or spending for food, Chinese friends seeking out one family rather than another, one family hitting the books hard, and another one "loafing." We learned now, if we had not earlier, that our halos were tarnished. They brightened up when we were farther apart from each other.

Life went on much as it had in Chengdu. Most of what we needed to eat could be purchased in the markets daily, and what we could not obtain was supplemented by the extra things we had brought from America: jellos, cake mixes, chocolate candy, etc. Milk was a problem. Whole powdered milk was expensive, and cows, unlike in Chengdu, were not available. The solution for the Simpsons was to get a herd of goats—three mothers and three kids. The initial cost of purchase was not high, and the only ongoing expense was to pay the herder and provide a little daily feed. The goats were not used to being milked and, at first, gave only two cups a day. Impressed with the results the Simpsons were getting, the Carrs also invested in a herd of goats. Linn Ann and Jeannie Simpson and Danny Carr were delighted to have the kids to play with. They also enjoyed getting rides on the Broomhalls' mule which grazed daily in a part of our outside courtyard.

Into The Work

The Lovegrens had rented a small chapel on a city street and began regular evangelistic meetings and worship services in December 1947. By now this facility was too small and soon after my arrival, with Lovegren still absent, it fell to my lot to rent a new and larger one. At first, as it might be expected where foreigners are thought to be both gullible and rich, the price was ridiculously high. Through patient bargaining, willingness to wait, and some degree of humor and cajoling, the rental price finally came down to what we had budgeted. We had only partial use of the property until July 15, but from the beginning there was room for a preaching hall, seating about seventy-five people when crowded, and living quarters for our two Chinese workers—Miss Hu Kaixiang and Mr. Niu. Later we added rooms for Bible classes, children's meetings, Sunday school, and inquirers' rooms.

Mr. Niu, who had travelled with Ida and Miss Hu from Chengdu, epitomized problems we had with outside colleagues. Even though he had received one year of theological training at the West China Union University Seminary in Chengdu, he was not too committed. The Lovegrens wanted him to run a book table at the chapel, but his heart was never in it. More than anything, he was appalled at the economic and social conditions of this desolate area. One day he abruptly resigned and returned to Chengdu, ostensibly to continue his seminary education.

With this expanded meeting place, there was something for all of us to do any evening whenever we had any left-over energy from day-long language study. Dan was particularly effective in playing a small Estey organ for evangelistic meetings or for our quieter worship services. Lucille and Ida, sometimes aided by Irene, helped in a variety of children's meetings with flannelboard, cut outs, and other types of visual aids. Ida aided in women's meetings, as did Lucille, but liked to spend as much time as possible in the many small rural villages surrounding the city. She and Miss Hu worked well together in this type of outreach.

Whenever possible, John, Dan, and I got our feet wet by speaking at prayer meetings or in Sunday worship services. Lee took much of the responsibility here, and he and Miss Hu took the lead in the many evangelistic meetings. My first "real sermon" was given on April 25, 1947. The Chinese love stories, and so I chose the passage about the paralytic who was brought to Jesus by his four friends (Mark 2:1-11). I am not sure who was more nervous, Miss Liu, my teacher, or me. If I did badly, no Chinese would blame me; the responsibility, after all, was hers! It would be a bad loss of face, and she might even feel it necessary to quit teaching me. No matter how dull this twenty-five minute message, it was "correct" enough, much to her relief. She did remark that it was "rather heavy."

Undoubtedly, in this context, the message was too long and too heavy on rather logical-type propositions. I did not utilize the story to its fullest potential, but was too interested in finding "truths." Shortly after this, I gave two short devotionals on the ten commandments to the servants working in our several homes. Once in these spring months I gave a prayer-meeting talk on our Attitude in Prayer (Hebrews 10:19-21). Again, these messages were too "heady" and not sufficiently motivational. Even when our language was under better control, we had to work hard to appeal both to the Chinese heart and mind.

Preparing messages was not easy for any of us. I usually fixed an idea in my mind, and then spent at least three hours, even for a very short message, on getting it into acceptable Chinese. The next step was to memorize it cold. Rehearsing it once or twice helped to get into the natural flow of the language. The Chinese are not the most expressive people and, lacking feedback, I often wondered whether any progress was being made at all.

The more serious inquirers, who had a developing interest in the Gospel, got far more from their listening when Miss Hu preached. At the end of the service, we usually got involved in helping to answer questions. I remember one night in particular. Miss Hu had just completed a moving sermon on the crucifixion on Jesus. As the meeting dispersed, numerous listeners gathered around the large poster which she had used to illustrate her message. She was busy talking to some of the women; so it became my happy privilege to answer questions others had and to explain more of the details of the poster. Included in the group were two Nosu who had wandered in out of curiosity. For most of the hearers, if they had any knowledge at all of Jesus, he was a Frenchman somehow associated with the Catholic church, whose presence in this area extended back to the mid-1850s.

Lack of personnel led to the ridiculous. As I became more literate in the reading of Chinese characters, it became my lot to help lead the congregational singing. No one was more unequipped for such a task. I could hold a tune after a fashion, but the haphazard waving of my arms was of no value to anyone. Fortunately, it was largely a matter of singing over endlessly a short chorus that we wanted to fix in the hearts of some of these first hearers of the Gospel message.

Beginning in late May, I started an English Bible class for some of the young people. Xichang was in a very isolated area of China, educational opportunities were not equal to those in other parts of China, and the demand for learning English was not high. Yet there were eight to ten students who came regularly, and we taught them portions of the four gospels.

Many people came to our meetings out of curiosity. Regular attendants began to gain a basic understanding of the Christian faith. The stumbling blocks were many, ranging from the very practical difficulty of giving up opium to religious issues such as eating meat or reincarnation. By mid-summer there were at least four believers. The most notable was Miss Zhu who had been a Buddhist for eighteen years. She found it difficult to believe, because friends and relatives had ridiculed her, and even made threats of physical violence.

Mixed in with our language study, some business matters, and the escalating number of meetings, we had good times playing tennis and horseshoes. On Saturday we broke the week's rigid routine of activities with special events. Once we joined the Upchurches for a picnic on the other side of Qionghai Lake. We left our home at about 10:30 a.m., walked for half an hour to the north edge of the lake, where we piled into one large row boat. It took an hour's rowing by the two owners of the boat to reach the other side. There we ate, swam a bit and rested, besieged as usual on such an occasion by a bevy of curious on lookers. We hiked partially up the mountain side and viewed the beautiful resort home of Generalissimo Chiang Kai-shek, certainly the equal of any modern home in America. This would have been his home had the capital of China been moved from Chungking to Xichang during the war of resistance against Japan.

Although our language study and initial evangelism were directed toward the Chinese, the Nosu people were never far from our minds. Dan and I spent three days in June at a student conference across the Anning River, about fifteen miles from Xichang. A part of this trip was done on horseback, and I concluded "never again." Both the horses—more like ponies—and saddles were too small for a foreigner. I could not cinch the saddles as I desired, and I had the sinking feeling that both the saddle and I were slipping.

The accommodations at the conference were adequate, but our preparations were not. Dan had forgotten to bring his mosquito net, and both his large frame and mine did not fit well under one net. As a result we both touched the net on the sides, and the mosquitoes feasted happily on us all night.

Since the conference site was within five miles of a Nosu village, we spent the day visiting there. We were most interested in the small school run for Nosu children. It was like an old, one-room, rural American school house, with the students ranging from five to twenty-two years of age. The Chinese schoolmaster was very discouraged and complained that the students were impossible to discipline. They ran home whenever they felt like it, and unless he himself went after them, they would not return. Much of the fault was probably his; only the poorest teachers, the left-overs, were sent to teach in these isolated, mountain areas. These Chinese teachers usually revealed their anti-minority biases, and the students responded in kind.

Jim Broomhall returned to Xichang periodically, and his presence always kept our interest in the Nosu burning brightly. Once, when he was in town to find workmen to help build the CIM home in Zhaojue, he told us of the current inter-clan warfare. A girl from one clan had promised to marry a young man in another clan, but then she eloped with a man in a third clan. The jilted clan started fighting with her home clan and the third clan to get her back and strangle her, the usual form of punishment. The two clans were willing to give her up, if the third clan would fork over a ransom amount in the equivalent of twenty thousand dollars. Unfortunately, we never heard the final chapter of this Nosu saga.

In this isolated area of China we felt separated from the life and death struggle that would determine China's destiny. The thunder continued, but its noise was muted by the mountains that surrounded us. For the many Kuomintang troops on the streets of Xichang, who frequently attended our street chapel services, there was to be no relief. In the last week of April 1948, forty military planes flew a division of the nationalist troops north to aid in the desperate fighting raging about Xian.

Farther Afield

Soon after the arrival of the *St. Paul* in early April, Lee took one of the newly-arrived couples, Jim and Virginia Garrison, to the city of Huili, 115 miles south of Xichang, but still in the Jianchang Valley. The Garrisons joined Esther Nelson, formerly of the American Baptist mission in West China and now serving with the Baptist General Conference in cooperation with CBFMS, in this new venture into China. Despite three steep mountain passes, hairpin curves, impossible roads, and the Chinese habit of putting trucks into neutral while they plunged down mountain roads with only poor brakes to hold them, the group got to Huili safely in one day.

Huili was much smaller than Xichang and might be called a small, mountain village. Although a seemingly insignificant city, its roots went back to the Ming dynasty. During the "long march" of 1935 when Mao and other Communist leaders headed toward Yanan in north China, the Politburo held an extended meeting here.[2] As in Xichang, the weather was very pleasant and reminded us of Southern California, albeit a bit more dry. High mountains were close by, but because of the slash and burn agricultural methods of the Nosu living there, everything was barren and unproductive.

The China Home Mission Society had commenced work in Huili as one of its outstations nearly thirty years previous. A few mature Christians remained from this early effort, but some had defected badly. One of the old members, for example, had become a Buddhist priest and faithfully rang the temple gong every day. Another disgruntled member occupied part of the church premises and refused to leave unless he was paid off.

For their first period of time in Huili, the Garrisons and Esther lived behind the church in small rooms with separate kitchens. First priority for them was to concentrate on continued language study with a teacher coming to the home. As time allowed, they became involved in English classes and many meetings for children. Even though their language was still insufficient, Esther, who had lived in China for many years, was available and did most of the speaking. Working through English in this part of China was frustrating. They wanted desperately to tell the Gospel message clearly, and yet their Chinese and the students' English both were too minimal for any real communication to take place. Looking back, we often think that in these early days it might have been better for us to do more listening and less speaking.

Meanwhile, arrangements were being made to invite a Chinese pastor, Wang Daoran, to assist in the work. He was a member of the China Home Mission Society, but would be working under the direction of the missionaries. Again, if we were able to redo this part of our past strategy, it would make far more sense to put inexperienced, still-learning-the-language missionaries under his direction!

Even before our party of missionaries had reached the Jianchang Valley, we had several poorly-formed ideas of what we might wish to do in the large area to the north of Xichang. The city mentioned most often was Mianning, about sixty miles directly up the valley and on the road to Yaan in Sichuan. Although it was largely a Chinese city with a population of twenty thousand, many Nosu lived nearby in the plains and mountains. In between Xichang and Mianning was the hub-city of Lugu, where the main road branched off to go toward Fulin and Yuexi. The latter city, two-days travel from Lugu, was, from the standpoint of nearness to the Nosu, the most ideal, but also the most dangerous. Chinese officials could give no guarantee of safety for people living there. Tianba, three days into the interior north-east from Yuexi, was in the very heart of Independent Nosuland, and, of particular interest, was under the control of a Chinese-educated Nosu chief, Lin Guangdian, who was favorably disposed to social work.

More distant possibilities were Yanyuan, four days west of Xichang through very rugged and heavily-timbered, mountainous country. To the northwest of Yanyuan was the famed Muli Kingdom, written up by Joseph Rock in *National Geographic Magazine* in April 1925. This kingdom was ruled by a Lama who permitted no opium. Reports indicated that there were about ninety thousand people of various minority nationalities in his kingdom.

Highest on the list of places where we wished to establish a Gospel witness was Mianning. We concluded that it would be wise to pay a visit there and learn more about this city before we made our decision. We left on Saturday, May 22, in an unlikely looking caravan—six rickshas, two for our baggage, one each for Lee, John Simpson, and me, and one for the servant Lee wished to bring along. We could have gone faster by walking, but travelling in this fashion saved our energy for times when we would have to walk.

As we came within ten miles of Mianning on our second day of travel, it was evident that we were in the middle of a "golden triangle." Poppy fields of opium spread out on both sides of the road as far as we could see. Farmers were scratching the poppy buds with their little three-bladed knives, while others were scraping off the hardened, brown substance with a crescent-shaped knife. In many yards, mats of poppy seeds were spread out to dry.

As we got nearer to the city, we saw fields where a row of wheat or millet was interspersed with two or more rows of opium poppies. When we arrived on the narrow, crowded city streets, we discovered that an opium festival was in progress! Everyone had opium. Some people carried it in rice bowls, either held openly in their hands or partly hidden in the long, broad sleeves of their gowns. Buyers were pushing sticks or knives through the dark, sticky lumps to see if they were pure opium or mixed with impurities. People buying almost anything were putting little bits of opium on scales for the purchase price. Smoking pipes could be found at almost any stall.

Most tragic of all, almost every other shop on the street was an opium den, where smokers ate or inhaled the black poison. Everywhere on the street were buyers, both Chinese and Nosu, who traded for large quantities to be shipped elsewhere in China.

Because of this extensive traffic in opium, prices in Mianning were nearly double what they were in Xichang. Opium was cheap, but that was all. So much land and effort were devoted to opium, that no space was left for the planting of necessary foods. This, apparently, was not the farmers' choice. Local officials, with some incentives from unknown higher-ups, were giving them poppy seeds and telling them to plant opium. If they cooperated, all went well. If not, they were forced, often under the penalty of being jailed, to do as directed. Some Chinese farmers complained that, in outlying areas farther from the city, the Nosu were forcing them to plant opium. Whoever was ultimately to blame, this was "opium city" China. As we stood on the majestic city walls and looked at the plains and valleys on all four sides, it was "mountain to mountain opium."

As we entered the city on the day of our arrival, rain was beginning to fall. Crowded by buyers and sellers of opium, all the inns were occupied, and we looked in vain for a place to stay. Finally, the local police chief (we did not yet know who he was), undoubtedly already wary because of our presence, arranged for us to have a spacious, private room, located very conveniently, both for his sake and ours, near the center of the city.

Apart from the evil traffic in black poison, Mianning was an attractive city. Typical of ancient Chinese cities, it was surrounded by a huge wall, penetrated only by four large gates which were always closed promptly as the sun sank beneath the surrounding mountains. Above each gate and at intervals along the wall were guard houses. Such precaution reflected the ongoing Chinese fear of the Nosu.

Well might they fear. Nosu crowded the streets, buying and selling their wares. Outside the city, they were armed to the hilt, often with rifle, pistol, and a full cartridge belt. All of their firearms were checked at the gates when they entered the city, but the Chinese could never be sure what other weapons might be hidden under their loose, sweeping clothes. When I was talking in Chinese with a Nosu man in a small eating house, he suddenly asked me if I carried a gun. After responding, "no," I asked him the same question, and, already knowing the answer, I followed it by asking why he carried a gun. With that open, frank look so characteristic of the minority peoples, he replied, "Why, to kill people, of course." The Nosu did not go about looking for people to kill, but "revenge" and "robbery" were two of the most important words in their vocabulary.

The Yi had more weapons than guns to deal with their enemies. Harrison Salisbury, who travelled through the Jianchang Valley in 1984 observed:

> Not far from Mianning rose a secret mountain spring, known only to the Yi. From this spring flowed a strange water with deadly effect on the vocal system. It acted something like laughing gas: People burst into laughter and could not stop. The Yi paralyzed their enemies with this water, making them laugh themselves to death.[3]

Word spread quickly that we were looking for a permanent home in the city. In the mid-afternoon of our first full day in Mianning, a man showed us some property which he owned and which was located in the southeast section of the city. The lot itself would have been suitable, conveniently located and about 100 feet wide by 150 feet long. The drawback was an old Buddhist temple, completely open on one side, that was on the land. While this decrepit building might serve as a temporary home for John and me while something permanent was being built for families, it was not a good long-term possibility. The need for extensive repairs or building, combined with the expensive purchase price of five hundred dollars, left us with little enthusiasm. We found nothing else in the city that was even as suitable as this.

The opium continued to interest us—too much, we learned. John and I had never seen it before, and even Lee in his years of experience in China, had never faced it to this extent. And so, almost like camera-crazy tourists, we took pictures for "the folk back home." People on the street asked us how we viewed the widespread use of opium, and we diplomatically replied that we were saddened by it. For whatever reason, that evening, an official bulletin was suddenly posted in the center of the city, noting that there had been illicit dealing of opium on the city streets and it must cease. Rather strange, since the growth, sale, and use of opium was already considered a crime punishable by death.

The next morning we headed out of the city in a southwesterly direction for about ten miles toward the large market village of Huilong Chang. Much to our surprise, we found we were accompanied by the man who had found the private room for us. He said we needed protection from unfriendly Nosu whom we might meet. This line seemed reasonable, until we noticed that he was beside himself when we continued to take pictures of farmers cultivating their opium fields.

On our way to the market town, we noticed three or four side valleys which led directly into numerous Nosu villages. At the market, everyone appeared to be Nosu and were very interested at the unexpected arrival of these foreigners. Genuinely friendly, they told us that we, like them, were Nosu. Never would they say this to the Chinese, from whom they sharply differentiated themselves. So outgoing were they that they urged us to take pictures of their beautifully-attired women, who, even then, were usually too shy to lift up their heads and look at us.

We thought no more about our "protector's" interest in our picture taking. That is, not until late that night! We had retired for about an hour or so, when an awful commotion of people banging on the door awakened us. Our benefactor in finding the room, our disturbed companion on the trip to Huilong Chang, now revealed himself to us as the Mianning police chief. He stood at the door accompanied by several deputies and armed soldiers. After some formal procedures of examining our passports and travel permits, he asked us to turn over our cameras, which, by this time, we had fastened securely around our necks.

This we refused to do, since he had no order permitting him to confiscate any of our belongings. The police chief ordered the soldiers to take them, but when they saw we did not frighten easily, this approach was dropped. Finally, after much arguing, we agreed to go—even at this post-midnight hour—to the local magistrate's office. The scene was scary: the three of us walking in front, followed by the chief, his deputies, and the armed soldiers. A stinging rain and blustery wind added to the drama.

When we talked to the magistrate at his court, we asked for proof that it was a crime to take pictures of non-military objects. He and several officials quickly disappeared, reappearing shortly with a large notice and its duly-affixed seal stating that it was unlawful to take pictures in China. Lee asked simply how the local magistrate had such authority to forbid picture taking in all of China, and this argument was dropped.

When it seemed impossible to resolve the dispute, another official was brought in and helped to make some sense of the impasse. He frankly stated that we had broken no law. The problem, he claimed, was that the city officials were new and had inherited the bad opium situation. They feared that we were opium inspectors posing as evangelists, and doubted our motives in taking the pictures. If this documented evidence of opium dealing were to reach outside officials, it could literally mean their "necks."

They had hoped to settle the matter more amicably, but the police chief, much to their chagrin, had jumped the gun and used gestapo methods. We learned that the middleman-official explaining all of this was a Christian of Anglican persuasion from the eastern portion of Sichuan province. He recommended that we take the film from our cameras, seal it in envelopes, and surrender it to them for delivery to He Guiguang, the Kuomintang general who was Chiang Kai-shek's personal representative in Xichang. He promised that when the film was developed, the non-opium negatives would be returned to us. We knew this was an empty promise, but it was a face-saving solution for everyone.

We were never sure which of several competing political groups (more of this later) were profiting from the use of opium. In some strange manner, possible only in old China, everyone was getting some cut. The tragic losers, although a small profit probably came to them too, were the common people, whose lives were being irreparably ruined by the black, poisonous glue that held the economy together.

We tried to analyze what had happened. Undoubtedly, we had made some bad mistakes. We should have realized the danger. On this first visit, it would have been wise to carry no cameras. We could have been less arrogant and overbearing when the confrontation did come. But, altogether apart from our obvious mistakes, our very presence might have triggered the same reaction. We had naively stumbled into a hornet's nest, and local officials, fearful for their lives, had reacted in a natural fashion. Our role, in this area of China seldom penetrated by foreigners, had been badly misunderstood.

We slept late the next day and licked our wounds. Officials to whom we talked assured us that this run-in with the police chief would not ruin any future work in the city. We felt better by Friday and, without our cameras, took another short trip outside the city. This time we went directly to the north along the course of the Anning River and then into a small valley to the west. At the foot of the mountain, on the north side of the valley, we found the city of Cala, inhabited by about two hundred Tibetans. Physically, these people resembled the Chinese more than the Nosu did. They were not under the control of Lamaism nor did the children and young people speak Tibetan. The people at Cala told us about a much larger settlement sixty or seventy miles distant, where the people followed Lamaism and the majority spoke only Tibetan.

We were thrilled at all of the potential ministry opportunities that we had turned up on this trip, but we were getting tired of travel. Our food had been good—lots of rice, vegetables, meat, and soya bean curd—but it was time to return. The main stop on our return trip was Lugu. We had not given much thought to it before, but with the lack of a good property site in Mianning and the "buzz saw" we had run into there, we felt the need to reconsider.

Lugu was a good "hub" city, almost equidistant from Xichang and Mianning. To the east was a narrow gorge leading toward Yuexi, and to the west across the Anning River was a long valley filled with

Chinese villages. At the end of the valley were two passes, entrance ways both north and south into hundreds of Nosu villages.

Wherever and whenever possible on this extended trip, we gave a witness for Christ. We carried a good supply of tracts and distributed these whenever we found someone who could read. More satisfactory in developing a good witnessing situation was to spend time at the ever-present tea shops. I think that if the Apostle Paul were evangelizing in China, he would spend a lot of time in these natural, community-gathering spots. We met people there, sipped tea, and talked. Time limits disappeared.

After a short stop in Lugu, we headed back on the one-day trip to Xichang. We had learned and experienced more than we had bargained for. Now it was time to make some crucial decisions. The foundations for the work in Xichang and Huili had been laid, and a spiritual building of "living stones" was being built. The next frontier was in the northern section of the Jianchang Valley.

Endnotes

1. Raymond Buker, Sr. pointed out to us that goiters and Cretins were to be found everywhere in the entire area, classified broadly as the "foothills of the Himalayas." He attributed it to lack of iodine in the water. Our letters spoke of its cause as no iodine in the soil. Ruth Laube hoped that we might get thyroid pills donated by doctors at home and dispense them without charge to the people. Ray objected strongly, feeling that such an approach would communicate that "pills were part of Christianity."
2. Salisbury, Harrison E. *The Long March: The Untold Story.* New York: Harper and Row, 1985, pp. 188-195.
3. *Ibid.*, p. 196.

7

You Can't Hurry the East—
The Uncertainty Deepens

Do Not Fear Going Slowly, Only Standing Still

A foundation had been laid for our work in Xichang, but from summer 1948 until early 1949, the spiritual building we were trying to erect on it proceeded ever so slowly. We already knew that you "can't hurry the East," but now that we were in China, the quaint proverb, *bupa man, zhipa zhan* (don't fear going slowly, only fear standing still), said it even better. We got used to going slow and praised God for any signs of progress.

Actually, it was not all that bad. We saw changes for the better in the work at the street chapel. If meetings were a sign of success, we had enough of them: meetings for passers-by, for children, young people, women, inquirers, and those who had entered the fold. I made as many of these as possible and took my regular turn in preaching on Sunday and at prayer meetings on Wednesday night. I would have started a Chinese Bible class, were it not for accelerating plans to head up the work in Lugu.

Miss Hu did most of the evangelistic work. She was in no hurry to rush people into the kingdom. After her preaching services, she patiently answered questions and urged on people the need to believe. She used no pressure, no manipulation, and no tricks. She wanted to be sure that inquirers knew what they believed, and that their conversion rested upon the power of God to change lives, and not on human persuasion. It was a lesson in evangelism to work with her.

In the late summer of 1948, a full-scale Daily Vacation Bible School was held for the neighborhood children. At least seventy attended this two-week event. Compared with children who would attend similar meetings later in Huili and Lugu, these kids had intelligent questions that showed their minds were taking in the message. Such classes were an easy way for us to make contacts with many homes, but it was not the most strategic approach. Ultimately, more solid decisions could have been made by the children had we been able to penetrate better the homes from which they came. This approach, however, would have demanded more maturity than possible at this time for our young group of missionaries. Much more time would be required, but time was the commodity we most lacked at this period in China's history.

Over the months, the consistent preaching and teaching of the Gospel brought a few results, although far from what we had hoped. Shortly after the new year, on January 9, 1949, we held our first baptismal service. Lovegren described the examination of the sixteen inquirers, twelve women and four men, ranging in age from eleven to sixty:

> Yesterday afternoon and evening (January 8), Ida and I sat in a committee meeting and heard the testimonies of persons who wanted to be baptized. You ought to have heard these testimonies! Some have come from Buddhist beliefs—one woman kept the Buddhist vegetarian vow for eighteen years; another for eight years; several had gone vegetarian for short periods from time to time—and one or two had come from a background of non-religious homes, but all believe on Christ and have experienced new life in Christ. Several have prayed for health and gotten it, and one, the oldest, had sore eyes and these are so much better, if not entirely well, that she kept mentioning them in her testimony before the committee. Practically none of these had ever heard of Christ only a year ago, December 21, 1947—and now they are rejoicing in their Saviour. Some found Christ last spring, while one was converted less than two weeks ago.

We had hoped for good weather in order to have these baptisms in Qionghai Lake, but it was cloudy and cold with extensive snow in the mountains. And so we resorted to the pool in our garden. Lovegren took some of the worst chill off the water by floating charcoal fires in two five-gallon oil cans and two Chinese deep stove tops. Dan, as the one among us most experienced in pastoral ministry, officiated at the baptisms.

On January 30, we organized a church with over twenty members, not counting the missionaries. Following this, there was a week's special evangelistic meetings during the Chinese New Year, a gala and festive holiday season when people have an extended period off work and are able to listen to and interact with the Gospel. Forty or fifty persons indicated their desire to follow in the Jesus way as a result of these meetings.

One woman's conversion was unique. She had come to Xichang from Mianning on a pilgrimage to the Lu Shan Guang Fushi, the temple on the mountain just south of Qionghai Lake. While walking along the streets of Xichang, she passed the church facility just as the daytime evangelistic meetings were being held. Attracted by the music and the general bustle, she stopped in to listen, and, following the message, prayed with one of the church members and committed herself to Christ. She did not complete her pilgrimage, but returned to her home rejoicing in her new-found faith.

The testimony of a rich merchant, Cao Linli, had a dramatic impact on many hesitant inquirers. After he confessed his faith, he thoroughly cleaned out his "god" room of its various religious paraphernalia—altars, religious scrolls, images, and incense. He burned the scrolls publicly—one half of them in our chapel and the other half at the Border Service church building.

Xichang was not the most desirable place in China to live, and our co-workers did not stay with us long. Mr. Niu had already left in the spring of 1948, and Miss Fu, with gifts suited much more to work with university students, returned to Chengdu where there was much more potential for this kind of ministry. Mrs. Han, a dedicated lay believer from the area, gave herself energetically to the work, and the new Xichang believers, zealous in their new found faith, carried many of the responsibilities of the ministry.

We were encouraged by the arrival of Yang Jiemin and his family in November 1948. The Simpsons had contacted him in Shanghai a year and a half before his graduation from the China Bible Seminary, in whose hostel they had stayed when they first arrived in China. A Baptist by conviction, Yang was loathe to return to his home in Shantung and work with missionaries whom he perceived as liberal in their theology.

Our earlier mission policy allowed for the possibility of each family having a "Chinese worker" to minister with them. John and Irene hoped that Yang and his family would accompany them to Lizhou, but the political crisis ended this possibility.

Mr. Yang was in his early 30s with enough experience and maturity to help us younger missionaries who were deficient in both. He and his very capable wife gave the most help in preparing for the baptismal services which we held in January 1949.

Even while there was a readiness to believe the Gospel, we sensed the need to respond to the social needs about us. In midsummer, 1948, Dan and I, accompanied by Bill Upchurch and the Chinese pastor of the Border Service church, visited a home for beggars a short distance to the west of Xichang. At this time, the home was more or less under the control of public officials, but we hoped that it might become a joint Christian project. The people were in desperate shape, poorly clothed, and many blind or crippled. Most tragic, many were children. The home in which these forty beggars were kept was really an old Buddhist temple that did not afford much protection from the weather. The escalation of the civil war ultimately kept us from implementing this needed joint ministry.

The needs of the Nosu, so visible every day in Xichang's crowded street markets, were never far from us. The CIM missionaries in Xichang were using a Nosu teacher two hours a day, and Lee and I made use of his time as well. I was not able to study more than two hours each week, but even this little bit whetted my appetite to jump into the midst of this work. Jim Broomhall invited me to go with him for a few weeks to Zhaojue, but even though I was poised to go, we never worked out a way when I could leave Xichang for an extended period.

We did not need to penetrate the deep mountain interior to see the hard realities of Nosu life. Returning from the post office one day, I saw a man carrying a basket packed with four still-bleeding Nosu heads. Another Nosu was being led along with a rope around his neck to the local government headquarters. I learned that a few days earlier, a group of wild tribesmen had tried to rob some Chinese soldiers of their guns. In the ensuing fight, two Nosu were killed, beheaded, and their heads hung up on a tree outside the post office. Two others were later captured and met the same fate. The other captive Nosu was executed a few days after I had seen him on the street. The worst part of these incidents was that the decapitated bodies were tossed outside the city gate, either to rot or to be eaten by the dogs.

Life Goes On

We followed with interest the November 1948 presidential elections back home. Truman won over Dewey against impossible odds. This unexpected turn of events hurt the Nationalists who expected Dewey to give them enough financial and military aid to defeat the Communists. Lucille observed that this was a "catch 22" situation. More aid might have meant a Nationalist victory, and yet what could such a corrupt government do for China? Was there really a choice?

The big family news of early summer 1948 was the birth of James Carr to Dan and Lucille. The medical care was not all we could have wished for, but Win Upchurch, a trained English midwife, Irene Simpson, a nurse, and a young Chinese woman doctor assisted in the birth. This, we believe, was the first birth ever of an American child in Xichang, but it would not be the last. We felt blessed that so many of the married and single women had had medical training and could care for deliveries and many minor ailments.

For any type of serious operation, it was best to go either to Chungking or Chengdu. John Simpson took his oldest daughter, Linn Ann, to Chengdu for a tonsillectomy during the fall of 1948, and, at a later time, Dan went to Shanghai with a serious medical problem. When the planes ceased to fly as the civil war intensified, we had to make do with the meager facilities and resources available to us.

Missionaries in the boondocks live a "fish-bowl" existence, with our lives intertwined with one another in ways it's hard for people in America to understand. Nothing showed this better than an incident that happened a few hours before Jimmy Carr was born. I had been having a few stomach problems, and at about 2 a.m. got up to go to one of the outhouses in the compound yard. At this hour there should not be many interruptions. Imagine my surprise then when the door of the outhouse was all of a sudden lifted off its hinges as by a tornado and disappeared! Dan, the culprit stealing my privacy at this hour, was equally surprised. With no word of apology, he rushed away hurriedly with the door, saying that it was to be used as a delivery table for his wife who had just gone into labor. Whenever we had down times in the months ahead, we retold this story, often with a few embellishments.

After several months, I moved into more adequate quarters on our compound. I was given two nice rooms right along the main road. One I used as a study and the other as a bedroom. Finally, I had a level wooden floor and a ceiling that could keep out some of the ever-present dust. We had screens on our windows and doors and made generous use of DDT, but the battle with insects—lice, mosquitoes, flies, and bedbugs—never ended.

The outside mud walls to our rooms were three feet thick, sufficiently large to build book shelves right into them. For me, with so many other symbols of my American identity gone, it was essential to have "my books." I had brought much of my considerable library with me, and weekly letters to my parents were filled with book and magazine orders. One of the most subtle dangers of missionary life, I was to learn, was to dry up intellectually. Particularly was this true when so many of the people we were working with were illiterate or poorly educated.

We did not suffer in our eating. We had thought, mistakenly, that Xichang would not rival Chengdu in the foods we could obtain. In the early summer we had corn, tomatoes, plums, and peaches, along with the ordinary range of vegetables. A bit later in the summer, apples came into season, and we were very glad for the thirty apple trees in our garden. We had planted lettuce in the garden, and since it was not fertilized by the "night soil," it was perfectly safe for us to eat it raw. By late October we had oranges and persimmons.

The only meat readily available to us was pork, and even this was scarce. Often this was because the government was trying to enforce a price level, and the meat sellers retaliated by keeping it off the market. We had less trouble in smaller cities, like Lugu and Huili, where the local officials had less clout to enforce the set-price level. About the only way we could buy beef was to find Muslims who were willing to sell it to us. Sick and dying water buffalo could be found, but we tried to avoid their meat.

Communication Problems

The Chinese often referred to the Ningsu area as *pian pi*, an out-of-the-way place. Roads and bridges were more often out than open. News was hard to come by. A short-wave radio brought in BBC or the Voice of America, but it was not easy to get news about China. Our only real connection to the outside world depended on the weekly flights of CNAC, which brought newspapers and letters.

A mail delivery made our day. Once we heard the noise of the departing plane as it flew over the city, two of us, usually one of our group and Bill Upchurch, hurried to the post office and offered to help the workers there sort it. No one at the post office could read English; so they welcomed our help in determining which pieces belonged to each of the four groups of foreigners (CIM, Church of Christ, Roman Catholics, and ourselves) in the city. This job usually took us an hour, but it probably saved us a whole day that would have been required for a home delivery.

Unfortunately, the plane seemed to miss more trips than it made. Bad weather was usually the culprit. The *St. Paul* on its trips was prepared to come in, even with a heavy overcast, if it could hone in on the radio beam. CNAC, however, very concerned over its safety record because of the spate of accidents in late 1946 and early 1947, could not come in unless there was a break in the clouds. The raging civil war also created factors that often led to the cancellation of flights.

For the plane not to come was more than a mere inconvenience. We could do without newspapers and letters. In fact, it was nice to get several weeks' supply at once. The critical factor was money.

Each plane brought in a load of currency for local banks. If the plane did not come, the banks had little money and no way to cash the checks our Shanghai agents were sending to us. In a pinch they would cash some checks, but discounted at 70%. So we were double losers—caught by inflation and then losing 30% beyond this.

Local politics also messed us up. General He had inside connections with some of the banks and frequently commandeered large amounts of local cash to invest in opium. Once Dan waited at a bank all day, insisting that we must have our money. Eventually he got it, but only because this bank borrowed the money from another bank.

The lack of money made it difficult to keep food on the table, and it also slowed up every phase of the work, whether to pay our Chinese co-laborers, to finish up chapel or home repairs, or to implement plans for starting the work in Lugu. Once we had the money, our problems were not over. If we did not spend it quickly, we would be victimized again by inflation and the wildly escalating prices. The government tried to enforce lower price levels on even more goods, but the people refused to sell. These products then were available only on the black market, but at a cost four or more times higher than the suggested rate.

If there was nothing that we needed immediately, we quickly put our money into something with a stable price value—two-ounce gold nuggets, silver ingots, or cotton yarn. We saved our money in this fashion, although it was a problem to use these directly to buy items, since the change would be given in the increasingly valueless paper currency. The national government made a token effort to turn the financial situation around in November, when it issued a new paper currency valued at four to one in U.S. dollars. Within a few days, scheming politicians in Nanking had manipulated this to twenty to one, and our newly-arrived missionaries in Shanghai, Bill and Flossie Simons and Ruth Laube, saw five hundred dollars reduced in buying power to one hundred dollars. Bill sent a letter to the folk in Chengdu stating, "WE ARE SUNK. We've overdrawn our salary for months." After a long debate, the board reimbursed the Simons and Ruth, even as it made clear that this was not to be policy. If there were further exchange losses, we would have to bear them.

We were grieved in the summer of 1948 to learn of the tragic death of our Shanghai financial representative, Dan Nelson, and his entire family on a short, routine flight from Macao to Hong Kong. The plane was hijacked by five pirates who hoped to hold the Nelson family as hostages for a large ransom. The only survivor of the crash was one of the pirates, who confessed the sinister plot.

Reinforcements from Chengdu

The big anticipated event of the fall months 1948 was the imminent arrival of our colleagues from Chengdu. Even as our first party was laying a foundation for our work in the Jianchang Valley, the Staffords, Coles, and Flora Mae Duncan had been continuing in language study in Chengdu. Now it was time for them to join us. The only question was, how could this be managed? The road from Chengdu to Xichang via Leshan and Mianning was as impossible to travel as when our first party came. The only alternative was to fly, but for five people with their children and their freight it was impossible to use the commercial CNAC.

Once again the only possibility was to use the faithful *St. Paul*. We hoped to work out a comprehensive package deal. Our three newly-arrived missionaries in Shanghai needed to fly to Chengdu. Bennie and Dorothy Benson needed to go from Chengdu to the orphanage in east China. Some of our Xichang group, both Chinese and missionaries, wanted to make short trips to Chungking or Chengdu, and we needed to fly our Chengdu group to Xichang. We hoped also to be able to recoup some of our costs by flying local Chinese passengers out on return trips of the empty plane. CNAC was not too happy about the potential competition this time, and so we negotiated carefully with them. They had been very good to us in numerous ways, and we did not wish to do anything that would destroy our mutual trust. Ultimately, we did reach an agreement that we could take sixty military police to Chungking. To have such a large group on a commercial plane would have disrupted travel badly.

We laid our plans carefully for use of the *St. Paul*, but then everything seemed to go wrong. We wanted the plane to bring the

Simons and Ruth Laube from Shanghai to Chungking, leave them off temporarily while it brought in luggage and freight to Xichang, return to Chungking to take the Shanghai group on to Chengdu, and then commence the several flights to Xichang. A prolonged streak of bad weather in Xichang messed this all up and made any planning hopeless.

The Simons and Ruth were delivered to Chengdu, but that was all. The plane ran on a very full schedule, particularly pressed to evacuate missionary personnel from the civil war areas. Once it left west China, we could not be sure when it would be back. The poor communication system made it difficult to tell what would happen next. Each day for several days, I biked the four or five miles to the airport in the hope that the radio operator at the field could update me. To telephone him from the city only gave a garbled message. When Jim Garrison and I biked again to the airport Sunday morning, November 1, three days after we had planned for the plane to come, we learned that it had flown from Chengdu to Shanghai taking the Bensons on the first leg of their trip to Ganxian. It was scheduled to return to Chengdu on Tuesday, November 3.

The days dragged on until the following Sunday, with most of us ready to interrupt our scheduled events at the drop of a hat. Finally, at 8 a.m. on Sunday, November 8, we received word that the plane was on its way from Chungking. It brought the luggage and freight that we had stored there as well as John and Linn Ann Simpson, returning from their medical trip to Chengdu. At this time we learned that the *St. Paul* had tried to come in on Saturday, the 7th, only to have to turn back to Chungking when it could not pick up the radio beam at the Xichang airport. This was probably par for the course, since there was only one operator on duty, and if he left his desk, even for a moment, an incoming plane would have no guidance.

Now that the log-jam was broken, the plane came once more that Sunday, twice on Monday, and the final trip on Tuesday. Each day was really bad for flying—CNAC did not come that week—but the pilots now seemed familiar with the field and expressed no fear in flying through the murky clouds swirling around the high peaks. The pilots stayed overnight with us once during these several days. Even as tired as they were from their heavy flying schedule, they and we both enjoyed a different type of camaraderie from what we usually experienced. We were to think often at how bewildered they were to be evacuating missionaries from north China, even as they were flying us into west China.

During these days of almost living at the airfield and then of trucking the freight into the city, we learned once again that planes are safer than trucks in China! As we brought in our last load on Tuesday, the truck went through a small bridge near the airport and nearly turned over. Riding on the top to hold down some of the loose stuff, I thought it was going to turn over, and I jumped. Fortunately, no one was hurt, and the truck was not damaged. This experience made me leery of riding trucks over bridges, but in the months ahead I faced much worse than this.

With this series of flights, all of us were now in either Xichang or Huili, except Flora Mae who stayed a while in Chengdu to help the Simons and Ruth get settled. For a few weeks our Xichang compound was overcrowded, and it was hard to find space for everyone.

For our new arrivals, the several plane flights brought all of their possessions. For those of us who had come earlier there were all kinds of goodies sent by friends and relatives. I had a batch of Christmas presents, but decided that I would not wait for December 25th to open them. Included were shoes, slacks, sweaters, and a watch—the kinds of things that could not be bought in any of Xichang's poor shops.

From the sixty passengers whom we flew out on the *St. Paul* we received twenty-four hundred dollars in Chinese national currency, a sum equal to six hundred U.S. dollars at the current four to one exchange rate. We learned to our grief that over these very days when the plane was flying in and out, the exchange jumped to twenty to one. Overnight our gain was reduced to $120, a loss of 80%.

In deciding what to do with this money, we acted in the same way for which we sometimes criticized Lee—using the exchange for our own benefit. We used this money to pay our salaries, but at the high exchange rather than the low. Lee protested this decision, but we outvoted him.

Our Jerusalem Conference

We had known for months that any attempt to have an effective witness for Christ in this area required careful planning. Until this point, we had not really had the opportunity. Yes, there had been meetings before we left San Francisco, on board the *Marine Lynx*, and periodically in Chengdu. But we had been so preoccupied with other matters or with language study that no more than one day—or even a few hours—could be spent together in planning sessions. We dealt with matters of the moment, urgent decisions for the next week. Not only were we lacking in time, but also woefully ignorant of first-hand facts concerning the Jianchang area and the opportunities awaiting us there. How could we make long-range decisions about which we knew virtually nothing? Lee Lovegren tried hard to fill us in, but even his patience was stretched to the breaking point.

And so with most of us in Xichang, we planned for a two-week mission conference, when we would formally constitute the Xikang Baptist Mission Conference and prepare strategy for the years ahead. We had never done this type of thing before, but Lee, drawing on his years of experience with the American Baptist Foreign Mission Society, guided us along.

These were solemn days, and we felt heavily the responsibility of being good stewards, not only of God's grace, but of the trust committed to us by our supporters at home. A verse that came to us all repeatedly and served to guide our daily Scripture meditations was Jesus' word to his disciples, "As the Father has sent me, even so I send you" (John 20:21). We focused on many themes growing out of this command: living as he lived; obedient as he was obedient; loving as he loved; pure even as he is pure; forgiving as he forgave; praying as he prayed; ministering as he ministered; meek as he was meek; suffering as he suffered. We knew that a ministry that did not embody this likeness to Jesus Christ would be worthless before the challenges confronting us.

Conference days were long and weary, but at least we could sense that we were getting into the work, that not all of our time in China was to be spent in never-ending language study. Almost anything was a relief from the daily grind of vocabulary, tones, grammar, Chinese characters, and memorization. We had two sessions in the morning, and then a longer one in the afternoon. Nights were kept free for committee meetings, digesting the day's decisions and, occasionally, some light game times. A few extra hours of sleep were always welcome.

Lying behind all of our discussions and decisions in these days was the goal of our mission work: it is our aim to preach the redeeming message of the Gospel of Jesus Christ to the peoples of Xikang, using every method of evangelism to promote the establishment of an indigenous church. We were to have many kinds of work—medical, translation, relief—but we saw these as having an ultimate goal in the on-going witness and service of local Christian communities. We, the members of the mission, were transition people, the scaffolding, but the agent of God's work after we were gone would be His church. And so we needed to be wise masterbuilders.

An immediate decision had to be made about Huili. We had already sent Esther Nelson and the Garrisons to commence work, but most of this was based on an oral agreement with the China Home Mission Society. Now Pastor Wang Daoran, the representative of this society, was in Xikang and brought with him a proposed contract for discussion. Beyond the contract, other strategic matters had to be faced. Was Huili, a bit further removed from Nosu villages, as good a place from which to do work among this minority nationality as other sites? Could we really work well with the China Home Mission Society, which had a checkered history working with other foreign mission agencies? Why not throw our weight behind the China Home Mission Society, without actually sending any foreign personnel there? Could we and the China Home Mission Society agree on Baptistic principles of work?

After protracted, detailed discussions over nearly every word of the proposed contract, we settled on a two-year agreement that spelled out matters of authority, finances, and personnel. Never did we lose sight of the fact that, ultimately, the local church would have final say in the matters we were discussing. Neither we nor the China Home Mission Society should interfere with the church as it sought to govern, support, and reproduce itself. After two years, if the present deteriorating political situation allowed, we could reevaluate and make any necessary changes.

The fact that most of us were now in Xichang did not mean that we were veterans, ready to jump wholeheartedly into the work. What were we—missionaries or language students? Without a doubt, we were still novices in the language, and we determined that certain sections of either the Chengdu or China Inland Mission language programs must be completed. This was expected to take another year for most of us, and even missionaries in their third year were expected to spend a minimum of three hours a day in language study. Our work was cut out for us, but we never doubted the wisdom of this decision. We made a tentative decision that if new missionaries came to China, they should be brought immediately to Xichang for language study, rather than spending time at the school in Chengdu.

We spent a major block of time determining the future of Lugu. Several of the men and I had already made several trips to the city since the time when we stopped there on our return from Mianning the previous May. The longest was at the end of August when Lovegren, Simpson, and I spent several days talking with officials, looking over possible property sites, most of them impossible, and taking short trips into the country. On the evening before our return to Xichang, we held a feast for the town leaders and gained repeated reassurances that they would help us in finalizing a deal for one of the sites we had found.

We heard a nasty tale at this time that we were never able to confirm. At the least, it indicated the feelings among the people. It seemed that in 1906 a vicious fight had broken out in Lugu between the Catholics and the Protestants, largely Baptists. The Catholics had rougher elements and killed over one hundred of the Protestants. The Catholic priest who sparked the massacre was later apprehended and punished. We found strong anti-Catholic sentiment in Lugu, and although a Catholic church building was still standing, there were no priests, no schools, and no ongoing services. Was this an embellished rumor to make us as Baptists feel happy, or was there some substance to it?

Within a month, Dan and I returned to Lugu and arranged the purchase of four acres of land on the top of a small hill, overlooking the city to the east and valleys in the other three directions. We also made initial contact with a prominent local banker, Xie Wendan, and gave him a New Testament to read. Motives are never easy to assess, but he showed a real interest in the Gospel and in our purposes in coming to the city. Everyone was delighted that we wished to use this large plot of land to build a hospital.

During another trip in October, we had rented an old inn on south street for evangelistic purposes. This property was forty feet wide and had numerous rooms which, with some cleaning and repair, could be used for the residence of two Chinese families and of a single foreign missionary. In common with local customs, the down payments on both pieces of property was reckoned in local grains: eight *dan* (a *dan* is equal to ten bushels, which, in turn, is equal to ten pints) of corn for the hill property and twelve *dan* of rice for the proposed chapel site.

In a sense, then, our conference discussions on Lugu were to ratify previous action and to plan the next steps. Everyone was satisfied with the property we had. We were concerned about two small houses on the hill property—the owners did not want to give them up. And how would we be able to clean up the street building when numerous rooms were filled with idols and other religious paraphernalia which we dared not touch? We needed the skilled help of a Chinese negotiator on these knotty problems and voted to appoint a fine Christian man from Huili, Liu Qinlang, to serve as a business manager with first responsibilities for these needs in Lugu.

Since Lugu was to be a center for Nosu work, we discussed special approaches that might meet their needs. A hostel, for example, might be more attractive for the Nosu than some of the local inns, where they were always suspicious that the Chinese owners might be cheating them. A small dispensary could care for minor ailments and serve to identify the Gospel with concrete deeds.

We voted on plans to build a wall around the hill plot in Lugu and to proceed with the building of two missionary residences, constructed in the same way as the Xichang homes—wood frame, mud walls, and tile roof. People, of course, were more important than mud and stone, and so we formally voted that our Lugu "team" would consist of Dan and Lucy, Elwyn and Becky Stafford, and me.

Pastor and Mrs. Yang Jiemin, still very desperately needed in Xichang, would work with us in the task of evangelism and planting a church.

Although the Yangs were needed in Xichang, he had gifts of evangelism that could better be utilized in the north. Furthermore, he had been blind-sided in the Xichang church by a dispute involving a missionary couple and new converts over the issue of how Christians should act at a non-Christian funeral. Were there not an invitation to work in Lugu, he wrote to me, he and his family would return to their home in Shantung.

If these ambitious plans for work in three cities were not enough, we talked about opening still another station. The place most usually mentioned was Yuexi, to the northeast of Lugu. Dan and Lucy were the ones to be assigned to this new station. We planned to take a special survey trip into this area in the spring of 1949. I suspect this planning was necessary, but, in retrospect, it was rather foolhardy—a measure of how far we were isolated from the realities of a rapidly-crumbling Nationalist China.

Order in our planning was very important. Properly speaking, we should work out a comity arrangement with the Border Service Department and the China Inland Mission, so that any future work conflicts might be avoided. When our ad hoc committee met with the Border Service representatives, they indicated their principal interest was in Xichang county itself, including Lizhou, about twenty-five miles to the north of Xichang, in the south toward Dechang, and in the west in Yanyuan county. The CIM expressed its main interest in the area east of the Daliangshan watershed, while we were committed to the territory west of this watershed. We did not seek any immediate agreement on the Tianba district.

Personal matters, particularly relating to the health of missionaries, were never far from our consideration. We gave attention at this conference to determining where the Garrisons should go for the birth of their first baby. Huili was never a possibility, and even Xichang was problematic. We feared there might be complications, and the only feasible place to deal with them was the fine medical facility in Chengdu. Even though this permission was granted to Jim and Virginia, they ultimately decided to remain in

Xichang. Mrs. Madge, a registered British midwife, believed she and the other nurses could care for any emergencies.

Over the next few months, Jim continued his language study there and preached his first sermon in Chinese. This delay, unwelcome as it was, furnished him an opportunity to gain a better foundation for the work he and the other missionaries would be doing in Huili during the next year.

A Strategy Decision

As missionaries, we had all been deeply influenced by Ray Buker, Sr., our foreign secretary, who was deeply committed to the so-called "indigenous policy." His own work with the American Baptist Foreign Mission Society in Burma had led him to believe that special guidelines needed to be followed to develop churches that could stand on their own feet.

In addition to Buker's impact upon us as young missionaries, we were also influenced by a spate of books that came out right at the end of World War II. One was a new printing of Roland Allen's well-known work *Missionary Methods: St. Paul's or Ours?* and Alexander Hay's *New Testament Order for the Church*. Allen's book was particularly significant, since he had been a missionary in China, and many of his insights came from what he deemed were mistakes in missionary practices in China. Another book to which most of us had been exposed was Samuel Clark's *The Nevius Plan*.

The Nevius plan, developed initially in south and north China and then implemented successfully in Korea, was the strategy we wished to follow. One of the motions passed in our two-week session read:

> The Conference accepts the principles of the Nevius plan as the field policy of the Xikang Baptist Mission Conference. These principles are understood to include:
> 1. Missionary personal evangelism with wide itineration.
> 2. The central position of the Bible in every department of the work. Systematic Bible study takes place for each Christian under his group leader or circuit helper.

3. Self-propagation: every believer becomes a teacher, and at the same time a learner from some one better versed than he in the knowledge of the Bible.
4. Self-government: every group of Christians works under its chosen unpaid helpers; who are later supplanted by ordained pastors.
5. Self-support: all church buildings are provided by the congregations; each group, as soon as it is organized, begins to pay toward the salary of the circuit helper or pastor; no pastors of single churches are supported by foreign funds.
6. Strict discipline, based upon Biblical teaching.
7. General helpfulness where possible in the economic problems of the people.

The key phrases here—the "three self" phrases, later to become famous in China's post-1949 church—are "self-support, self-propagation and self-governing." We did not wish to bind ourselves to a human plan, and yet we felt that these principles best epitomized the spirit of Paul's work and that of the early church. The phrase "self-support" was a critical one. When this principle is rigidly applied, it means missionaries do not open any building for evangelistic purposes which is supported by foreign funds. This could be applied to a street chapel, such as the one in Xichang and the one proposed for Lugu. For when people become Christians, they might think of the chapel as a church, and the first step of self-support would be ruined. Some of our missionaries felt strongly that it would be best to start in homes, the tea-shops, the streets—anywhere, in fact, that had no connection with foreign funds.

We were serious about implementing these seven indigenous principles. Our newly-established evangelistic committee met after Christmas in 1948 and developed specific guidelines to carry out each one of them. The biggie was self-support, and we engaged in a lot of hair splitting. One of our motions, for example, stated that "street chapels be not included in the phrase 'church building,' provided that church functions such as Bible study classes, prayer meetings, Sunday school, and church worship services are not held on the premises." We never asked ourselves how we might pull off this impossible ideal.

How would we see to it that all of our group had a common understanding of indigenous principles? By requiring each person to read Merle Davis' *New Buildings on Old Foundations* and Clarke's *The Nevius Plan* and giving them an examination on the two books!

Buker applauded our commitment to Nevius and his strategy. He added still another angle—why continue to buy and build houses, whether in Xichang, Huili, or Lugu? "If you rent," he argued, "you may pay more, but you will retain your mobility and be more apt to move here and there as the need dictates, rather than getting bogged down in ways that will make local Christians depend on you for everything." He kept the ideal before us, but in the last analysis gave in to our property requests. The money involved was not much, not quite fifteen thousand for all three stations.

Unfortunately, even this relatively little amount, when multiplied by the needs of the many new fields acquired by CBFMS, could break the bank. To meet the pressing needs on many fields, the CBFMS Board in October 1947 gave the green light on the "Millions for Missions" campaign. The aim of this campaign was to bring in $500,000 for recurring annual needs worldwide, as well as another $500,000 for emergency needs for property and work needs in each field. We in west China were to receive $70,000 of this latter amount.

Despite all the hard work, prayer, and commitment, it was clear by mid-1948 that the plan was not working. Very little money had come in, and much of this had been eaten up by promotion efforts. Buker confessed in one letter that the staff had never really liked the plan but could not dampen the ardor of the "enthusiastic preachers on the board." This short-fall reduced us to skimping along in everything we did.

The Nevius plan was good theory, but, at this point, there was no real proof that it could help us. Later missiological thinking would refine both Nevius and Allen and show that their principles worked well only when there was ripe soil for the Gospel message. The "indigenous church" was not so much a method, or a set of principles, but rather a goal. Following them would not produce a church; in fact, in unresponsive areas, whether China or Korea, the Nevius plan hindered the work. We later consoled ourselves that neither the Nevius plan nor any other method of work would have produced much in the way of results in the rocky soil of the Ningsu area in these pre-Communist years.

Crossing Some Bridges

At least half of our time was spent splitting hairs over the constitution that we needed to direct the work of our field. As Americans, we felt we needed to put ourselves under the rule of law, and not mere whim or personalities. Certainly some of this was needed—we required order in our work. But the net result was a full-blown constitution that would have done justice to a much larger group of missionaries. Our mission agency in Chicago wanted us to have at least a framework organization, but the main impetus for our prolonged discussions came from Lee's years of experience with the West China Baptist Conference of ABFMS.

And so we worked out eleven single-spaced pages with minutiae about membership, officers, committees, station councils, and amendments. The by-laws, as would be expected, went into even more detail. We worked out the powers and duties of seven separate committees (for sixteen people!): executive, property, language study, evangelism, promotion, auditing, finance, and furlough. We developed extensive procedures for voting by correspondence, a frequent necessity since we were usually separated at several locations. Only once a year at conference time were we able to get together.

We wrote one by-law denying a conference vote to new missionaries arriving in the Ningsu area. Buker told us to delete this provision, sarcastically reminding us that if we had the wisdom to vote, could we not give it to others who arrived after us? The board, he affirmed, saw this as the inalienable right of Baptists!

Many of the actions we took would be necessary for a larger conference of missionaries. And, sooner or later, even our small group would need to face some of the issues we considered. But some of us thought it might be better to cross our bridges when we came to them rather than try to anticipate every little matter in advance. The board at home did not help that much when it sent back to us an extremely detailed interaction with nearly every jot and tittle of our document. Once again, the executive committee had to wrestle with putting into final shape what would never be more than a paper document.

A Bombshell Drops

All that we were doing—plans for Lugu, Xichang, Huili or Yuexi, matters of constitutional order, a strategy for work—all paled into insignificance with the telegram that came Saturday morning, November 20, during our business session. It was sent by the Chungking American consulate and read:

> Please inform all Americans your neighborhood following notification issued by authority American Embassy. Quote. View generally deteriorating. Situation and likely means of exit from China may later be unavailable. Americans in Chungking consular district not prepared remain in areas where now residing under possibly hazardous conditions should plan at once to move to places of safety. Facilities for movement being arranged and will be announced shortly. These facilities will probably be available for only short period; therefore persons intending take advantage this opportunity should do immediately on receipt information time and place of availability of transport. Unquote. Americans should inform consulate Chungking by telegraph name and sex each American desiring take this opportunity to leave. Vandenarend Consul General.

Needless to say, we altered our afternoon agenda. As we discussed our options, we did not doubt that mothers with children should go when the opportunity was presented for them to do so. We wired this decision immediately to Chungking. We were not certain about the men and single women and postponed action until the next day. We had no further light after a night's sleep and much prayer, together and individually. We recommended that the men and single women make their own decisions, with no sense of compulsion from anyone else. This, of course, was easy to say, but obviously none of us wanted to do anything impulsively that would reflect on the courage or wisdom of others. The Garrisons, with a baby due soon and uncertainty about the medical facilities they might need, put their names on the evacuation list.

We wished that we were in a larger center where we might consult with other missionaries. We wired to Simons and Ruth in Chengdu, informing them of our action and requesting them to let us know what their response might be. None of the men or women in Xichang decided to evacuate. Personal danger was of little concern in this decision. We knew that this was the Roman Catholic response, and we had heard that many missionaries already living in Communist-occupied north China had not left. We did not wish to be a stumbling-block for local Christians, but the jury was still out on this question. In one letter to a supporting church, I commented:

> Where would the Church of Christ be today if everyone had pulled up stakes and run whenever the going was rough? It is difficult to know just what the future will bring for China, all of the native Christians, and the foreign missionary, but the Lord guides the future and He is our rock and fortress. I feel that the consulate was just ridding its hands of a little responsibility and that really there is yet no danger in this area of China.

In one sense, previous history made this a reasonable judgment. No Chinese government for at least 150 years had controlled this area of China—why should the new government have the power to do any differently? Compromises might be made with local warlords that would be satisfactory both to the new central government and local officials. Life would go on as before, and we would still have the opportunity to continue our ministry. Little did we know that we were at the beginning of a new era in China's history. Our work would continue, even with many indications of success, for another two years, but the handwriting was already on the wall.

Farewell Service in 1946 for China Missionaries (C.B.)

Ruth Covell with students in her Bible class in Chengdu

Language study with Teacher Pan in Chengdu

George and Hannah Cole

The Covells' outdoor wedding

Lugu home for Covells and Carrs

Dan Carr treating some Nosu illnesses in our Lugu home

A black Nosu wife

Lucille Carr with a black Nosu wife

Dan Carr and Bill Simons at Hannah Cole's grave in Fulin

George Cole leaving Hong Kong with his four small children

Lee Lovegren with Ida and daughter Mildred
on the day of his exit from China

8

Keeping on Keeping on– A Long 1949

The Beginning of the End

Keeping on keeping on is at the heart of the missionary task. Nothing is more important than perseverance—that ability to tough it out when the going gets rough. Very few among us are brilliant. Our strategies, no matter how well conceived, will not win the day. I do not mean that we "somehow muddle through." God does not reward unwise plans or lazy thinking. But that ability to hang in there and move forward trusting Him is a pearl of great price.

The telegram we had received in late November (and more were to come) made it abundantly clear that our days of effective work in China were numbered. We were at the beginning of the end. This did not deter us in our daily living, nor did it mean we were about to stop our work. Even after "black Saturday" with its ominous warning, we held a festive Thanksgiving together, and then, a few weeks later, celebrated Christmas. Church members and some of us rehearsed endlessly, both for the children and adult programs on Saturday the 25th. The children did particularly well in putting on a pantomime of the birth of Christ. We even had Christmas trees, cut down by Dan and me in the mountains behind the normal college and hauled home ingloriously on the backs of our bikes.

We celebrated our Christmas dinner at noon, in between the morning and afternoon meetings at the church. The missionaries had fun and frolic with games, songs, and refreshments in the evening. Even my birthday, once missed entirely on our trip across the ocean on the *Marine Lynx*, was worked into the evening get-together.

If normalcy continued in our daily lives, so was it with the work. The first baptisms and the formation of the Xichang Baptist Church came in January 1949. We had just completed what we hoped was only the first of many annual field conferences. And we were continuing plans to open a new station in Lugu, with all the time, energy, and money that this might require.

Even as we did all of this, we began to see that the telegram was only the first of many signs of the impending end. Christian refugees from north China showed up in many of our church services. News continued to trickle through of missionaries coming through Chengdu on their way out of the country. People to whom we talked and preached were more apathetic. Change was coming in China, and they did not know how we and our "foreign religion" fit into the total scheme of a new future.

Local politics, long smoldering on the back burner, were ready to boil over into open conflict. In the Xichang-Lugu area four different armed groups, only one of which belonged to the national government, tried to control the turf. China's government at this time was very weak, even as it had been most of the time since the beginning of the Protestant missionary movement in 1807. It held nominal sovereignty over all of the country's provinces, but only because Generalissimo Chiang Kai-shek had surrendered some of his power to ruthless war lords.

The national government was represented locally by General He Guiguang and the Jin Bibu. He was opposed by the Qin Bianbu (Border Guard Division), the Ten Kenhui, a kind of agricultural society, and the 24th Army group. General He's unwise actions provoked a minor war between two groups of Nosu, which made the trip to Lugu by bike, or by any other means, a risky venture. When in Nanking, General He had promised Den Teguang, twenty-three year old son of the famous Den who had organized the forty-eight families of Nosu, that he would support him as leader of the Nosu around Xichang. However, after he returned to Xichang, he switched his support to Sen Silin, a close friend of the Den family. Rumor had it that this abrupt turn-about was sweetened by a gift of eighty ounces of gold.

On one of my frequent trips between Xichang and Lugu, armed men blockaded the road and threatened me with levelled rifles. They did not wish to harm me nor to steal the several dozen heavy ten-ounce nuggets of silver I was carrying. They only wanted to know which side of the two Nosu factions I supported. My answer that I was neutral and really knew nothing of their affairs seemed to satisfy them.

To demonstrate in a concrete fashion that we were neutral meant that we must court all factions equally. This led us to pay many polite visits to men in power and to hold endless feasts where we communicated clearly that our motives were religious, and that we were interested in the welfare of all people in the Ningsu area. A part of our problem in the picture-taking episode in Mianning in June 1948 stemmed from the constant conflicts among these four groups. It was a no-man's land, filled with many booby traps. We had stumbled into one unawares.

The clearest sign of our impending trouble was that we were constantly out of money. In December 1948, we received word from the Lutheran World Federation in Shanghai that its representatives could no longer serve as our financial agent to transmit money to Xichang. Even after we found a new agent in Hong Kong, our problems were not over. We had checks, bank drafts, and many other proofs that we had money. The difficulty was that the bank had no cash to give us. If the planes did not fly—and increasingly it was clear that this tenuous life line would soon be severed—no cash was being brought into the area. This lack of money slowed things down in Xichang, but the biggest crunch came in making it impossible to start the work in Lugu. Even enough salary to keep food on the table was a worrisome issue.

We grasped at any possible solution. One hope was to get hold of some greenbacks. This would enable us to buy stable local products—something we could not do with checks—that did not lose their value overnight as the local paper money did. And so it was decided that John Simpson and I should go to Kunming and use our American checks to buy U.S. currency and bring it back with us. Easier said than done!

Transportation south toward Kunming was non-existent. The road to Huili, although filled with awful ruts, broken bridges, and dangerous landslides, was open, and we travelled with the Cole family as it returned home after the mission conference. To say that this two-day trip was precarious is an understatement. John and I sat on top of the truck and fended off low-hanging telephone wires that threatened to knock both us and the baggage to the ground.

From Huili to Kunming, a distance of about two hundred miles, we depended on our two feet. Travelling with a team of twenty-three pack horses and their drivers, we covered about twenty miles each day. We could have gone faster on our own, but we needed protection from gangs of robbers lurking in the mountains. We ate and slept with the men throughout the trip. The food was coarse and the sleeping accommodations were rough, but it showed us another dimension of Chinese life. The mountains along the way were breathtakingly beautiful and rugged, particularly on both sides of the Yangtze River, called the River of Golden Sand in this western part of China. During the day as we walked, the weather was warm and pleasant, but in the Yangtze area we had to don heavy coats.

One day we travelled through the CIM station at Salawu, where we visited with Arthur and Alice Glasser. There had been a people movement to Christ in this area among the dependent Nosu of Yunnan province. Many thousands of these people had declared their allegiance to Christ and a translation of the Bible had been prepared. We learned of a recent church gathering at Salawu where two thousand Nosu had crowded out the building as they met to memorize and study Scripture. We breathed a prayer, not yet answered, that this might occur some day in the Ningsu area.

We arrived in Kunming on January 11 and stayed in the CIM home, where always there was a welcome to unannounced strangers. We were famished by this time for something other than our coarse Chinese diet of the past two weeks. The food at the CIM home that first evening was delightful, but not quite enough. As John and I went out on the street in the evening for a short stroll, we saw some delicious-looking *bao zi* (meat or sugar filled dumplings) and gobbled down a few. Eating *bao zi* at the end of the day, even when the climate is cool, risks picking up spoiled meat filling. So we should not have been surprised that we woke up sick the next morning and lost some of our precious time in Kunming. Our CIM hosts were very concerned and wondered what of their meal the previous evening could have made us so sick. We did not have the nerve to tell them what had really happened.

Our four days in Kunming were hectic—a dental checkup, physical exams, buying some of the things we could not get in Xichang, such as 1250 airmail forms. First priority, of course, was to get the money we needed. We purchased $10,000 in U.S. currency and squirreled it away safely in our suitcases.

While we were in Kunming, we met Mr. and Mrs. John Nance who had carried on an independent Baptist work in Kunming. They wished to affiliate with CBFMS, and John and I encouraged them to write to Ray Buker. A few months later, Mrs. Nance, home for a short visit, presented their application papers to the Board. The Board decided not to accept them, citing an insufficient educational background, but Ray agreed that the door might still be open. Before this could happen, most Kunming missionaries were leaving China.

We had prayed that we would be able to arrange safe transportation back to Xichang. At about the time our business was completed, we learned of a six-truck military convoy that was leaving for Xichang. We received permission to go along and set out on January 17th. We never let the suitcases out of our sight. Since they were tied on top of one truck, we rode right with them during the day, and slept there in our sleeping bags when the convoy stopped for the night. One of our Chinese fellow-riders asked me, "Why don't you and your friend come inside and sleep in the inn where it is more comfortable?" I replied that we liked it outdoors better, hardly a sensible answer for the bitterly cold nights. Undoubtedly, some of the men suspected what we were carrying, but no one bothered us. Travelling this way was not the smartest, but God protected us and the money.

The first 150 miles of our return was west along the famed Burma road, and then, near the city of Chuxiong, we turned north and wound our way over numerous high mountains to the Yangtze River. Here the goods on the trucks—largely gasoline and military uniforms—were ferried across the river and put on other trucks which would carry them to Xichang.

The ferry was pulled by a small gasoline-run tug boat. On the first trip across, just as we were preparing to turn into the main current of the river, the drive shaft broke. With some herculean effort on the part of the crew, we were able to return to the shore. A few seconds more, and the entire load of freight and passengers would have been swept down to some nearby rapids.

The trucks were badly overloaded, and those of us riding on top feared every time a bridge approached. I failed to pay enough attention at one point, and when the rear end of the truck cracked through a weak bridge, I was thrown off by the sudden lurch. My right foot was bent under me when I landed, but fortunately it was nothing worse than a strain.

Later that same day, we got over a long, high bridge just outside Huili, but the truck immediately behind us went through it. No one was hurt, but this accident kept us in Huili for two days, while the Chinese fretted and fumed as they extricated the heavy truck from the broken bridge. We relaxed with the Coles and gained new courage for the final two days toward home, when we went over 110 precarious bridges. The drivers used more caution on this leg of the trip, unloading the truck whenever it seemed that there might be danger.

Wednesday, January 26, three days before Chinese New Year, we arrived in Xichang. Were we (and the money) ever welcome! Now waiting plans and dreams might be implemented. Not only did we bring money; we also had arranged for Mr. Savage of the English Assemblies of God to be our financial agent in Kunming. Each month he arranged for ten horse-loads of *yangsa*, ten-pound bundles of cotton thread, to be sent to us. This staple good, conveniently prepared in twenty-two skeins, enabled us to buy what we needed.

Another sign of the beginning of the end, although we learned about it only later, was a meeting on January 7 at CBFMS mission headquarters in Chicago of executives from eighteen evangelical mission agencies. They deliberated on the future of mission work in China even as John and I walked toward Kunming. A number of important matters were discussed. First, the representatives of several agencies reported that their missionaries had been told by Chinese leaders and pastors that their missionaries should remain on the field. This, some affirmed, was true even in those areas that had already come under Communist influence. At least one mission agency, the China Inland Mission, announced that it was officially encouraging its missionaries to remain at their posts of duty.

Second, these representatives talked about the possible need, if a severe crisis developed, for the evacuation of all missionaries. At this point, about 30% of the total north American missionary force had left its areas of work, but some had relocated to less-threatened areas within China. These leaders agreed, rather gratuitously it would seem from the outside, that missionaries should not "leave in a hurry," but rather plan carefully with Chinese leaders how their churches might deal with the impending crisis. The hope was expressed that an entirely indigenous church, meeting largely in homes, could continue to have an effective Gospel witness. Some leaders suggested that funds be left to subsidize certain institutional work, such as Bible schools, for one year.

In general, the spirit of this gathering was upbeat, planning for the worst but hoping for the best. The general mood was that the mass of China's "population was so huge that no nation had yet succeeded in consolidating its conquest of this land for any length of time."*[1]* The basic assumption of this statement can be questioned: was it indeed another nation attacking from the outside, or was it Chinese themselves who desired to create a new China?

Had we known of this meeting, it probably would not have influenced any of our decision-making in China. All of these options were in our minds. The ongoing task that occupied us daily tended to push these "signs" to the side. God had called us to China; the work was well under way; it could hardly be God's will for us to leave China with so much of the harvest unreaped; and we felt relatively safe physically, since the high Daliangshan mountains shielded us from the agony in other parts of the great Middle Kingdom. And so we "kept on keeping on" in each of our areas of work.

Further Progress in Xichang

Lee and Ida were central figures for the work in this capital city. They spoke the language far better than any of the rest of us and were familiar enough in the culture to avoid the problems that could bother us. When Miss Hu Kaixiang left to do student work in Chengdu, she had been replaced by Mr. and Mrs. Yang Jiemin. These two fine workers had Bible school training and were mature and spiritual. They entered into all phases of the work very well, and church members rejoiced to have this kind of stable leadership. This stability was to last for only a time, since it soon became apparent that the Yangs were more urgently needed to develop the work at Lugu.

One vexing matter that we chose to implement at this time was to insist, in accord with the Nevius plan, that the Xichang church assume responsibility within a period of six months for the rent, lights, and servant of the building it occupied. Otherwise, we concluded, it should find other quarters. In retrospect it would seem, that though this might be an important goal, it was not the focus needed at this critical juncture for a newly-formed church.

Even with the loss of valuable workers like Miss Hu and the Yangs, the Xichang church had capable lay leaders. Mrs. Han continued to give herself unstintingly to the needs of the brothers and sisters. Mr. Lo Binjiong, a former Baptist evangelist who had served with the West China Baptist Mission in Yaan, came to Xichang during the winter months to work in the Superior Court. He gave much-needed help, until late summer 1949 when he returned to Yaan. Pastor Wei Danchen of the "Spiritual Seminary" across the river from Chungking came for six weeks in the fall and, had it not been for the worsening political situation, would probably have moved to the area. The deacons of the church, not really that mature for the most part, arranged for all of the evangelistic services and enlisted some of the new members to do the speaking.

Lack of trained leaders meant no fewer meetings. Each week the church ran one Sunday morning preaching service, two or three evening evangelistic meetings, one women's meeting, three children's meetings, three Bible classes, two prayer meetings, several sessions for inquirers, a meeting in the prison, several home meetings, and frequent home visits. Unlike churches in America that give little attention to members and new converts between Sundays, Xichang's meetings were intended daily to strengthen, nurture, and develop the faith of all who had made a commitment to Christ. In a city like Xichang, with no competing meetings and no "night life," the church meetings became the focal point of a new community for young believers. Without this rather hectic round of activities, they would have lacked the social network to develop their new life in Christ.

In July 1949, with the help of several of the missionaries wives, the local Christians conducted a three-week Daily Vacation Bible School with attendance running between seventy and one hundred boys and girls. One boy made a definite decision for Christ and was accepted for baptism. However, because of the strong objection of his mother, his baptism was postponed.

Working with children gave an entering point with families, but it was not as effective as in America, where we stress individuals acting independently from their families. The best strategy, where possible, was to evangelize within a family network. One good example was a Mr. He. Soon after he had shown interest in the Christian faith, he got tracts and Bible portions and carried them back to his home, about fifteen miles from Xichang. He told his father and other family members of his new-found faith. Within a short period, the elder Mr. He, the young man's sister, and his own wife had made professions of faith and were baptized.

Missionaries took part in the services as they had time and their language ability permitted. I was not stationed at Xichang during most of the year, but when I made business trips to get money and supplies or to sit with the mission executive committee, I was pressed into leading meetings. I may have already used a certain message once at Lugu, and the opportunity to give it again to a wider audience in Xichang fixed the vocabulary and style more firmly in my mind.

As a result of this considerable activity, the message reached many Chinese in Xichang. By the fall of 1949, Pastor Wei from Chungking baptized twenty-three more persons, raising the total church membership to forty.

One of the best places for outreach was the local jail in Xichang. The weekly meeting was held on Saturday, and the participating church members met first at the church mid-morning and then went as a group. Compared with what we might have expected, the prisoners were not dressed that badly, nor did they look poorly fed. Possibly 20% of the group were women. One in particular stood out—obviously a lady of some class who was imprisoned for trying to smuggle out opium on the plane to Chungking.

A surprising thing was that some small children were with the prisoners. In one instance, at least, the prisoner was a widower, and there was no one else but himself to care for his infant daughter.

Nothing was unusual about the service: a few short choruses sung from large song sheets tacked up on the courtyard wall; a testimony from one of the group who had confessed Christ; and two short messages. Mr. Lo spoke on "the salt of the earth" at one service and brought along a couple of ounces of salt for each inmate to illustrate what he meant.

The range of crimes represented included murder and robbery, but opium seemed to be an ingredient of most offenses. Legally, to grow, sell, use, or transport opium was a serious crime, but the victims of the law were those too naive or poor to get away with it or to buy themselves out of trouble.

One criminal had a unique situation. He and his wife both had leprosy, not an unusual situation in the Ningsu area. In accordance with a tradition often followed in this area when a wife with leprosy seemed about to die, the husband killed her by burning her to death, and then cremating the body. In this instance, the infant son of the woman also died in the incident. Officials felt that an older son might have done the killing, since the father was blind. However, in the trial, the father assumed all the blame. At the time, there was no separate facility in the jail where this prisoner with leprosy could be kept, but jail officials were planning to build a separate room.

Ida and one of the women converts, Yang Kaimin, made short forays into the country areas. Witness here was difficult, because of the depth of Buddhist belief. Once they explained the Gospel to a ninety-two year old woman, whose belief centered on calling on the name of the Amitabha Buddha. This name in Chinese comes out as *amitofu*, and she repeated it endlessly. When Ida mentioned the name of Jesus to her, she immediately replied, "Jesus, *amitofu*." Or when she told her that Jesus can forgive sin, it came back as "Jesus saves from sin, *amitofu*." One telling, or even several, of the Gospel story did not penetrate a lifelong worldview. The name of Jesus made no sense, or else his name was added to the list of buddhas or saviors whom they felt might be able to help them.

The Xichang station was the hub for receiving and distributing Christian literature in the area. During a medical trip to Chungking, Lee Lovegren arranged for the *St. Paul* to fly in an entire plane of Bibles, Testaments, and Gospel portions. Ernest Madge, one of the English Baptists serving with the Border Service Department work, was the local representative of the Bible societies which provided the literature and paid for the high price of its shipment.

Problems in Huili

No sooner had the George Coles and Esther Nelson returned to Huili after the November 1948 conference, than major problems arose in our mission's agreement with the China Home Mission Society. One question concerned travel expenses from Shanghai to Huili for Wang Daoran and his family. Another issue was the money needed to evict a Dr. Ji, who stubbornly refused to move from the church property. George's understanding was that the CHMS was to pay this, and its hesitancy reinforced what he had heard from others that it was a "pauper" mission.

Because CHMS felt that "you (CBFMS) want everything according to your ideas," an attitude it found "troublesome," it wished that we take over things on a trial basis for two years. It agreed that after this period, with the concurrence of an Australian church group that had been funding it for some time, it would give us the entire work.

The conditions we had laid on CHMS were probably more harsh than necessary, a decision pushed more by the younger missionaries over the objections of the more experienced "old China hands," Lee, Ida, and Esther.

For the first time we learned from this CHMS letter that it still had a contract, with two years left to run, with the Foreign Mission Board of the Australian Churches of Christ, by which it paid them two hundred pounds sterling a year to operate the station. CHMS had apparently been dealing with the Australians and us at the same time. Our Xichang executive committee immediately sent off a letter to Australia to clarify this muddle.

From the secretary of the Australian mission we learned that it had, in cooperation with CHMS, taken over the work from the ABFMS when it could no longer maintain its long supply line from its main centers of work in Chengdu and Yaan (then Yazhou). When the Australian board reduced its help to the annual subsidy, it proposed that the CIM, with its strong tribal work in Salawu, take over responsibility for Huili. This did not prove feasible, which is why it seemed natural to relate the Huili work to our center in Xichang.

The Australians hoped that we could straighten out our tangle with the CHMS, but this was not to be. Unfortunately, by summer 1949, it seemed necessary for CBFMS and the CHMS to go their separate ways in the task of evangelizing this small Chinese city. The mission rented the He Chen Bank building on South Main Street and commenced a full schedule of preaching services on July 3. From that time on, the missionaries discontinued all meetings at the West Suburb Street Chapel with Pastor and Mrs. Wang, although they maintained cordial relationships and worked cooperatively whenever possible.

In the first part of 1949, before this separation occurred, the new missionaries kept diligently at their language study, helped Miss Nelson in the children's and women's work, and supported Pastor Wang in preaching services. A local Christian woman, Mrs. Tu, helped as she was able, as did Peter Liu who, despite the protests of the Huili group, was often diverted to Lugu for business matters.

From March until June, the missionaries held Saturday evening Youth for Christ meetings. These were bi-lingual, with George teaching choruses and preaching in English and Dr. Chang, a local physician, interpreting. At the beginning, attendance crowded out the chapel's seating capacity of two hundred people. Once, at an outdoor service, over four hundred were present. Within a couple of months, however, after the closure of one of the large schools and the starting of a conflicting meeting for singing at another school, attendance dropped off, and the meetings were discontinued. This was also true of the Sunday afternoon bi-lingual meetings for students held during the spring. In February, George accepted an invitation to teach English one hour a day in the Xian Zhong Middle School. This continued until school was out in June and gave many fine opportunities to form friendships with young people.

The entire Ningsu area had many homeless and helpless children. This led George to propose that the Huili missionaries establish a small orphanage to care for these pressing needs. By this plan the children would attend local schools and not be separated from their culture. Even though he did not project a large school, he hoped that it would care for needs in Lugu and Xichang as well. Buker was not impressed that we ought to start such projects in unstable China. Our Xichang Executive Committee vetoed the plan since, unknown to George, there was already an orphanage run by a Christian man in Xichang.

The Garrisons returned to Huili in May 1949 with Judy, their first born, and with Jim having given his first sermon in Chinese at the Xichang chapel. Since Cole's language facility had improved and Flora Mae, who had arrived with the Garrisons, was ready to participate in the meetings, everybody felt the occasion was right to begin a full range of services. At this time, they opened the new meeting place, simply named the Christian Chapel.

Between them, George and Jim took on the heavy load of preparing and preaching two services each during the week. This covered the Sunday morning and evening services and the Tuesday and Thursday evening evangelistic services. George, Jim, Esther, and Flora Mae handled the four different sections of the Sunday school. Women's and children's meetings during the week, as well as the August DVBS, were conducted as the Lius and Mrs. Tu were available.

Jim and George were never sure how much of their preaching the people in the usually-crowded chapel understood. Peter Liu was often available to give a recapitulation of their messages, but, even then, they were not sure. To be able to preach twice weekly was a boon to them spiritually. This is what they had come to China to do. To see the earnest faces of listeners, who, until this time, may never have heard the name of Christ was a great thrill. Whether or not this was the best way to reap a spiritual harvest is questionable. None of us foreign missionaries had fluent Chinese at this stage of our ministries, and it was presumptuous to think that being filled with the Holy Spirit, as we often prayed, compensated for the boring experience it must have been for the Chinese to listen to our child-like language.

Another problem bothered the Huili missionaries. Peter Liu was a likable chap, very capable in business matters, always willing to go out of his way to serve. His wife was a fine helpmate. But he had several distasteful habits—smoking, drinking, and gambling among them—that the missionaries did not feel commended the Gospel. They suggested that we should review his status at the second annual field conference. If this type of conduct disqualified one from being a church member at Xichang, could it be tolerated in a business manager and part-time church helper? This type of situation confronted us wherever we worked throughout the Ningsu district—left-over Christians from previous groups who were not really following the Lord closely, but who yet wanted to be involved in what we were doing. They were used to working with foreigners and knew how to get along with us and serve our every whim. We knew the difficulty, but what real choice did we have?

A highlight of the summer was when K. Y. Chen, a teacher at the Southwest Bible School in Salawu, Yunnan, some three or four days to the south, came with several students and conducted four days of special evangelistic meetings. The good interest in the Gospel, rather different from what the missionaries had seen to this point, only intensified the need to have the regular services of a Chinese evangelist.

Some adults had professed to believe, as had four girls in Flora Mae's Sunday school class, but none of these was actively preparing for baptism. Glad as we were for specific evidence of interest, we knew only too well that baptism was the seal, the final commitment to Christ from which one did not turn back.

An attempt was made once again in September and October to conduct bi-lingual services for students on Sunday afternoons, but these only lasted for a few weeks and had to be discontinued for lack of interest. Jail services were held weekly in October, and, along with the Gospel, food and clothing were distributed. Esther made two three-day trips to outlying villages distributing medicine and literature. The Nosu village of Mamagu was one in which they felt that there might be a continuing interest in the future. The mission was also involved in a small school at the village of Xiaohechin, a former project of the Border Service Department and CHMS, but when a number of students left and Mrs. Liu resigned, the missionaries decided not to continue it.

During these months, life had its ups and downs. The Garrisons were very happy with their new baby, and, on July 11, Hannah Cole gave birth to their third child, Gary. The Coles' good friend, Dr. Chang, was the attending physician. Gary was probably the first foreign baby born in Huili. Dr. Chang had western training and was in charge of the government hospital in Huili. George and Hannah witnessed regularly to him and his wife, a trained nurse, but he was totally indifferent to the claims of Christ.

In an isolated area like Huili, communication with distant America was difficult, expensive, and often garbled. When the group broke with the CHMS, some new housing was needed, and the missionaries sent a telegram to Chicago to request the needed amount. When it arrived at the home office, it read: "Recommend purchase of Huili property under BREN dollars." The Board asked Western Union to clarify it, and the second attempt read "H00 dollars." Finally, this was corrected to the right amount of "500 dollars." The Board approved it.

Depending on the zigs and zags of the dollar exchange, telegrams could be expensive. At one time a six-word text cost $100 U.S. When the Coles were expecting their third child, they wrote the Board ahead of time giving the full names of a boy or girl. When the child was born, all they needed to send was one word, "boy."

The only serious health problem in Huili was when Virginia came down with a light case of typhus. This disrupted Jim's preaching schedule, since for two weeks he was nurse to Virginia and the baby. This illness reminded us all that, even though we had all received the prescribed shots, these were inoculations only, and not guarantees! Typhus-producing fleas were everywhere, and despite precautions, insect repellents, and the use of DDT in our homes, we faced health hazards daily from which only the Lord could deliver us.

Huili, much like Mianning to the northern end of our field, was an opium center, and it was tragic to observe its deadening effects on heart, mind, and body. We were told that as many as 90% of the local populace were addicted in some measure to the black poison. Money continued to be a problem, although the missionaries always had a two- or three-month supply of yarn. Unlike hard metal money that could be placed in almost any safe spot, yarn had to be stored with care. Mildew got at eighteen bundles of the *yangsa* in late August, and Huili members could do nothing but absorb the loss. The economic future did not look good, since our financial agent, Mr. Savage in Kunming, felt the need to close his work and left us once again with uncertainty about our continuing money supply.

By the beginning of August, another warning came from the American consul in Chungking, and this, along with stone-throwing at the chapel and some signs of a mob spirit, caused the missionaries to think once again about evacuating women and children. Jim and Virginia tended toward leaving, while George was ready to send his family to safety. Esther said she would stay, and Flora Mae wished to go elsewhere in China. This "go or not go" ambivalence stayed with the Huili missionaries to the end.

Along with this pessimistic picture were some naive statements by local people that "it will be a long time before the Communist control is felt in Xikang." Isolation and a weak government in Beijing had convinced them that life in their area could not be disrupted by the zigs and zags of the national destiny. My own estimate was no better. I wrote to my parents in early February with the profound observation: "I don't think Communist armies will ever come here. There would be no point in it. They will grab the government and control things that way." We would learn shortly how mistaken we could all be.

Moving Ahead in Lugu

Although we had acquired a street chapel and the residential property on the hill in Lugu, some of us had been travelling back and forth from Xichang since August 1948. No foreign missionary resided there permanently until I moved from Xichang on February 3, 1949. For most of that month, I lived half-settled in two large rooms above the chapel and spent my time making as many friends as possible, studying, and supervising the workmen who were remodelling the rest of the chapel. I ate with Zhou Lianbe, another man who helped the mission in business matters.

We would have liked to use Mr. Zhou more actively in evangelism, but his complex marital situation made this unwise. A graduate of Biola in China at Changsha, Hunan Province, he had originally lived in Xichang. When he returned to this area for a short visit, his relatives put pressure on him to take a second wife, since his first wife had given him only daughters. He gave in to their demands, but this marriage, although producing the desired son, gave him no satisfaction, and he separated from his second wife. He now wanted his first family to join him, but the Communist drive had cut roads from Hunan, and he did not have the money to bring them by plane. As a mission, we did not feel that we could help him.

Living in this fashion in Lugu meant an all Chinese diet, which, for me, translated into nine average-sized bowls of rice daily, along with the vegetables and meat that go with it. Small items like cocoa or bread served to supplement the Chinese food. I learned, though, that it is better to eat either Chinese or Western food rather than mixing the two—just a personal prejudice. By late March and early April 1949, fresh cherries could be found everywhere. We could buy two pounds for an equivalent of about five cents and had a bowl or two with every meal. When the cherries were gone, we had loquats. Some type of fresh fruit always seemed to be available.

My apartment, if you want to call it that, was not much. The floor was of uneven planks, a crude mat covered the ceiling, and the windows were pasted over with a very poor tissue-like paper. The walls had large cracks through which the wind and dust came in huge gusts. I had placed a charcoal-burning stove in the middle of the room, and, if I put on enough layers of clothing, I was reasonably warm. Ordinarily I was bothered by charcoal fumes, but the cracks allowed most of these to escape, and it did not make me sick. One decrepit wooden chair, a rattan chair, a make-shift book case with my few precious books, a crude box-like closet, an old army cot, and a nice, local desk made up the furniture. A small washroom was at one end of the large room. The commode, the usual Chinese squat-fashion type, was downstairs, not at all convenient to get to in the middle of the night.

The rest of the chapel was no better than this. The downstairs room where we held meetings, when white washed and decorated with a few Gospel posters, looked tolerable—even beautiful to the passers-by. The inner rooms on both the first and second levels were hopeless, but what else was there in this kind of a city? With faith and hope we went ahead in trying to remodel them for Elwyn and Becky Stafford and their two girls, who were expected to join me shortly in Lugu.

We not only needed to remodel some rooms; we had to arrange for the "proper" removal of what was in them. In one room there were several "gods," and the old woman in charge was not about to move them until a propitious day came along. We finally persuaded her, but, in the end, she made some special sacrifices to these small wooden and stone images, including burning incense and candles and offering paper religious money.

Peter Liu replaced Mr. Zhou in late February, and the two of us together were able to start a weekly children's meeting and one evangelistic service. We opened the chapel door and welcomed passers-by to browse through our books and to buy Gospel portions. Preaching in such an environment was a new experience for me. Crowds of people coming in off a busy street were never well-behaved. But Lugu set new standards in unruliness. People did not sit still for more than ten minutes. When they left they rose, said something polite (or otherwise) and made their way out, often taking several friends with them. Some came right up front, shook my hand, commented about something I said, and then went on their way. We learned how to prepare short messages and repeat them three or four times as we spoke. In this way the early-leavers or the late-arrivers got a total message. This "preaching in circles," something I did not learn in seminary, was the only way to get a message across.

The mission's plans for others to join me in Lugu went awry. Elwyn had already made several trips to help in the planned renovation and to bring some pieces of freight. Then, with little warning, his wife, Becky developed a severe depressive psychosis, and Dr. James Broomhall advised her and the entire family to return to America. Otherwise, she would be a continuing care for those in Xichang, and her own condition would get worse. She became totally disoriented and was not able to relate even to Elwyn or to their girls. Stress is always present in varying degrees as one works in another culture; some because of temperament and personality make-up are able to handle it better than others.

The personality tensions on the Xichang compound undoubtedly contributed to the stress. The group there recognized this and tried earnestly by prayer, confession, and some frank talks to resolve the problems. The relief was only temporary and would not be settled until each unit was at its own station and involved in its own ministry.

The Stafford family flew to Shanghai on March 24, and Becky was placed in the Shanghai Mental Hospital. She improved remarkably in a few days, and it appeared that they might work with Youth for Christ, go to the east China field, or even return to Xikang. These hopes never materialized, and they had to return home. Dan and Ida accompanied the family as far as Shanghai and hoped to return shortly. Ida made it back in six weeks, much slower than Lee had hoped, but Dan was delayed by various problems until mid-October. His delay hindered what we wanted to do in Lugu, since, with the Staffords' return to America, it seemed natural for the Carrs to be stationed in Lugu. But was it wise for Lucille and the two children to come alone to Lugu? Or would it be best for the Simpsons to move to Lugu? This was not impossible, although tentative plans—we learned that all plans are "tentative"—were for them to go to Lizhou, a city about halfway between Xichang and Lugu.

During these days of remodelling, of starting a few services, of arranging for the Staffords to return home, I was constantly biking the thirty-five miles between Lugu and Xichang. As the Chinese said, it was either *nie feng* (adverse wind) or *xun feng* (accompanying wind). If the former, the trip took five or six hours and left me totally exhausted. If the wind pushed me along, it was as short as 3-3/4 hours. Once when my "foreign horse," as the rural Chinese called a bicycle, "dropped an anchor," a quaint Chinese way of saying it conked out, I pushed it about fifteen miles. High streams, broken bridges, horrible ruts, gangs of marauding Nosu always made the trip interesting and produced a few more war stories.

The local children in Lugu were much less disciplined than those in Xichang and in Huili. Many came from uneducated families with high illiteracy rates, and they had never gone to school. They devised every conceivable way to irritate me. My response was not always what it should have been. As I studied at night in my second story room, reading with the kerosene Aladdin lamp, children going by on the main street below threw pebbles or even stones against the paper windows. Quite a few came through, and I was afraid these could break the lamp, or even start a fire. So every once in a while I hurried downstairs and tried to catch the more rascally ones. This, obviously, only added fuel to the fire. Eventually, some of the neighbors intervened to help the children behave in a more orderly way.

With all its problems, being right in the center of Lugu had great advantages. We quickly made friends with many neighbors. They did not see us as avoiding Chinese life. In fact, that was what made Elwyn willing to put his family temporarily into the remodelled chapel, while something more adequate was being built.

We were initiated quickly into life all about us. Once a number of Daoist priests came to the door and offered, for a high price, to cast out all of our resident demons. I politely told them we had none, and they went quietly on their way. At another time, I was awakened at about 3:30 a.m. by frightful wailing in an upstairs room in the building sharing a common wall with my bedroom. This kept up intermittently until dawn, when, to an accompaniment of clanging crude brass instruments, the funeral procession began. We were reminded sorrowfully of the multitudes who have none of the comfort or hope of those who die believing in Christ.

I learned something about loneliness in these days in Lugu with no other expatriates around. Life was Chinese the whole way—all Chinese meals, Chinese language all day long, fluent Chinese dreams at night, Chinese books and literature as I studied it and distributed it. Not that I did not have some good English reading. Particularly helpful were the classics *Behind the Ranges* by Mrs. Howard Taylor, *By My Spirit* by Jonathan Goforth, and a book entitled *Praying Hyde*. Many times I asked myself, "How did I ever get myself into this situation?" And it was a situation: isolated, no missionary companions, single with little apparent hope of change, strange food every day, people about us who did not know why we were there, a deteriorating political situation that threatened to blow us away at almost any time, local wars involving Nosu and gangs of bandits, uncertain finances, and this pesky Chinese language on which one never made enough progress!

The stress became more intense as I tried to deal in a rational way with all the winds of rumor and superstition that swirled about us. A classic one was about the "golden ducks." We foreigners, it was affirmed by the local people, had extraordinary eyes. That is why we had bought the rocky property on the hill where our new residence was being built. We saw that far below the surface of the ground there were several flocks of golden ducks. These eventually would surface and we would sell them at an immense profit. How do you deal with this?

A rumor at about the same time, starting first in Xichang, where John and Irene Simpson heard it, was that two missionaries were overheard discussing what they had heard on the radio the previous evening. The news broadcast was that two eminent Chinese had visited America and had brought back five atomic bombs. They had returned to China, and one bomb had been dropped on Nanking, killing all the Communists there. This made the local people think that the Nationalists must be winning the war, and so the prices of *yangsha* (cotton thread) and silver dropped dramatically. For the most part we listened carefully, declined to discuss, and tried to switch the topic of conversation.

Some hope came to our Lugu work when Pastor Yang and his family joined me on May 1. I felt a close kinship with Pastor Yang and his wife. We held long conversations on many subjects—about him, his family, his dreams and hopes, and about me and the mission. Why did we operate the way we did? What would happen to China? How best could we evangelize in the countryside around Lugu? He was not much older than I, rather quiet by nature, deeply-committed to his family (their fourth child was born shortly after they came to Lugu), and willing to bear the brunt of working with foreigners in his own land.

This was not easy for him. We worked, prayed, travelled, faced hardship, and ate together, but the barriers preventing complete fellowship in Christ never totally collapsed. Some of these were cultural, most economic. The Carrs and I did not live high on the hog, but even when we tried our hardest to identify with the Chinese life-style, we still failed to "live as comrades."[2] We like to think, falsely I fear, that we no longer have this problem in Christian missions. If our national church leaders dared to be frank, we would soon learn otherwise.

The political situation had heated up considerably, but we found it difficult to keep pace. I had no radio, we did not want to ask direct questions to local people, and the planes, after virtually stopping for about two months, were flying only sporadically. So we had no outside newspapers, and our mail from the states followed a circuitous route that took it by air to Chengdu and then overland to us via Fulin and Mianning. We did know that Beijing, not the capital of the country at that time, had fallen to the Communists, that Chiang Kai-shek had made a token resignation, to be replaced as president by Li Zongren, and that negotiations were going on that might bring a Kuomintang surrender. By mid-May Shanghai fell to the Communists, and we were all concerned for Dan who had gone there for medical treatment. His first problem was a persistent cough that was corrected only by a dissection and interruption of the superior laryngeal nerve. Then, as a result of a fall while still in Shanghai, he suffered a complete rupture of the left supraspinatus tendon. This was treated by the application of a shoulder spica.

You can be sure that in these tense days, on the national scene and locally, that our parents at home were frantic with worry. We frequently encouraged one another by noting that it was harder on them than it was on us. We knew what was going on, at least locally, but they had no idea what was happening. Nor was the mission board able to help them. Some of the wives, to keep their parents from anxiety, did not even tell them about important things, such as a pregnancy.

With the arrival of the Yangs, we intensified our evangelistic emphasis, and Mrs. Yang began meetings for the women and the children. She had natural abilities for this, and with the help of flannel-board and other visuals prepared for her by the missionaries in Xichang, she did very well. One day in mid-May 1949, Lucy visited Lugu with her small son, Danny. The presence of this light-colored little foreigner increased our chapel attendance dramatically that evening. We had a larger-than-usual group of Nosu, and they listened very attentively. Both Pastor Yang and I noticed that they listened better to a foreigner than they did to Chinese, for whom they have a centuries-old enmity.

The difficulty we had in preaching in Lugu was to determine our audience level. Only lower-class people came to our street chapel meetings. With so few having any educational background and with the illiteracy rate so high, we had to be repetitive and use simple, homely illustrations. Those conscious of their higher position in the social hierarchy felt it below their dignity to attend.

We tried to offset this in a couple of ways. First, we called on a large number of local officials, explaining carefully why we were in Lugu. Then on Sunday afternoons, we held a special class for those who wanted to look more deeply into the Christian faith. For three weeks fifteen or twenty of these men came quite faithfully, led by our banker friend Xie Wendan. I gave my testimony one week, and another time presented basic doctrinal lessons on topics such as the person of Jesus, the new birth, and salvation. Yang gave a more intellectual-type lecture each week. Their interest may have run more to various philosophical questions, such as man's nature—is it good or bad? One man commented to a friend later, "We weren't interested in more superstition." And, like officials and intellectuals everywhere in China, they wanted to know what the Christian faith had to say about a person's fealty to his parents, a very important tenet in Confucian thought. At any rate, the early good attendance waned, and, after three weeks, it was useless to continue to meet as a group. We did see some of the individuals regularly. I always had the feeling about these meetings that they need not have ended this way. The fault could well have been ours in not scratching where these men itched. Or it may have been that these men, largely of the gentry or official class, saw clearly the "handwriting on the wall" and felt it unwise in days of pending political upheaval to be identified in any way with Americans.

In early June, Yang and I took evangelistic trips to three neighboring farm villages. We took several posters along and started by spreading the poster on the wall or on the ground and explaining it to one man. Gradually, others came from the fields, where they were busy transplanting rice, and listened. None had ever heard the name of Jesus, and even after a half-hour, they could do more than merely repeat it. Often Pastor Yang was more discouraged than I was. He was from Shantung province in north China and had an accent hard for local folk to follow. I, although a high-nosed foreigner, had learned the local patois, and the people understood me better than they did him. In fact, much to our mutual embarrassment, people sometimes asked me what he was saying!

With this brief country itinerating whetting our appetite for direct evangelism, Yang and I spent six days on an extended trip which took us on foot about eighty or ninety miles through nine of the thirteen town-village areas of Mianning County. Not a really large geographic area, it was inhabited by about fifty thousand Chinese, and, in the nearby mountain areas, by many more Nosu.

We had two carriers to help us with baggage. Each day we walked several hours until we reached our principal destination. After finding a suitable room, spreading our beds, hanging our nets, and getting some rest, we visited the local magistrate and then went to local schools to meet the principal and teachers. We had tracts and books for these people and usually had the opportunity to give a short witness. We were never treated impolitely, and often there were those who were receptive. We sensed a hesitancy on the part of many to show too much interest—China's political turbulence caused thinking people to adopt a "wait and see" attitude.

Rural people were deeply immersed in their local beliefs—a strange mixture of primitive animism, Buddhism, and Daoism, along with an ethical Confucian veneer. They understood what we said, but it was not relevant to them. Why was Jesus needed when you had door gods, kitchen gods, local earth gods made of wood, mud and stone, and *amitofu*? And *Guanyin*, the saviour (boddhisattva) of mercy, was always ready to help the women.

Our preaching was simple, utilizing basic Biblical truths and communicated through local proverbs which served as starting points. These proverbs, widely known by nearly everyone, always elicited smiles of recognition when we used them. Two common ones were: "we are in a sea of suffering; but turn around and you are at the shore" or "evil has an evil reward and good has a good reward; it is not that there is no reward, the day of judgment has not yet come." Hanging Biblical truth on these ancient sayings caused our message, while strange and new in many ways, to take on local flavor.

Both Yang and I were impressed with the large market towns of Ho Bian, Fu Xinchen, Shi Longchang, and Mianning itself. Markets were held in a three-day rotation cycle at these centers and afforded the opportunity to contact the same people in a more intensified fashion than if we went to only one market once a week. Repeated hearing of the Gospel message was the key if it were to sink deeply into the soil.

During this rainy season, the weather was very changeable. Local people said there were only two seasons in this area: the hot weather when it did not rain and the cold weather when it did. The rain, though creating messy roads, at least kept us cool. In these summer months, whether wet or dry, the bugs came out in their biting splendor, particularly bed bugs and mosquitoes. They were a pest as you travelled, and even at the home base. I tore my cot apart one morning after a bad night, and found about forty fat bed bugs that thought they had it made.

We carried a large supply of tracts with us, but were frustrated in knowing how to give them out. At least 90 to 95% of the people were illiterate. Before we ever gave out a tract, we asked "Can you read?" If the answer were negative, we followed this up with "Can your husband read? Or a son or daughter? Or a neighbor? Or anyone in the village where you live?" If the answers were all negative, we did not give the tract. If people responded that they could read, we urged them to gather village friends about and read it to them.

A couple of weeks later, Yang and I travelled to the south of Lugu, visiting the towns of Qilong and then Saba. This latter town may have been as large as Lugu, but it was well off the beaten path. We learned that twenty years previous the American Baptists had worked there, apparently with no lasting results. We did not sense the degree of welcome on this trip that we had experienced when travelling to the north. Food was always poor on the road. Rice was plentiful, but finding much that was tasty to go with it was difficult. We could not even find the apricots, loquats, and blackberries available to us in Lugu. We got all the hot water we needed in villages, but during long, country walks we drank water, mixed heavily with halazone (chlorine) tablets, directly from filthy rice paddies.

When the home on the hill was completed in late July, Lucille and her three children, along with their fine Bible woman, Mrs. Jiang, moved to Lugu. We were uncertain whether this was a wise move or not. The road was still cut periodically by local wars, and we were afraid for their safety. Travel was arduous, and we did not reach the outskirts of Lugu until well past dark. We were challenged by soldiers guarding the city and had a few tense moments, until we were identified to their satisfaction. The weather on the day of their arrival was impossible. They travelled by rickshas, and I was on the bike. At times, in fording rivers, I went through water up to my waist. At each really bad point, I hired someone to carry the bike. The children and Lucy had to be carried over several of the swollen rivers.

Another factor to be considered in old China was the propriety of a married, foreign woman living in the same area with an unmarried foreign man. The Chinese imagined many things. So although we consulted on many matters and even had two meals (western!) a day together, we were careful to do it with many people around. I always left the hill and returned to my home on the main street of town well before dark.

When Lucy and Mrs. Jiang arrived, it gave new impetus to the work among women and children. The work in Lugu itself was expanded, and we commenced new meetings in four small villages located a short distance from the city. Having Lucy play our little Estey organ for the street chapel services was a tremendous help.

Sometimes we wondered if we were spreading ourselves too thin. Why not just stay within the environs of Lugu city itself and concentrate on needs there? When these questions bothered us, we remembered that Lugu had been selected as a site for mission work, not because of its own importance, but because it was a hub for all of Mianning county. We had to have a base somewhere, and this was it.

Even as the national news continued to alarm us—large groups of Communists in Yunnan, Chungking about to fall, armies advancing on Chengdu, possibly half of the foreigners in China leaving—the local Nosu war was settled. Much confusion accompanied this, with nearly three thousand soldiers coming to Lugu, about equal to the population itself. Many big feasts were held to celebrate this happy occasion, and we were invited to most of them.

We had ardently hoped for more in the way of results. To our knowledge, three people had believed, but they were hardly ready for baptism. We comforted ourselves with other "results." People now understood why we were here. Certain ones regularly attended all meetings. Attitudes of suspicion, both in the city and in the outlying districts, had begun to break down. We found it easier to preach than in the early stages of the work. And people were excited to think that we had plans to start a medical work in the near future.

Lucy was very worried, as all of us were, about her husband Dan. Nobody even knew where he was. Caught in Shanghai during the liberation, in transit via Manila, in Hong Kong, where? An encouraging note at the end of the summer was that China Air Transport (CAT), the airline run by General Clair Chennault of Flying Tigers fame, began to fly weekly on the Kunming-Xichang-Chengdu route. This gave us a better sense of communication with the outside world, particularly since the CNAC planes were totally unreliable at this point. We presumed that, in many instances, their planes were commandeered by the government to fly troops here and there.

We needed to take advantage quickly of this service to Kunming. Our financial agent in Kunming had left, and we had to make new arrangements for getting money. And so, in late August 1949, John Simpson flew to Kunming to see what could be done. Alarmed to learn that most missionaries were evacuating Kunming, and that they thought CBFMS also ought to get out while the going was good, John wired to Lovegren at Xichang, asking what he should do. Was it wise to sink more money in thread when we risked losing everything? Lee phoned me at Lugu, a clumsy process that took three hours, and together we wired John to go ahead. Why back out now when we had already nailed our flag to the mast?

With this confirmation, John chartered two planes to fly cotton thread from Kunming to Xichang. This cost us $7,500 in "transmission fees," but we now had 112 bales of yarn, with each bale containing nine bundles, and each bundle having twenty-two skeins. This massive amount of yarn was stored in our Xichang warehouse and cared for our financial needs over an extended period. At this time we also set up a reserve fund of silver ingots, silver dollars, and U.S. currency for either an "ordinary" or "extraordinary emergency."

John also reported that the missionaries evacuating from Kunming were most concerned about their children's education or the difficulty of getting money. The CIM policy, affirmed in many other areas of China, was to stay on as long as its personnel were in no danger from the fighting itself or were no embarrassment to the Chinese churches.

As the summer of 1949 moved toward the fall and the following year, we knew we needed to make some decisions that would be important for our own welfare as well as for our Chinese colleagues and the new believers.

Endnotes

1. Mimeographed "Report on China Conference," January 7, 1949.
2. For this term see Daniel Johnson Fleming's fine book, *Living as Comrades*.

9

Liberation at Last

Birth of the People's Republic of China

On October 1, 1949 Mao Tse-tung, standing on the balustrade of Tian An Men Gate before a crowd estimated at 200,000 in the square below him, inaugurated the People's Republic of China as the only legal government of China. This marked the culmination of a revolutionary process that had commenced in 1911 with the overthrow of the foreign Manchu Dynasty. China was declared officially to be liberated from the ravages of feudalism, capitalism, and imperialism that, according to her new leaders, had held her captive for ages past.

Most of China had indeed been freed by the "liberation army," as the conquering troops were called. Pockets of resistance, largely in western and southern China, continued to hold out. To subdue these outposts was the military agenda for the rest of 1949 and into the early spring of 1950. The first major city in the west to be liberated in early December was Chungking, the new Kuomintang capital. The Nationalist government quickly proclaimed Chengdu to be the new capital, but that city was abandoned precipitously on December 8, and the capital shifted again, its fourth move, to Taiwan. Concurrent with this move to Taiwan, the Kuomintang transferred its military headquarters to Xichang. Contrary to some of our early predictions, it appeared that the stage was being set for a major military showdown. Kunming and all of Yunnan were at the point of defecting to the Communists, and Xichang was the only major, reliable airfield in all of China controlled by the Nationalist forces.

Even Xichang, however, was having its problems. On December 11, General Liu Enhui, the governor of Xikang, taking advantage of Communist victories in Sichuan, sought to use his 24th Army to stage a coup. He instructed his son-in-law, Wu Peiyin, a general in Xichang, to seize control of the Xichang airfield and obtain the surrender of General He Guiguang of the Jinbibu. The Jinbibu, loyal to the Kuomintang, intercepted this message and arrived first on the scene at the airfield. General He appeared ready to surrender and then, upon the advice of his junior officers, turned the tables on Wu and chased him from town. Serious fighting took place about Lizhou to the north, and many soldiers in the 24th Army were killed. As a result of this abortive coup, both the 24th Army and the Tenkenhui were dissolved. Magistrates over the entire area were fired and replaced by men loyal to General He. He was wise enough to follow the advice of local authorities in these appointments.

So although we were "solidly in Nationalist territory," to use Lovegren's words, we were not sure how long the security would last. In fact, it lasted just four months, and on March 26, 1950, we too were liberated and joined the rest of the nation in the new people's republic. The story of these intervening months was revolutionary, but we will hold it for a while as we retrace what was happening to our missionary group in the Ningsu area.

Reinforcements Arrive

Bill and Flossie Simons, along with Ruth Laube, had been living in Chengdu for one year, intensively engaged in language study. Apart from the final few days of their stay when they camped out at #51 Huaxiba, they lived in what we called the Dwan home, just outside the campus proper and across from a large radio tower. They could tell a long story about their many and varied Chengdu activities: hard days of study, weekly Bible studies with interested Chinese students, some commitments to Christ, the social whirl of the language school scene, and the making of many friends.

A serious problem arose in April when Bill had a short attack of polio. With care and exercise, he recovered well from this. Another discouraging note was that even while they were waiting for the plane to take them inland to Xichang, there were members of the Scandinavian Alliance Mission (now TEAM) waiting for the plane that would take them out of China to Hong Kong and on their way home. These evacuating missionaries did not necessarily wish to leave China. But, having lost their own fields of work up north, where now elsewhere in China could they go? Some had large quantities of medical supplies, and Bill brought some of these with him to Xichang.

The Simons and Ruth felt more decision-making pressures in Chengdu than we did. First, while it was nice not to be alone, the many other missionaries coming and going had so much conflicting advice that it confused them. We might have been wrong in Xichang, but we were not confused!

Second, they saw the deteriorating financial picture better than we did. Inflation was running wild, and in the frequent conferences which were held among the mission treasurers in Chengdu, they got a gloomy picture of how desperate the situation had become.

Third, even more ominous, when the Chungking Consular District of the American Embassy sent out its second and third warnings to American personnel in the area, it sent consular officials to hold public meetings. This added several-fold to the urgency of its warnings: "persons who have not yet made a decision are urged to make one immediately by which they are prepared to abide in all eventualities;" "you are urged to consider whether you are prepared to remain in circumstances in which your access to food supply and sources of obtaining funds might be stringently limited;" "the opportunity for the Consulate to render representative or protective services may be limited or rendered impossible." Hearing these severe warnings directly from American officials caused the Simons and Ruth to wonder, rightly so, whether those of us in Xichang were living in a dream world.

Another serious decision concerned Ruth. Was she to go to east China and help in the orphanage where there were serious emergency needs? Or should she continue to go as planned to Xichang? After months of indecision and numerous memos back and forth among Chengdu, Chicago, Xichang, and Ganxian, it seemed best for her to stay where she was in Chengdu and then go with the Simons to Xichang.

The original time of departure for the Simons and Ruth had been September 7 or 8, 1949. However, they faced every conceivable delay. First, the *St. Paul* was very busy evacuating people from China, and the crew felt that these people had first priority. They could not be too hasty in this task without facing incredible dangers. In fact, this *St. Paul* was not the same plane as the one which had flown our missionaries earlier. The original version had crashed on landing in north China, and although the crew escaped unscathed, the plane was a total loss. To the credit of the Lutheran World Federation, it arranged for the purchase of another C-47 (DC-3) and flights continued.

Weather always caused delays in getting into Xichang. Murphy's law was at work in the third kind of delay. About September 18 it looked as if the flight could be made, and the plane took in one load of freight and luggage. After landing in Xichang, crew members were surprised that the plane was met with soldiers holding rifles and bayonets. The soldiers refused to let them unload and indicated that they must return immediately to Chengdu. It seemed that, without their knowledge, their permit to land in Xichang had just expired. Fortunately, a high-ranking officer was at the field, waiting to return with the plane to Chengdu. He persuaded the soldiers to allow the plane to unload its cargo and proceed on its return flight. The situation was not helped when one of the missionaries with the Border Service Department "shot off his mouth" and angered the soldiers. He was not allowed to leave the airfield until he had given a written apology. The unforgivable sin in dealing with Chinese is to lose your temper. Although they do not always follow this maxim themselves, it is still the Confucian ideal.

Renewing the plane's permit, throwing in a few more bad flying days, and allowing for further evacuation flights resulted in more delays until the morning of October 4, four days after the founding of the new Communist government. Foolhardy? Possibly. But they and we felt that God still had a task for us to do. With the plane came lots of supplies that we needed: four Estey organs, Bibles and literature, medicine that could be used for the proposed dispensary or hospital at Lugu, and 125 gallons of kerosene for our Aladdin lamps.

Bill also carried two hundred kilograms (about 450 pounds) of silver dollars from Chengdu to Xichang as a special favor for the 136th Chinese Army division. We all felt nervous about this—another catch 22 that would hurt us eventually whether we agreed or not to help. Just to be in China at this time meant being put in these kinds of boxes.

The Lost is Found

Dan had been gone from the Ningsu area for seven months, and, with the rupturing of many normal communication lines, no one was really certain where he was. During the course of his medical stay in Shanghai, caring both for a throat problem and a tear in a shoulder tendon, he had spent several months in the China Inland Mission Nursing Home and the Country Hospital. While he was at the latter facility, the city was liberated. The Kuomintang leaders did not wish to give up easily, and for several months they conducted nuisance bombing raids, trying to disrupt all return to normalcy. Seeking to protect themselves, but in reality only becoming sitting ducks, the liberation forces placed anti-aircraft guns on top of one of the hospital buildings, breaking all rules of international warfare.

Once Dan was healed, a difficult thing for a person put together so unpredictably, he tried to get out of the city. After many tries, he managed to get an exit visa but missed an opportunity to sail on the General Gordon, because he lacked an entrance visa to Hong Kong.

A few days later, two American freighters ran the Nationalist blockade of the harbor and came into port. Dan's Hong Kong visa had arrived by this point, and he obtained passage on one of the freighters, the *Flying Clipper*. The two ships were unharmed by a sudden Nationalist bombing raid at the wharf area, but they had no luck in getting out of the harbor again through the Nationalist blockade.

And so three Nationalist gunboats and the two American freighters tried to stare each other down for two days. A British warship sailed close by one day but refused to be involved in an international incident. The captains appealed to the American Navy at Okinawa, but the best the navy could do was telegraph its deepest sympathy.

Both sides faced a common danger—the water level above the bar was very low, and they must move to safer water. The gunboats led the freighters to the southern coastal port of Chusan, just off the main island of Tinghai. Fortunately for Dan and all the others on the two ships, the Communist forces were in the process of capturing the Chusan Archipelago, which made it possible, after a few days, for the two freighters to escape surveillance and sail on their way to Hong Kong. Little wonder that the Nationalists wished to stop them—they were carrying millions of dollars worth of Communist cargo.

One day after his arrival in Hong Kong, Dan found room on the *St. Paul* flying to Chungking; the next day he reached Xichang on the same plane. He had been detained a long time by an incredible series of circumstances, but now very suddenly the door was open to return to his family. He had already been liberated once, and in a few months, like others of us, he would experience a second liberation. Dan's arm was still in a cast, but he got this off in a couple of months and entered fully into the work at Lugu.

Life Goes On

We all had our fears, but seldom did we confess them to one another. No one doubted that we were getting backed into a corner in China's hinterland, but it helped to keep busy and have as much fun as we could in the process. We did not socialize much in either Lugu or Huili—the cities were smaller, and the opportunities were much less.

But in Xichang something was always cooking. Each month there were monthly prayer meetings which brought folk from the CIM, Border Service Department, and us together. We felt strengthened to pray for our common needs in work and witness. Frequently, our group hosted afternoon teas to which the others were invited, or we were entertained at the Upchurches or Madges.

On our own CBFMS compound, Flossie never tired of planning fun nights: an evening of "pick-up-sticks" or a Halloween party for which we had makeshift costumes. Irene and Ruth surprised the Simons with a party celebrating their fifth wedding anniversary. The Simpsons and Lovegrens took turns having Ruth or the Simons over during the period when they were getting settled.

The mission expected, even demanded, that we have a month's vacation each year, but this was easier said than done. Flora Mae and Esther combined a dental trip with pleasure in going out to Chungking. The trip lasted longer than they expected, and they narrowly escaped being liberated in both Chungking and Chengdu. Irene and John Simpson took a week off and went to Lugu just to get a change of scenery. Most of us gave up on vacations as an improbable luxury in these troubled times.

Crisis situations create unusual bonds of friendship. In each of our stations of work, we had pleasant relationships with French Catholic missionaries, most of whom were affiliated with the Paris Evangelical Mission (PEM). Two Catholic nuns were available to help with Judy Garrison's birth in Xichang, and when the Garrisons returned to Huili, they got their daily milk from a Catholic dairy farm. Dan was an avid chess player, and the only person he found in Lugu as a partner was the Catholic priest responsible for the Lugu-Mianning area.

Far more than the fun which helped to relieve the tensions, the sense of God working through our ministries kept us going. Meetings continued unabated in Xichang during the fall of 1949, with many inquirers seeking to learn more of the truth. Much of this, humanly speaking, was due to the meetings which Pastor Wei conducted during September and October.

This pastor, mature with a wisdom even beyond his fifty years, was a great tonic to all of us. He helped me gain a more balanced sense of the missionary role. One day when I came down from Lugu, I mentioned to him that a couple of us missionaries had been doing some rural evangelism. After patiently listening, he asked a pointed question, "Do you think it best for a Chinese to hear the Gospel first from a foreigner?" While I was racking my brains for a suitable answer, he continued: "The other day when I was preaching, I happened to give an illustration that made mention of an American and an Englishman believing in Jesus. After I finished my message, an elderly woman came up and exclaimed: 'Do Americans and Britishers also believe in Jesus?'" Then he drove home his point: "Why not wait on rural evangelism until the Chinese can do it with you, or, even better, by themselves. It may slow you up at first, but in the long run it will work better."

Pastor Wei practiced what he preached. As a part of his meetings with the Xichang church, he instructed new converts in Bible truths, sent them into the streets in groups of four to sing and testify, and then helped them when they returned to the chapel to deal with the difficulties they had encountered.

Wei Danchen had been a pastor for over twenty years, and, at present, he was teaching and acting as principal of a small "junior" (undergraduate) seminary in Chungking. Run by the Border Mission Committee of the Southern Baptist church in China (an early third world mission agency), this seminary desired its graduates to work in China's frontier areas. Even after liberation, one of its graduates came into the Ningsu area in an effort to start an independent Baptist ministry.

Pastor Wei, however, hoped to work with us. He had refreshingly new ideas. Like many other Southern Baptists, he interpreted Matthew 28:19 to mean: make disciples (converts), baptize, teach." In addition to giving minimal instruction to assure that converts had been born again, Wei wanted to do most of his teaching after baptism.

He believed there were three categories of church officers: deacons, elders, and pastors. Pastors had more general responsibilities and should work in outlying districts. The elders were to be chosen from the local church members by the pastors (or missionaries), with the approval of the church members. These elders were responsible to care for the local church in the absence of the pastors. They were to be paid a salary by the local church, although the ideal would be for them to be self-supporting. Pastor Wei emphasized strongly that local churches must be self-supporting, self-propagating, and self-governing from the very beginning.

I had a long conference with him about the possibilities of his joining our team in Xikang. I think we could have worked out some differences in our views with more time. In the long run, the worsening political situation proved to be the greatest deterrent.

Our executive committee had been thinking about the need for better trained workers. One idea that several of us advocated vigorously was that such Chinese co-laborers as we had should meet with us in our next annual meeting. We made the point that they were involved in the work and should be participants in the decisions made. No longer could we operate with any kind of a "they-we" dichotomy. When this action was taken, it was assumed that our meetings would be in Xichang. When we had to move the site to Huili, probably an unwise decision for these days of turmoil, we could not include our co-laborers.

Another idea we began to play with was to open a Bible school in Xichang. The change in government made it impractical for us to send students out of our area to schools in Chengdu, Kunming, Salawu, Chungking, or any other centers. Acting on the premise that we might be isolated from control by the new Communist government, why not grow a school locally? Wei Danchen would have been the ideal principal. We voted the money and the personnel, as needed, but that is about as far as it ever got. Such action, at least, kept our vision high and prevented us from slipping into a passive mode in these disturbing days.

We continued our wide itineration about Lugu, largely to evangelize among the Chinese. I was concerned that we might never get to the Nosu. In one letter to a supporting church, I dreamed out loud, as it were, that maybe the time had come for a single person like me to move into a Nosu village, taking no more than a "toothbrush," and concentrate totally on learning the language. A step like that might have been a move of faith; it might also have been presumptuous. God has his time table, and it is usually much slower than ours.

On alternate weeks, Yang and I spent three days in Hebian or Fuxinchen. Our usual procedure was to preach and distribute tracts on the street and then find a quieter place, often an abandoned Buddhist temple, where we could give more systematic instruction to any who were interested. People's motives varied. Sometime their first interest was that we might help them find a job. Local people were accustomed to the approach of Roman Catholics who had been in this area much longer than we had. Their policy, when one person professed to believe, was to transplant the entire family to Catholic property, to give them work, and then to oversee them on an ongoing basis.

Whenever possible, we tried to develop better social relationships with people we saw regularly. In Fuxinchen we played volleyball with the teachers in the local middle school. They were friendly and open, but the principal, very outgoing in his welcome on a previous visit, was now much more reserved. For such people we used booklets rather than tracts. We carried many copies of the four Gospels, but these were for sale at a very cheap price, and not for free distribution.

In Lugu itself, we were sure that several women had believed. We knew, however, and so did they, that the proof of the pudding was whether or not they were prepared to forsake their false gods and their vegetarian vows. The Gospel is "good news," but it begins with the bad news of repentance.

Still Another Conference

The first annual conference had been held in Xichang, and it seemed logical that the next one be in Huili. But this was a five-day trip south for the majority of the mission members. Furthermore, if there were a sudden deterioration in the political situation, it would be much more difficult to evacuate from Huili. Another consideration was that our national workers could not meet with us in Huili. John Simpson, the current treasurer, was also unwilling to leave our large supply of cotton thread in the storehouse, unguarded for the three-week period required for the travel and conference time in Huili.

All this notwithstanding, a majority voted to go to Huili. The decision motivated John to say that he would not attend. Such an abrupt decision caused George Cole in Huili to circulate a correspondence motion requiring "all male members of the mission to attend the conference." This motion was roundly defeated, although a few voted for it. Dan facetiously appended a note to his affirmative vote "but what if I get double pneumonia?" To those of us who knew a bit of Dan's medical history, this was not a laughing matter.

With all of the pre-conference caucusing out of the way, we got ready for the conference. Missionaries at the Huili station were put in charge of the devotional portion of the meetings and prepared an outline based on the book of Ephesians with a focus on The Church and Jesus as Lord. How important was such an assurance when all familiar structures were crumbling in China! We needed to see things from God's perspective—that his son, Jesus, was indeed in control of all that was happening in China and sovereign in our lives as well. He would build his church in China, and all the powers of hades would not be able to thwart His plans. We believed it by faith then, and, now, nearly forty years later, faith has become sight.

The biggest preparation was just to get ourselves to Huili, a hard, five-day, 120-mile trip over all but impassable roads. Occasionally, truck travel was possible, but we opted for rickshas and bicycles. We divided into two groups, in order not to crowd out the inns in the small villages where we would stay overnight. The Simons family, Ruth and I made up the first group, and the second group of Carrs and Lovegrens came a day later. I rode my bike, which gave me more freedom, but it also meant that I had to adjust my pace to the much slower rickshas. My role, however, was to act as interpreter for the other people which meant that I had to stay with them most of the time. Our first party had six rickshas, and the second group had eight. Some of these carried luggage.

We started out by 6:30 each morning and reached our day's destination well before dark. We did not have to pay the Nosu any "protection" money to keep bandits away on this trip, but we did well not to press our luck by night-time travel. We did well for food. Rice and noodles were available in abundance, as were soya bean curd, fruit (tangerines and persimmons), some vegetables, and boiled eggs. We carried along enough other goodies to supplement local products.

A good place to sleep was harder to come by than was adequate food. We were never free from myriads of peering eyes, both outside and inside our rooms. The rooms were public enough to be not only walkways for people, but also for horses, cats, or dogs. Rooms in these inns were frequently placed over pig sties and were very smelly, with lots of grunting going on through the night hours as the pigs rooted here and there.

We had some nice accommodations, notably one evening at a Catholic mission home where we found that there was real glass in the windows, and another evening in the facilities of a pottery factory. One day, to relieve the weariness of the ricksha pullers, Ruth walked the entire time. This was the general rule in going up long, steep grades and when going over a series of streams. Frequently the pullers had to co-opt other travellers to carry their rickshas over swollen rivers.

Our fourth night out we were overtaken by the group that had left a day later. Mighty embarrassing for our pullers! But the second group had some younger pullers and were accompanied by a Chinese business manager who urged them on better and who hurried up other aspects of travelling.

After a weekend of rest and two stints of preaching for Lee and me, we settled down for a relatively short conference, only ten days in length! During the weightier discussions of the first few days, we talked ad infinitum on what the Nevius plan meant for us. In fact, our very first motion was to reaffirm that the two books *New Buildings on Old Foundations* and *Principles of the Nevius Plan* be read before our next meeting but "that an examination not be required."

Now how to apply this theory? We were all too preoccupied with methods, rather than goals. We presumed to declare confidently that Nevius would not have approved of an organized church holding its meetings in mission-rented property, without at least paying part of the cost. We likewise felt that he would probably not want any of us to make personal use of a national worker.

A knotty problem for us was to determine how much Chinese language study should be done by those going into work with the Nosu. Those in Chinese work must complete four sections of the CIM or Chengdu program. Should it be the same or less for those who were planning to learn still another language? Lee monitored our language progress carefully and kept track of who should be ready when for what exam. In fact, just before we left for our Huili conference, he gave an exam to Ruth. For those planning to work with the Nosu, we determined that the character-writing requirement of the third section would be waived. For a wife working with her husband among the Nosu, the entire third section was eliminated.

We voted to enter into negotiations with Baptist Mid-Missions about the placement of two of their young missionaries, Louise Marqueling and Helen Moose, who were beginning Chinese language study in Chengdu. When Ruth and the Simons had been together with Helen and Louise in Chengdu, a Nosu chief from Tianba, Lin Guangdian, had asked the whole group to start Christian social work in his area. Helen and Louise apparently thought this invitation was directed particularly to them and communicated it excitedly to their board.

In a letter that he wrote to Arthur Fetzer, a Council Member of Mid-Missions, Lee indicated that we had worked out a comity agreement with the CIM for this area, and that, if China's doors remained open to missionary work, we wished to go there. He suggested that the best arrangement for the young women might be to work with us, in the same way that Esther Nelson of the Baptist General Conference was doing. In fact, our board in January 1950 signed an agreement with Mid-Missions similar to the one it had with the Baptist General Conference. Lee asked Jim Broomhall to write a letter to Mr. Fetzer to reinforce the need for cooperation. Jim could not have been much stronger in his recommendation: "Tianba is no place for single women. The people are very wild, warlike, cruel, ambitious, arrogant, and backward. Lin Guangdian has education and is a civilized man, but his own relatives are like the Nosu here (Zhaojue)." In hindsight, we hardly needed to have worried whether we, the CIM or Baptist Mid-Missions, or anyone else were to have first rights to Tianba!

We spent far too much time working out details of term lengths, furlough times, and vacations that would never be. We wasted a lot of breath arguing the pros and cons of transportation. A nice issue to talk about, but the problem was the roads—not the vehicles that might run on them. The purchase of a jeep approved several months earlier, was vetoed, but we approved George Cole purchasing a motorcycle with the money that had been given to him for a jeep. Even this was questionable. Dan had bought a motorcycle in Shanghai, and it never proved to be that useful. When working, which was only rarely, it made good time on some sections of the road, but was much more clumsy and heavy to carry over a four-foot deep stream than a good old foreign horse!

A knotty problem was to work out an equitable salary scale for national workers, one that would not be a millstone about the neck of a local church wishing to employ them in the future. The agreed amount, worked out ever so carefully in silver and thread, was such a pittance compared to what we made that many of us felt guilty in even discussing it. Who were we really to be determining the livelihood of a local person? We worked closely with our Chinese co-laborers, and yet this financial disparity precluded that we could ever be partners, save in name only.

We had a pleasant day's respite from conference business with our Thanksgiving break. Turkeys were hard to come by in old China, but goose was a good substitute. Just to be able to relax with a large dinner, a few games, and casual conversation made the following few days of hard conference business to go more quickly.

Jim Garrison had the misfortune to be elected treasurer for the coming year. Dan and John had preceded him in this thankless task and found it to be almost hopeless. Altogether apart from the tricky issue of finding an agent outside of our area through whom finances could be transmitted, was the more perplexing problem of keeping rational records. How do you figure out what to pay a person for his salary, for example, when he may want to have it given in various amounts of gold bars, silver nuggets, thread, silver dollars, or silver half-dollars?

All of this was compounded by a run-away inflation. During the early months of 1950 right before liberation, the exchange rate between one dollar U.S. and Chinese notes had risen to twelve million *yen*. We were instant millionaires and did not like it. If we used notes to go on the street to buy anything (and we needed them for certain things), we carried them in a suitcase or two, particularly when the biggest bill being printed was for fifty thousand *yen*.

We needed Chinese notes to buy postage stamps. An air form to the States required three million *yen*. The biggest denomination of stamp was fifty thousand *yen*; so you needed sixty stamps of the biggest denomination, and the local post office might not have that many this large. We all had the experience, after a letter had the proper number of stamps, to find that the stamps had made it overweight! So a special flap of stamps had to be pasted on to the letter! We wondered how any of our letters ever made it. So did postmen in America.

Despite the problem with stamps, however, the Chinese postal service did a remarkable job of getting mail and packages to us. The latter might take months and have to pass in and out of Nationalist and Communist-dominated areas several times. Both sides had a sense of pride in Chinese ability to deliver the mail and gave it priority even while they were killing each other.

The last conference action before we headed back to our stations of work was to send off a telegram with fraternal greetings to the Bensons and Ruth Mayo in Jiangsi. Being much closer to the coast and in south China, they had already been liberated. The last letter we had from Bennie came in June 15, 1949. He noted that the three of them had made a specific decision not to be evacuated, but to "go behind the curtain" and carry on as best they could. He reported the encouraging news that he had baptized twenty-eight converts the previous Sunday and that these would be the nucleus of a new church.

At conference time Hannah Cole, our conference statistician, added up numerically what had been happening in our various ministries. Though paltry and focusing more on *activities* than *results*, these statistics give a rough idea of the work we were doing:

Statistical Report for West China
1949

Meetings	Xichang	Lugu	Huili
Church Services (Christians)	52	3	--
Evangelistic services	110	66	83
S.S. and children mtgs.	155	35	32
Prayer Meetings	80	--	--
Weekday classes (Bible study)	200	6	58
Women's meetings	45	15	18
Home meetings	150+	--	--
Prison meetings	10	--	15
Village meetings	15	45+	several
Evangelistic trips	--	?	--

As soon as the conference was over, the Simons and Carrs left to return to Xichang. Ruth, because of Hannah's serious illness, stayed on to help as needed. Lovegrens and I waited for a few days and then set off together for Xichang, they travelling by ricksha and me by bicycle. We stayed together for the first day of about twenty-five miles, and then early on the morning of the second day I went alone to Dechang, a small city about fifty-five miles away. Despite the usual rough roads and a blustering, opposing wind, I arrived about an hour before sunset. I spent a nice evening of fellowship with Mr. and Mrs. Sen who cared for the Gospel Hall of the Border Service Department. The next day, with a following wind and much more level terrain, I covered the forty-five miles on to Xichang shortly after noon.

A Time for Romance

No amount of disturbing national and local news or of conference meetings prevented people from seeing that something was brewing between Ruth and me. Even our parents at home were asking hard questions about "that young man" and "that young woman." If this were going to happen, and they and many others had been praying that it might, they hoped that it might not have to take place ten thousand miles away. Ruth and I were not predisposed to be interested in one another—our common friends in the States had not encouraged her about me, and I was still daydreaming about Anne.

I first met Ruth shortly after she and the Simons arrived from Chengdu. After that I found more and more reasons to spend as many weekends as possible in Xichang. Usually, I found legitimate business—leading a Sunday worship service, meeting with other members of the executive committee or getting more money for the work in Lugu. We had no way to keep any large supply of money in Lugu; much better to get it in Xichang when we needed it.

These weekends gave us both a chance to become acquainted better. We did this most often by taking walks up the hill behind the mission compound. One Sunday afternoon we biked beyond Qionghai Lake and explored the temple on Lushan (Deer

Mountain), as well as Chiang Kai-shek's elaborate home. Often, on the hill walks, we ran into groups of Nosu with whom we conversed as much as our poor Mandarin and theirs would allow. The women particularly, dressed in their long, full, flowing and very colorful dresses, were anxious to explore how Ruth's clothes were put together. They had no sense of embarrassment, and Ruth had to restrain their curiosity.

As we travelled the five-day trip to Huili, we saw each other in far-from-ideal circumstances. During the conference, we had free time, but the more rascally, less-restrained behavior of the curious kids in Huili gave us less freedom to be alone, even on walks into the hills. Finally, we hit upon a unique solution—why not go into the large cemetery near the city? Here we were really alone. Fear of the spirits, thought to be lurking about the grave sites, kept everyone at a distance.

The time we were together at Huili, away from our usual places of work and study, was just what we needed to seal our relationship. We pledged our love for one another on December 21, two days before my birthday, and then tried to figure out a way of letting her mother and my parents get the news directly from us, before anyone else could tell them. With the mail so erratic, this posed a problem. The best solution was to write home immediately and postpone our announcement on the field for awhile. And even when we told everyone, we pledged them not to write home about it for two or three weeks.

I did not let Buker in on the secret until late March 1950 with a short remark: "Cupid has joined our staff out here (no salary for him—don't worry) and is ridding you of two single missionaries." Unknown to us and before any announcements were made, our colleagues were busy sending signals here and there. Lee wrote to Ray Buker for his "personal and private information" that a wedding was imminent. Lucy, in a more mysterious vein, wrote her mother that the home being built in Lugu needed to be larger, because Ralph was "going to bring a girl to live with him!"

Can you surprise anyone in the "fish bowl" atmosphere of a compound of missionaries who already suspect that something is going on? Despite my usual lack of imagination, I went down to the telegraph office, got a regular form, wrote out an announcement of the engagement in a telegraph style, and had the gate men take it into the entire group as they were having afternoon tea. With mock surprise, they all joined enthusiastically in congratulating us. They, like us, recognized the dangers of getting engaged in this kind of atmosphere. Was it because we were both lonely, because there were no other real possibilities, because we felt it was now or never, because we both needed more security? All the possibilities were there, and yet we felt God had matched us in an unusual way and was leading us into the uncertain future.

Our field had a dispute with the board interpreting its marriage policy. It read: "Any missionary who is not engaged prior to his leaving for the field is requested to delay plans for marriage for at least one year unless otherwise agreed by the board." We all read this to mean ". . . at least one year *after arrival on the field*, while Buker assumed it meant ". . . at least one year *after engagement*." He wrote hurriedly his advice to us: "I can only tell you two now that you've probably done wrong, but nobody is going to penalize you for it." We both had been in China for at least one year, and with life becoming more uncertain daily, we did not wish to postpone the wedding too long. Too much hurry, however, in the Chinese environment would appear unseemly. We finally selected the end of May as the best date and hoped that the changing political scene would not force a postponement.

Liberation Approaches

With conference over for another year, we all returned to the work before us. We had a sense of urgency, knowing that the "night was coming when no one could work," but we did not wish to be impulsive and precipitous in our decisions. We could afford to wait on God.

The next three months brought two important holiday seasons. Christmas had meaning only for the small band of Christians, but it was important for them, in both Huili and Xichang, to sing carols, to gather at the church for special meetings, and to try to introduce their neighbors to the meaning of this strange holiday which celebrated God coming to earth. Chinese New Year, celebrated on

February 17 in 1950, was the annual festive blow out for all the Chinese people. Life came to a stop for two weeks, as each household observed religious rites, gathered for family feasts, visited relatives, and just wiled its time away relaxing.

This period of frolicking, the only extended holiday in the year for most Chinese people, was a wonderful time for evangelism in each of our cities. We noted a difference this year from previous times of winter evangelism. In all of our chapels, there was an influx of Nationalist soldiers with a keen interest in the Gospel. Many of the troops were from central China, and some had been marching for months to escape the pursuing Reds. In some cases, the troops had done an 180 degree turn and hardly knew what side they were on. This was the case with a General Jiang who marched into Huili with his troops. Some two months earlier he had joined the Communist ranks, but now with his twelve hundred men following, he returned to the Kuomintang fold.

In Xichang, many of the forty members of this one-year old church spent a large portion of the two-week New Year celebration preaching, testifying, giving out tracts, and selling Scripture portions, both in the city proper and in the country environs. Noon and evening services were held daily in the chapel with many more wanting to hear the Gospel than there was room for. Hundreds requested prayer, and many remained after services to pray with the workers.

In the Lugu area we hoped to get a couple of things accomplished during this winter holiday season. One was to make an extended visit into a Nosu village. This would give first-hand practice with the language, far more than I got from occasional visits to Xichang to learn from a very part-time teacher. Even more important, it would produce some friends for future visits to the same village.

The son of Xie Wendan, the Lugu banker, had a friend in the Nosu village of Wan Gendi, about twenty miles north of Lugu above the city of Ma Fanggou. He agreed to go with me for a twelve-day stay. We both travelled lightly, taking only what would be most necessary for sleeping. The people had so little, particularly on cold winter nights, that we did not wish to burden them with the need to furnish us with any special hospitality.

Mr. Xie and I left on February 1, but we quickly met a disappointment. Unexpected fighting in the area about the Nosu village meant that the leaders could not guarantee our safety. Equally as serious, an unexpected sickness occurred in the Nosu home where I would be staying. The family was preparing to sacrifice countless sheep, cows, and pigs, and we thought it unwise to intrude on it when all of its religious forces were concentrated on finding out what curse or enemy was responsible for this.

Having travelled this far, I continued on in the valley to Mianning to make plans for the extensive evangelism we would be doing in that city over the New Year period. Never could I recall it having been that cold, with snow covering the ground. Just as well, I concluded, that I wasn't facing this deep freeze in a drafty, mountain home.

Two weeks later, Dan, Mr. Yang, the Christian son of the Carr's cook, and I headed to Mianning for a nine-day evangelistic trek, the most ambitious of any that we had tried. We lived near the center of town in a nice inn, which, we discovered later, was really a gambling den. The accommodations were comfortable, but noisy. The rattling of the *mah-jongg* gambling chips went on endlessly, and we did not rest well. We borrowed a hall, facing right out on one of the streets, for our evening preaching. During the day there were two preaching services on the street, with two of us speaking at each service, a children's service at five o'clock, and an evening evangelistic service.

The town was laid out systematically—four main streets, running north, south, east, and west, merged at a large drum tower in the center to form a perfect cross. Our daily preaching rotated to each of these main streets, so most of the townspeople were exposed to the Gospel.

Street preaching was never easy. Crowds were not hard to get, particularly with Dan pied-piping them with his accordion and booming voice. The message got across best when we used a picture chart illustrating what we said. We used stories constantly, and it helped even more if these tied in closely with the lives of the passers-by. In fact, at times the preaching was almost dialogical—bantering back and forth with people in the crowd, trying to draw them actively into the story.

Each day we were distracted by the presence of multicolored paper dragons, usually preceded by various types of drums, horns, and other noisy instruments. One of these dragons intruded into the preaching hall once, demanding some money from us, but we refused politely.

The people responded poorly to this intensive evangelistic effort. We could find many reasons for this. We put most of the blame on superstition that had hardened the hearts of the listeners. People had leisure during these days, but they were also easily distracted. The time may not have been right for people to think about serious matters; far easier to play with dragons and their gods. Presenting the Gospel by street preaching may not have been an appropriate way for China then, or at any time. Evidence many years later, long after Marxism had won the day, indicated that if we had shared Christ personally, friend-with-friend, it would have been far more effective. Such a method, however, required that we spend more than nine days in Mianning.

Superstition certainly blocked belief with many, particularly in rural China. In a small village a short distance from Lugu, we had carried on weekly meetings with much success. One week, however, it was different. The people had heard, falsely, that on this day we were going to take pictures of them. Rumor had it that whenever we took pictures, everything shown on the print—houses, land and people—would belong to the foreigner. Consequently, they refused to come to the meeting, and their former attitude of welcome changed entirely.

Some old tales never die! One young woman was right at the point of believing, until a friend told her that if she became a Christian, her eyes would be plucked out at death. Mrs. Jiang, one of those working with us, sought in vain to reply that she had believed many years and nothing had happened to her. The answer that came back was that she had not yet died, and that we were just deceiving her until that time.

Mixing as intimately as we did with the country people, we knew how ready they were to be a part of liberated China. To them, China had always been fighting. First, it was the war with Japan and now the interminable, internal strife, Chinese fighting Chinese. People were weary of this and did not care who won. Rural peasants were badly oppressed by landlords, in some cases owing future harvests to them for a ten or fifteen-year period. They were ready to welcome anyone who promised a better future, particularly when it held out the hope that each family might have its own land and a better livelihood.

Equally as important as this reasoning was the gut feeling that Chiang Kai Shek and his Kuomintang followers had lost the "Mandate of Heaven." It was Heaven who put emperors in place and brought them down. Dynasties, or presidents and parties, lasted only as long as Heaven bestowed its favor. Evident corruption, hopeless inflation, inept officials, failure to gain victory in the civil war—all of these were omens that Heaven was displeased. Therefore, it was out of Chiang's hands, and the people could do no better than bow to the will of Heaven.

In the period before liberation neither we nor the board did well in avoiding military or government contacts. In early February, a month before liberation, George Cole hosted a family dinner for General Gu, commander of newly-arrived Kuomintang troops, well-known for his victories over the Japanese. George's purpose was to give a Christian witness, but this explanation did not wash with the Communists.

The board found it difficult to avoid compromising relationships with the U.S. State Department. Ray Buker wrote to Lee Lovegren in early March 1950 that "we have some contacts with the government, and your letters coming to us recently have been some of the first information they (sic) have had concerning the situation in that area." This type of contact, meant only for our safety but subject to a sinister interpretation, had been going on since August 1949.

In a special memo to members of its member mission societies and marked "strictly confidential," the Evangelical Foreign Mission Association (EFMA) spelled out the conclusions of a private meeting that state department personnel had had with representatives of the International Missionary Council, the Foreign Mission Conference, the EFMA, and the Roman Catholics. The following information was given:

1. The U.S. is planning to close its consulates at Chungking and Kunming.
2. The state department invites all mission boards to make use of its confidential communication facilities in sending advice to its missionaries. This means that the material will be coded and will not be understandable to the Chinese Communists. Direct such messages to the missionary, c/o U.S. State Department, Division of Chinese Affairs, Washington 25, D.C.
3. The U.S. government anticipates its relations with the Chinese government will deteriorate; its does not anticipate recognizing the Chinese government. Americans in China may be subject to unusual pressures.
4. A tentative plan is being made to launch an evacuation ship from Shanghai about September 15, 1949. The state department wishes to know how many missionaries are hoping to leave. However, the state department is not encouraging people to evacuate China.

The Day Comes

During February and March we were convinced that the Kuomintang forces were going to make a "life and death" stand at Xichang. Otherwise, why all of the military flights, possibly as many as 180, from Hainan Island and Taiwan to Xichang, loaded with new American weaponry? We heard rumors that some of the supplies, surely not that much, would be given to arm the Nosu who were reportedly being pressed into government service.

These C-46 military flights, usually ten or fifteen a day, always carried along many extras. The pilots were underpaid, and they added to their scanty salary by bringing in such things as watches, canned and powdered milk, sugar, raisins, cloth, flashlights, batteries, yarn, and many other things not easily found in Xichang. Possibly each plane brought in a thousand pounds of these miscellaneous items. Whenever possible, we used U.S. checks to buy two-ounce gold bars that we then negotiated in Xichang. The pilots always reminded us that they were returning empty, either to Hainan or Taiwan, and that they could find room for us and all our belongings.

But we had made our commitment to stay, and found this to be no great temptation.

These daily flights ceased in the middle of March 1950. Sun Kechang and Pan Fuchang of the Jinbibu said that the 10th Air Force would be making similar flights to Xichang very shortly. On Saturday afternoon, March 25, four planes roared into the area, making a low pass over the city, and we surmised that a new phase of flights was beginning. Immediately we went down to the newly-established military hostel to see if it were possible to buy any products that the planes brought in. We were surprised to see the doors locked and barred and to hear that the flyers had been taken into the city.

By the next day we knew that something was up. Troops all through the city had been organized into marching units and were preparing to leave. A rumor spread like wildfire through the city that Communists troops were approaching from the south and had already reached Dechang. We saw no more reason to believe this than we had countless other rumors that had been filling the air in previous weeks.

This rumor had substance. By mid-afternoon, many of the Nationalist forces had left the city. At about 6 p.m. General He and the other high-ranking officers piled into their cars and trucks and beat a hasty retreat to the air field. Only then did we recognize how serious the situation had become. The four planes that had flown in on the previous day along with General He's plane, parked for several months on the air strip, took off that evening at about 9 p.m.

The night was pitch black as we stood in our compound and watched the planes fly over, with their small blue, red, and white night lights piercing the murky darkness. How these brave officers must have rejoiced in their narrow escape, even as their soldiers were left leaderless and hopeless with all of their new American armament to face the oncoming Communist army!

We had business to do before the new army came. This was a vacuum period—one group had left and the other had not yet arrived. Another rumor going the rounds was that a group of five hundred Nosu had come to the north gate of Xichang and were preparing to plunder the city. With this possible threat facing us, we decided to distribute our hard money—particularly the lumps of gold—around the compound. We thought about doing this with our yarn, but the warehouse was fastened securely. Some of the yarn had been loaned to local banks, hard up to get their hands on money, and it had not yet been returned to us. If plunderers broke into the warehouse, they would not get everything that we had.

After we had taken this precaution, we all went to bed, although not without some apprehension of what the night might bring. The next morning as we cautiously poked our heads out beyond the compound gate, we saw that different soldiers were walking about on the street. They apparently had come at about midnight and had uniforms very similar to those whom they had displaced. The insignias, however, were different—on the front of their caps was a five-pointed red star in which the numbers *bayi* (81) appeared, and above their left front pocket were the words *jiefangjun* (Liberation Army). We felt no different, and very little had changed, but we had been liberated. We, too, were now a part of the People's Republic of China. And it had happened, despite Taiwan's claim to the contrary, with hardly one shot being fired. All of the fine weaponry, paid for by the American people who had been given the line that we had betrayed China, now belonged to the Communists.

That first morning was an exciting one for us. About 9 a.m. Mr. Tan, our business manager, and Pastor Lo Zaixin, a new addition to the staff in Xichang, came to the compound and explained the notices that already were being pasted on the walls about town. Some declared that foreigners were to be protected if they obeyed the law and did not engage in spying. Other notices urged the people to use the *renminpiao*, the "people's money," gave rules for the conduct of soldiers, and explained the purposes of the liberation army.

Propaganda posters went up quickly, maligning He Guiguang and Fu Zhongnan, the two Kuomintang generals who had formerly controlled the area. What a contrast these were to the notices of a few days previous, also scrawled like graffiti on every available space, declaring that Mao Tse-tung was a *hanjian* (traitor). Soon pamphlets appeared explaining the government policy on opium, the possession of fire-arms, and many other issues.

I had originally planned to return to Lugu later in the week, but the sudden turn of events made it seem best to return immediately. Pastor Lo and Mr. Tan accompanied me as far as Lizhou, where we had just rented two pieces of property, one for a chapel and the other as a residence for the Simpsons. They wished to see how these events might have changed the property situation.

On the road to Lizhou, we noticed two or three abandoned military trucks as well as a sedan. We saw no fleeing Nationalist troops until midway between Qilong and Songlin. Just before reaching Songlin, I spotted a number of soldiers coming out from a compound to the right of the road. They stopped me and questioned me for a few minutes. They were most interested in what had happened in Xichang, the number of Communist troops coming along the road, and their nearness. They still had their arms, but they were very fearful and did not want a fight.

Beyond Manshuiwan, many soldiers were straggling along the road. A large truck, formerly the property of CNAC, had been abandoned because the road was so narrow that it could go no further. All of its load of ammunition had been turned over to some soldiers, who took it to Lugu. When I reached Lugu, I found it crowded to overflowing with Nationalist soldiers. Sentries were posted everywhere, and it was difficult even to get to my chapel home.

The next morning at 10 a.m., the first Communist troops entered Lugu. I had now been liberated twice on successive days! At first, the local residents were very frightened. All of the stores on south street were shut down, their open fronts boarded up, and the heavy doors bolted. Gradually the bolder people reappeared on the streets, and within a day or two it was business as usual.

Dan and Lucille had a big scare at the home on the hill. Lucy and the children had been out walking around the home, as they often did, when they noticed soldiers shouting and racing through the cemetery next to the compound. Not wishing to be caught in the squabble, they hurried back to the yard and barred the gate. Dan, somewhat like Peter, was a bit impulsive. He reopened the gate quickly to see exactly what was happening and found himself staring into the barrels of five American-made tommy guns. Immediately, he saw these were not Nationalist soldiers. They intended no harm, and when they saw the Carrs were not harboring any hiding Nationalist soldiers about to jump them, they went peacefully on their way.

Things did not go well for the fleeing Nationalist troops. Many tried to escape into the mountains, where they were fleeced step by step by the Nosu out of both their arms and clothes, until they were left, absolutely naked, for the pursuing Communist forces to capture. Later they were taken back to Xichang for preliminary indoctrination, and, if amenable to this, sent into other areas to serve with the People's Army. Local people were fickle. Only a few days previous, they had depended on the Nationalist soldiers for their protection. Now as these defeated soldiers were lined up naked for a mile or two along the road, marching single file before their captors, the people giggled, calling them "those with bare buttocks."

Liberation in Huili differed little from either Xichang or Lugu. The Communist forces appeared as if from nowhere, and, within hours, were in control of the city with no fighting or resistance. George Cole was caught out in the street buying some household goods, but the soldiers allowed him to return home. People were impressed with how orderly the new soldiers acted, in stark contrast to Nationalist soldiers, often underpaid, who had to rely on getting food, lodging, and other necessities from the local populace.

Business was damaged more badly in Huili than in Xichang or Lugu. Shops were closed for about two weeks, and everything came to a stop for six weeks. The new soldiers brought in the new currency, but the business people wanted nothing to do with it. They had been fleeced before and feared that the exchange rate between the silver in common use and the bills would fluctuate, and they would be the big losers. Some of the shops nearly went bankrupt. Hundreds of people depended on weaving cloth for their daily living, and for this six-week period, the market had dried up.

A new day had dawned for China and for us. By faith we had decided to remain and face this new day with the Chinese people. Only the months ahead would show if our decision had been wise or foolish.

10

An Uneasy Interlude From Liberation to Chinese Volunteers in Korea

After Liberation—Now What?

After we had been officially liberated, we felt a great sense of relief. United as we were now with the rest of China, our mail might come through better, not only from China, but from the States, even though air flights into Xichang had been suspended. The long period of waiting, trying to anticipate what would happen to us and Chinese Christians was now over. Whatever would be was right on top of us.

The shape of this future, however, was still unclear. Not too much change came in the first several months of liberation. The mail came more regularly, although by slow overland routes; life quieted down; no more local wars bothered us; the roads were safe; inflation stopped; corruption was dealt with speedily; opium disappeared; and the soldiers, rather than scaring people with their demands and raping women, were ready to help in anything. They often dropped in to local preaching services, and some seemed genuinely interested. Local civil government continued, often with the same officials, while the new military authorities took a "wait and watch" attitude to discern what they needed to change.

Our work continued almost uninterrupted until the middle of November. When the Korean "war" started in June, we were scrutinized much more carefully and harassed more intensely. This was an interlude between liberation and the heightening of the Korean war, when Chinese volunteers stormed across the Yalu River, the border between China and North Korea.

We hardly needed to be prophets to know that certain plans must go on hold. Despite the hopes that Ruth and I had that our move to Lugu would be for only a six-month transition period that would prepare us to go to a more strategic Nosu center like Yuexi, this now seemed highly unlikely. The Simpsons were poised for their move to Lizhou, but this, too, had to be shelved. We had already spent money renting two pieces of property, held a large feast for the town fathers, and prepared for other details of moving, but now the clear signal was "no go."

No longer did we talk of a Bible school in Xichang, and there were no plans B or C to find co-workers in our three cities. Pastor Wei from Chungking could not plan to join us. Pastor Chen, about to commit himself to join the team at Huili, had to reconsider because the Southwest Bible Institute in Salawu would remain open. A young man, Lo Zaixin, who had originally intended to work in Zhaojue with the CIM, joined us for the work in Lizhou. Now, it appeared, he would stay in Xichang.

We were still committed to a medical work in Lugu, but it would have to be scaled down from the grandiose plans that included a hospital. The huge piles of foundation rocks that had been carried to our hill property for the projected building now served as mute, forlorn markers of dashed hopes.

Even though we hoped to remain in China, we all began to talk with one another and write to the board about where we might go "after China." Terms lasted for six years, and it was too soon to go home. Our plans varied widely. Carrs talked of the Ivory Coast, Garrisons of Latin America, Simpsons of India, Coles of India along the Tibetan border, Lovegrens of Japan, Simons of the Philippines, and Ruth and I of the "Chinese world." Flora Mae hoped to stay in China, but wanted to work more directly with students in a large center like Chengdu or Kunming.

We were disappointed in another task that we had not done well: to prepare the church ideologically for the coming of the new government. Before liberation we had taught the church members, even as other missionaries had done all over China. But the sound of the trumpet was not clear. We had assured the church folk that God would not permit the Communists to come. After all they were atheists, and God would not allow them to thwart his plan of evangelizing all of China's unreached hundreds of million peoples.

We instructed them simply in some tenets of Marxism and how to make a case for theism and refute atheism. None of this was too helpful—the battle was not over philosophy and "isms." We regretted now in our post-liberation quarterbacking that we had neglected so many basic Biblical truths: God's sovereignty and the fact that he often allowed difficult times to come on his people; the way in which God often used unbelieving nations to do his will; the role of suffering in discipleship; how to witness graciously in a hostile society (I Peter 3:9); that even unbelieving people may do many very good things in society; that God's purposes for China were good; that the early church had lived triumphantly for God in a totalitarian state; that it was proper for the church to love its government and to involve itself in constructing a better country; and the role of being salt and light in society.

Obviously, we had not neglected all of these things; neither had we given them the weight they deserved. How we wished that we had some of our pre-liberation time back, when we might have been able to do a more adequate job. Most of our classes still went as usual, but now we had to be much more discreet in what we said. We did what we could in personal conversation, but this was very limited.

If we had been able to see how the church was faring in other parts of China that had been liberated for a longer period, we would not have felt as hopeful in our local situation. Already in larger urban areas, some church property had been occupied, church buildings had been seized, obstructions of one kind or another had been placed in the way of religious work, and church leaders and members had been intimidated by local officials. Because of these problems, several teams were formed in Shanghai to visit churches and Christian leaders in four or five specific areas to analyze and evaluate what was happening.

The visiting team to North China, in addition to meeting in a four-day conference with church leaders, had the unusual opportunity to discuss church problems with Chou En-lai, the new premier of the People's Republic of China (PRC). He met with them altogether for thirteen hours, the last time for an extended period lasting from 11 a.m. to 4 p.m. All were impressed with "his frankness and sincerity, his tolerant spirit, and his interest in an independent Chinese church."[1]

In essence, Chou declared that the church's problems were not from the outside, from the opposition of the army, government or nonbelievers. The difficulty, he affirmed, was from within. The churches had become the pawns of feudalism and imperialism. These must be eliminated from her life. Once the "church had put its own house in order," then the government might be prepared to issue a special edict guaranteeing protection for her religious life and activities.

This was not the first time the church in China had been accused of "imperialism." But when Chou emphasized it in this famous conference with church leaders, it gained new currency. It did not take us long to learn that we were "imperialists" and that those who followed us, i.e. church members, were "running dogs of the imperialists." And so we asked ourselves what our new friends meant by this term. The range of meaning was wide and included much of who we were and what we did, both good and evil.

First, imperialism meant an actual military invasion of China. This had been done by the armies of eight nations after the Boxer rebellion in 1900, but it had not happened often in China's relations with other countries. However, when the accusation was made that missionaries carried on "spy" activities, these covert actions were thought to be the prelude of a military invasion. To make maps (for missionary itineration), to have a short-wave radio (often misunderstood as a sending set), to record weather observations, to have a telegraphic code book, all fell under this category.

In early February, 1950, the Kuomintang sent its planes from Taiwan to make bombing raids on Shanghai, resulting in the death of many people. This was viewed as an act of "American imperialism," because America had supplied the planes and weapons for this atrocity. And, since many missionaries were from America, this was also an act for which the missionaries were blamed.

Second, imperialism was defined as a cultural invasion of China. When the missionary movement and churches promoted schools, hospitals, orphanages, and other types of social institutions, it was seeking, critics claimed, to dominate and enslave the Chinese mind. By these means missionaries and their Chinese friends introduced into China western values and ideologies that would undermine Chinese culture. In his talk with the Chinese church leaders in Beijing, Premier Chou specifically mentioned "democratic individualism," a term prominent in America's White Paper on China.[2] This is why PRC leaders reacted so negatively to a speech made in the United Nations at the end of November 1949 by the U.S. representative, Warren Austin, in which he attempted to prove America's friendship to China because of these various institutions.

In the inflamed atmosphere prevailing after liberation, missionary leaders found it difficult to do anything right. The Baptists' University of Shanghai is a good example. Immediately after the new government came into power, a few professors in the school accused church leaders of attempting to control the university by "their money" that was being poured into it. Then, when the mission board took definite steps to reduce financial aid to a minimum, these same professors cried out in rage that America was attempting to ruin the university by cutting off funds.

Third, imperialism was broadened to mean that the standard of living of many missionaries was an affront to the Chinese among whom they lived. It denigrated the more simple-living Chinese and tempted them with too high a level of rising expectations.

Fourth, imperialism meant that missionaries reflected the political viewpoint of the country from which they had come. This allied them with oppressive forces who were taking advantage of the common Chinese person. Thus, without seeking to analyze the Chinese situation concretely, the missionaries favored the Kuomintang, did not criticize the economic alliance between Chiang's government and America in 1947, and opposed the Chinese Communists who were seeking to liberate the Chinese people. And, in being silent and not opposing the Kuomintang's corruption and oppression, they had, in effect, adopted a specific political position and were not neutral, as they liked to claim.

Fifth, imperialism denoted that the missionaries gained their initial entrance to China because of the "unequal treaties" imposed by force on China as a result of the opium wars. Some Chinese said,

"You forced on us opium and Christianity, neither one of which we wanted."

Sixth, the Communists called the missionary movement imperialistic because of the alleged privileges which they claimed missionaries received from the Nationalist regime. This happened, they claimed, because many of the leaders of the Kuomintang government had been at least nominally Christian. They felt badly that the former government had given a free rein to missionaries to do more or less what they wanted to do in China and had not kept a tighter control over them.

Seventh, Christian missionaries, for the most part, came from imperialistic countries. Critics pointed out that the very Reformation of the church under Martin Luther was coterminous with the birth of capitalism, colonialism, and imperialism in western Europe. Thus Christianity, as it was propagated in China, was a capitalistic and imperialistic Christianity.

A few missionaries were naive enough to take all the Communist promises at face value. Among these was Dryden Phelps in Chengdu. With characteristic exuberance he wrote a personal letter which a friend published in *Soviet Russia Today*. In this he stated that liberation was "the most profoundly religious experience I have ever been through. I absolutely believe this to be the most comprehensive renaissance the human spirit has ever experienced and the most dynamic change in human history. God is working alongside of these Communists." This was too much for the ABFMS, and in mid-December it took "immediate and unanimous action" to bring Dr. and Mrs. Phelps home to explain their statements.[3]

His favorable views of the Communists did not help him get an exit permit any faster, and he did not appear before the Board of ABFMS until January 22, 1952. He submitted his resignation effective at the end of January, even as he asserted that he was not a Communist and that his views were not meant for publication.

Life and Work as Usual

In our relative isolation from both political and ecclesiastical tensions, we tried to live normal lives and do our normal work. Jim Broomhall of the CIM, even more isolated in Zhaojue, four days foot travel farther into the mountains from Xichang, said it memorably in a personal note to Lee Lovegren who handled his business affairs in Xichang:

> As for prospects!? Who knows? All that matters is that the Lord knows, and He has said, 'Stay put and await further orders!' Our present outlook is—stay, till driven out, and if furlough means no returning, then furlough on the field or none at all. Hope you are having as much encouragement in your work as we are having nowadays.

We on the field lived by hope and were irritated with the board attitude that impressed us as having given up on China. "Why," I asked Buker, "is the board not accepting more candidates for China? We are staying here at great risk because we don't think the situation is hopeless. And yet, by turning away candidates, you are saying it is. This discourages us." Ray's reply stated it simply, "We can't help it. The state department is giving no passports even to Hong Kong. How would we get visas?"

The group in Xichang were encouraged at what it saw happening in the work of the church. Liberation did not require that any services be cancelled or that any ministry activities be curtailed. Wisdom dictated that church leaders move all evening services earlier so that they could conclude before dark. By May 7, another group of five men and six women were prepared for baptism, after having gone through an intensive four-week training session. During April and May, I spent as much time as possible in Xichang studying Nosu, and for two out of the five evenings helped in teaching these inquirers. Pastor Lo and I taught them Bible truths for one hour, and in the next hour I helped them to learn how to pray. The most significant aspect of the baptismal service, conducted by Pastor Lo and Bill Simons, was that the group included a Mr. and Mrs. You, the first couple to come into the church together. Following the ceremony in the muddy, little pool in our compound, all of us gathered together to partake of the Lord's table. More than anything else, this gave us a real sense of our unity in Christ.

The two-year contract on the church building had expired by this time, and the church, recognizing that it could not depend on us for continued financial help, rented a somewhat smaller facility at a monthly rate within its ability to pay. Members were concerned to find a pastor who would be able to shepherd them, but this need would not be met as easily as finding an adequate facility.

Studying Nosu in Xichang was not ideal, but at least I could find teachers more easily than I could in Lugu. I had to adjust to my teacher's own very busy schedule. This got me up to study one hour right at the crack of dawn, and then I tried to find another hour in the afternoon. In between, I beat my poor brain analyzing the material I had accumulated. It was confusing, what with tones, a vast number of pictographs, and a grammar far different from Chinese. I often led prayer meetings and preached at least every other week at the church services. This was great to give me more fluency in Chinese, but the Nosu language and Chinese tended to get mixed up in both my mouth and brain!

Ida continued to make bi-weekly trips with several Xichang Christians to the small rural village of Zhuan Xinpu, three or four miles outside the city. In addition to the house-preaching services that were held, John Simpson went along occasionally to take care of some simple medical ailments. No specific place had been allocated to him where this kind of a ministry might be carried on, but when he put out his medicine and dressings in front of almost any building, the people quickly gathered with all kinds of complaints. Eye ailments were the most common, and these were simple to care for with a boric acid solution and some sulfathiazole ointment. John charged three or four coppers, even a pittance in their own economy, so that the people would recognize the value of the treatment and be ready to follow directions in taking their medication.

The big event of the summer was the Daily Vacation Bible School held in August, directed by Flossie and Irene. For both of these busy mothers to get to this stage in their language use and to plan and implement this ambitious program was a major accomplishment. Given the increasingly tense climate for living, it was hard to predict how many families might allow their children to come. How surprised everyone was, when throughout the two-week period, seventy children, ranging in age from five to fourteen, showed up every day.

The theme song was "Bringing in the Sheaves," and the theme chorus was "The Wordless Book Song." The program was a full one: object lessons, class periods for Bible study and memorization, organized games, handwork (embroidery for the girls, making rice-straw fans for the boys, coloring for the smaller tots), singing, and group memorization of the day's verse written on a big red heart. The leaders asked the children to bring an offering whenever possible, consisting usually of a tiny handful of rice, peanuts, beans, or a copper coin. When the DVBS was ended, these were given to a few of the many hungry children of the city. We cannot assess the results of such an educational effort. Many of these young people were exposed to the Gospel message, and several of them declared their willingness to follow the Saviour.

In the early fall, yet another group was prepared to confess Christ openly. John, assisted by Bill, conducted this service as five women and two men followed their Lord in baptism. This brought the total membership of the Xichang church to sixty. The level of interest was high, and even as the result of this public testimony, several others indicated their interest in entering a training class.

One of these new inquirers was the father of Mrs. Yang, a deaconess in the Xichang church. She and others had prayed for the father over a long period of time, with no apparent results. One day he was far from home, alone in a rural area harvesting rice. In the early evening he heard shooting, a good sign that robbers were coming in his direction. He knew he must get away, but where? Just then, he remembered that his daughter had often told him that Christ was a refuge for those who trusted in him. Almost without knowing it, he uttered a simple prayer, "Find me, Jesus, the place of refuge." He had already left his original place of harvesting and had reached a hillside. Continuing to walk and to utter his prayer for help, he reached a very poor home with nothing but a twig-thatched roof and mud floors. These poor people invited him in and reassured him that he would be very safe, since no one would bother to molest their humble home. For three days he took refuge in this out-of-the-way place, finally coming back to the city when the roads seemed safe.

The uncertain days ahead did not lessen the motivation of the several mothers in language study. Flossie took one giant step forward in her missionary saga when she led her first prayer meeting in Chinese in early October. Held at the chapel on West Street, the upstairs meeting was attended by only a handful of folk. But even that is scary if it's the first time! Somehow she struggled through it, closing with a humble declaimer, "My Chinese is not good, my pronunciation is also poor, but God's Word is perfect. Please take this outline home with you and study the verses of Scripture we have been discussing."

Babies continued to come regularly to our missionary families. Martha Jeanne joined the Simons family in May, and in September Marilyn Jean was born to the Carrs. These were not the last of the "liberation" babies; others were yet to come to the Coles, Simpsons, Garrisons, and Carrs. Ray Buker wrote to us once, tongue in cheek, asking our field personnel just what they were doing continuing to add family members. Bill Simons, claiming to speak for everyone, wrote back in the same vein, "What else is there to do?"

At least in the early days of liberation, the new government allowed age-long traditions and customs to continue. The Dragon Boat Festival, celebrated usually in mid-June, was one of these. We were in the wrong place to see the boat races, swimming events, and many aquatic sports, but people took the day off to *shua*—just to play, walk or spend their time doing nothing in particular. Eventually, this kind of wasteful use of time would be condemned, and the people would try to forget these feast days.

By October and November, as the "volunteer" action in Korea heightened in its intensity, the government imposed tighter restrictions on us—limited itineration, evening curfews, registration of those attending meetings, activities geared to compete with our meetings, close surveillance of everything, and house searches. Soon we ceased writing prayer letters to our supporting churches—there was nothing more to write about.

Although the PRC was a responsible government, not a gang of marauding guerilla bands, it could not guarantee personal safety in these chaotic days. Frank Perry, the business manager of the CIM in Kunming, a man who had helped our mission and with whom George Cole had often corresponded, was robbed and then brutally murdered in his office in mid-May 1950.

The biggest American villain to the PRC was President Harry Truman. Compared in popular rhetoric to Hitler, he was maligned in every possible way. One day, in fact, local officials in Xichang came to our missionaries and borrowed Lee's black suit in order to make an effigy of Truman to be hung up near the post office. Fortunately, the effigy was not burned and Lee got his suit back. He was not amused at being linked with Tu-lu-man, the Chinese pronunciation of the President's name.

The sequence for the work in Huili was much the same as in Xichang. A big boost for the work following liberation was that Pastor and Mrs. Lo Zaixin, graduates of the Chungking Bible Institute and recently a part of the team in Xichang, were assigned to the Huili work. This was a great encouragement, since all earlier plans for someone to come up from the Southwest Bible Institute in Salawu had fallen through. Joining this fine couple was a Mr. Guo, a Christian man from north China, who, although untrained formally, contributed significantly to the work.

This additional help not only strengthened the city work but enabled George and Jim to form two teams for country evangelism. The plan was to reach out to every rural village within a day's travel of Huili. Because of poor roads these would be a day's *walking* distance, although the men purchased a horse, which they described as "peppy," to help in some of the itineration.

This initial attempt at rough, country evangelism was not encouraging. June is one of the rainiest of the rainy season months, and the roads were a quagmire. Often when they reached small villages, they found no one at home—every member of the households was busy working in the fields. And when they went to the fields, the people were too busy to talk. The team members reluctantly concluded that it was best to postpone these forays until the fall months when it might be possible for them to keep at it for a week at a time.

The late summer months were filled to overflowing with intense evangelism right in the city itself. The visiting evangelists were from the Southwest Bible Institute, not that many walking days from Huili. As our southernmost station, Huili had the advantage of being a bit more accessible to the outside world, and since travel permits were still easy to obtain, at least for the Chinese, it was possible to hold such meetings.

Pastor K.Y. Chen, Pastor Li, a Nosu who pastored a church of three thousand members in Salawu, and three students from the Bible school reached Huili in July and conducted an intensive evangelistic campaign. Each of the pastors preached once a day for eight days, with the students assisting in leading the singing and talking with the inquirers. Attendance at each of the services exceeded anything that the missionaries had yet seen in Huili. Even more gratifying, the great majority of the listeners stayed right through each of the meetings, even when the preachers went on for more than an hour. Many made a profession of faith, about half from Huili itself and the other half from nearby rural villages. Twenty of these, mostly adults, signed up for the baptismal preparation class which Pastor Lo commenced immediately after this week of evangelism.

After the two pastors returned to Salawu, the students stayed on for another month preaching in most of the small villages around Huili. One of these students was Chinese, one Lisu, and one Nosu. This gave them almost immediate rapport with anyone whom they might meet. George and Jim had hoped to accompany them in this work, but since the official attitude of the government was increasingly anti-American, it was better for them not to go along. The Gospel had enough forces opposing it without adding this political opposition.

Even without the missionaries, this team of young evangelists had problems. When the men reached Mosoyuin, a large village of several thousand people about thirty miles to the north of Huili, they were questioned closely by soldiers from the newly-arrived Liberation army. The soldiers did not forbid them to preach, but, in view of their clearly hostile attitude, the students thought it best to return to Huili. Later they learned that the reason for the suspicion was that a revolt was brewing among the Nosu of that area, and the army was fearful of any strangers, no matter who they were. In the next few weeks, this revolt grew to formidable proportions with the addition of former Kuomintang troops, still hiding out in the mountains.

One of the most interesting incidents of this rural evangelistic effort was a visit to a group of Lisu minority people living near Lixi. A few thousand of these were serving as virtual slaves of the Chinese who owned the land. These Chinese landlords had to give permission before any of the Lisu could even think about becoming Christians. The permission was finally given, and several of the Lisu indicated that they were prepared to follow Christ.

In early October, Pastor Lo baptized the first group of seventeen in Huili. Included in this group were both young and old. The Cao family saw three generations—a grandmother, mother, and daughter—baptized. Another family included a mother and a son, both from a Muslim background, as signified by their name Ma (the Chinese word means "horse," but the sound of the name carries over the first syllable of Mohammed, the founder of Islam).

Only one man was included in the number baptized. This pointed out the problem of reaching men in those days; they lived in fear of getting in bad with the government if they accepted the *yangjiao*, the foreign religion. One young man, probably a believer, did not wish to add to his problem with government officials, already suspicious of him because of past connections with the former government.

These seventeen people became founding members of the Huili Baptist Church. Pastor Lo had already drawn up a covenant to be signed by all of those wishing church membership. Largely a negative statement, communicating much more law than grace, it specifically forbade smoking of tobacco or opium, drinking, gambling, and lying. Without doubt, these were serious problems in Huili life and had been stumbling blocks for the previous church founded by the China Home Mission Society. As a statement of the life-style of Christians, however, this list was little different from comparable "do-nots" to be found in Buddhism. It did not convey to believers or unbelievers anything of the uniqueness of the Christian revelation.

After three weeks, eight more people were baptized, bringing the total number to twenty-five. This time, Mrs. Wang, eighty-three years old and long a practicing Buddhist, confessed her faith. She had been scheduled to be baptized with the first group, but literally got cold feet at the last moment. She was afraid of water and also dreaded having to unwrap her bound feet in front of a large crowd of people. After hearing that baptism was a simple kind of ceremony, she went ahead joyfully.

At times, George and Jim might have questioned the motivation of some being baptized. One man and wife, for example, made a decision for Christ after promising that they would believe if God would bless their home with a child. Very quickly the wife was pregnant, and they saw this as answered prayer. This family's post-baptismal walk with God seemed to indicate that their conversion was real.

By mid-fall, attendance at most of the meetings had dropped dramatically, and George and Jim decided that, with regulations increasing, they needed to use time in an intensive training program for new converts. The planned program was to last for three months, starting with a month of classes, followed by practical involvement in ministry projects, and concluding with a final month of study. Nine students were enrolled, three of whom were among those recently baptized. George, Jim, and Pastor Lo divided up teaching responsibilities, with such topics as Life of Christ, The Five Books of Moses, and Romans. December was the month of ministry, and plans were made to start classes again in January. By this time, however, the full crunch of the Korean war was evident, and even these types of activities ground to a halt.

Christmas was the last opportunity for the missionaries and local Christians to fellowship in a free way with one another. The church was decorated in a simple, but effective way, with everyone taking part in the festivities. On the afternoons of the 23rd and 24th the young people went around to people's homes caroling and relating the Christmas message to those whom they met. On Christmas morning a worship service was held, after which grab-bag type gifts were distributed. On Sunday afternoon Pastor Lo was ordained; the missionaries hoped that in Huili, as well as in all of China, this type of service would symbolize a new phase in the life of the Christian church.

During the last days of active ministry in Huili, a potential serious medical problem increased the stress. Georgie, the Coles' oldest child, ran a slight fever for about two months, and Dr. Chang feared that it might be tuberculosis or undulant fever. The aureomycin brought from Kunming did not bring relief, and the

Coles applied for a travel permit to take their son to Kunming. Had they been granted this, Flora Mae would probably have gone with them to care for a chronic medical ailment, and the Garrisons and Esther would have followed suit. The likelihood of any of them returning to Huili was almost nil. All of these various complex possibilities were avoided when the local officials refused to grant them a travel permit. In due course of time, Georgie's ailment seemed to care for itself. We all thanked God for his intervention in Georgie's illness when all human possibilities were exhausted.

Whether in Lugu, Huili, or Xichang the rumors multiplied daily. One was so pervasive in May 1950 that we wrote to Buker and asked him to confirm or deny it. "Is it true that Japan and the USA are preparing to wage an immediate war against China? Local soldiers are spreading this report and claim that 500,000 Japanese troops tried to make a landing at Shanghai." Ray denied it quickly, chiding us that we could give credence to a report putting our government in such a bad light.

Later in the fall, we at Lugu heard that several thousand American paratroopers had landed near Xichang. The local people were excited to think they were about to be liberated again.

The First Marriage of Americans in Xichang

The prime social event of the year was my marriage to Ruth on May 26, 1950. From the time of liberation until the wedding, Ruth and I were caught up in many activities, a frenzied merry-go-round of language study, travel, ministry in Lugu, and preparations for the big event.

Ruth continued to study Chinese six or seven hours a day, preparing for some section exams and her first message in the Chinese language. With me, it was Nosu study, even as I consolidated my Chinese. While I was in Xichang, either the Simons or Simpsons provided meals for me and often included Ruth as well. Business matters took me back to Lugu every week or so, but with Pastor and Mrs. Yang and the Carrs there, I was not really needed that much in the work at the chapel. Travel was more difficult now with soldiers guarding the road much more tightly. Rare was the trip when I was not stopped one or two times to explain my business.

We continued to use silver dollars to pay workmen for repairs they were making on our home, but increasingly we had confidence in the new "people's money," now current through all of liberated China.

Ruth went with me once or twice to Lugu to plan our new home. I had entertained some hopes that we could live together in my "suite" at the chapel, but all of the missionary wives dismissed this as "hopeless." I knew they were right, but I thought that being there might communicate to the Yangs that we could live in a community spirit with them.

The home on the hill was hardly ostentatious. With mud walls whitewashed with white lime and a sturdy tile roof, it was a two-story building divided into five sections. The Carrs already had three sections, and Ruth and I would have two. The Chinese-style toilet facilities were outside, and a six-foot high wall, topped with pointed glass, just like in Chinese homes, surrounded a small, barren courtyard. A small, four-foot high wall divided our yard. Oiled paper covered the windows, kerosene lamps furnished our light, and the water was hauled from a stream several hundred yards away. Compared with stateside standards it was nothing; for Lugu it bordered on being a mansion.

Numerous problems confronted us in our planning. First in importance was to get a travel permit for Ruth, allowing her to move to Lugu. This explained why I travelled back to Lugu as often as possible; I did not want local authorities to think I was living in Xichang. They might have wished me to come to Xichang where they could watch me better, rather than allow Ruth to move north to be with me. At first, the officials gave no decision, but when they were convinced that we were really getting married and that this was not an "American trick," they granted the permit, although not until the last moment.

We also needed permission for the wedding itself—not to be married, but to have this kind of a public gathering. The military authorities were very suspicious of any large meeting, particularly where foreigners were involved. This problem was resolved, when the men responsible for "assemblies" decided that they could send one or two representatives to be sure that nothing illegal was done. It helped that the ceremony was to be held outdoors in the compound courtyard. Nearby was a temple housing soldiers, and groups of soldiers were regularly stationed on two other sides of the courtyard as well. It would have been difficult for things to get out of hand!

We faced the legal problem of registering our marriage with the U.S. government, which no longer had any representatives in China. We filled out several carbon copies of homemade forms, all properly signed by witnesses and affixed with the mission seal, and sent them to Hong Kong. One copy of this served as the only proof of our marriage, until two years later when we reached Taiwan and the U.S. Consulate gave us a properly notarized marriage license.

Wedding invitations were also a problem. With mail service badly disrupted, no invitation would reach America before the wedding date. And so we compromised. The English portion, printed rather poorly right in Xichang, was an *announcement* of the wedding, and the Chinese portion, intended largely for local friends, was an *invitation*. Apart from the missionaries, probably none of our friends, American or Chinese, noticed the difference.

As soon as we had permission for Ruth to move, we began to send her belongings and furniture to Lugu. Lacking good roads where trucks might be conveniently used, we resorted to rickshas, which can carry a huge load. We had a faithful ricksha puller named Mr. Yu (Mr. Fish), and we put him in charge of several, separate small ricksha caravans that carried Ruth's things to Lugu. For each trip Mr. Yu had to be sure that he had a permit showing why and for whom he was transporting this luggage.

Ruth's biggest concern through these months was to have a nice wedding. Flossie, an expert in all domestic affairs, was more than happy to be a surrogate mother, even when her own second child was imminent—Martha was born about a month before the wedding. She designed and made the wedding gown and veil, made several things for Ruth's trousseau, planned and managed the wedding reception meal, baked a six-tier wedding cake, made the bouquets, and arranged the decorations. Irene Simpson, Ruth's maid of honor, and Ida Lovegren helped in many other ways.

May 26 was a beautiful day with hardly a cloud in the sky. The ceremony was held at 11 a.m. on the compound in front of two large trees by the Lovegren home. Nicely arranged flowers made for a beautiful background. Because of the unsettled political conditions, only the Xichang missionaries were present, although Bill and Win Upchurch came up from Dechang, and Dan from Lugu. Locally, the Madges as well as Janet Broomhall and her children joined with our CBFMS family. About sixty Chinese attended, most of whom were Xichang church members. The day warmed up well, and before the service was over, most of the people put up umbrellas to protect themselves from the sun.

The wedding was western in style, although Pastor Yang read the Scripture in Chinese, and Bill, who performed the ceremony, used both Chinese and English in the exchange of vows. Bill and Flossie sang two duets in Chinese and English, "I Love You Truly" and "O Perfect Love." We used a phonograph recording of "Because" for another musical number. Dan, my best man, wrote both the music and words of the consecration song which we used as we committed our lives anew to the Lord for his purposes for us in China.

Following the ceremony, we moved the chairs away and held the reception right in the courtyard. Nothing amused our Chinese guests more than our cutting of the wedding cake. That may have made the day for them. Originally we had planned to take a week or so honeymooning in one of the rooms of Guangfu temple, half-way up the mountainside opposite Qionghai Lake. Our new political friends would not permit this, and so these plans were cancelled.

The wedding, reception, and picture taking were finished by two o'clock, but we were tired and decided not to try to bike the thirty-five mile-trip to Lugu that afternoon. We were able to get an early start the next morning, and by noon we arrived at what would be our home for the next nine months. We had one scare along the road. While bicycling past what I thought was an empty guard house, we heard someone shout in Chinese. We kept right on going, even though the command was repeated twice. Undoubtedly, a soldier, standing guard along the road, had tried to flag us down for questioning. Fortunately for us, he did not make an issue out of our not stopping. If we were not foreigners, it might have been different. Already, it was apparent that the new government was being careful not to harm foreigners physically.

Lucille, who had not been able to leave Lugu because of her pregnancy, gave us a royal welcome and helped us set up housekeeping. We tried to be as lazy as possible over the next few days as we rested and unpacked. When Dan and Pastor Yang returned from Xichang, our entire station of workers was together for the first time, and we set our minds and hands to the task before us.

During the post-liberation months when I had been spending so much time in Xichang, the Carrs and Yangs had been busy in many different ministries. They had carried on meetings at the chapel with children and adults, both men and women, as usual. With Dan back in Lugu after his long time in Shanghai, now was the time for us to commence a small medical work. He had had first-aid training as a chaplain in the Navy, and with the help of Mrs. Yang, who had been trained as a nurse, a small dispensary was set up in the chapel.

Although started in pre-liberation days, the urgent need for medical help was most apparent right at the turn-over time. As pointed out earlier, there was no significant fighting between the Communist and Nationalist troops, despite Taiwan radio's claim that a "fierce struggle" had taken place. But the Nationalist troops and their sympathizers, who retreated through Lugu, met their "Waterloo" about a day's journey to the north at the hands of Nosu warriors, who stripped them of their clothing, and then stoned, captured, and killed a number of them. The arrival of Communist troops at this opportune time probably prevented a much greater slaughter.

Following this mountain ambush, refugees poured into Lugu for days. Most were stark naked, and we were able to use "white cross" relief clothing as temporary help. Dan and Mrs. Yang treated as best they could those who had been stoned, beaten, and shot by the Nosu. Members of the newly-arrived liberation army were not too happy to see us "helping the enemy," but they did not give us any direct trouble. They had no reason to complain, since we also gave medical help to wounded Communist soldiers.

Most of the simple treatments were for malaria, cataracts, venereal disease, simple colds, stomach ailments, and opium addiction. On some days people showed up who claimed they had been walking four days for medical attention. The news of our medical "magic" spread through the mountains as well. One day Dan and Lucy were surprised to be visited by a Nosu chieftain, along with his five wives, children, and a whole retinue of armed attendants. They wandered through the house and then squatted on the ground outside with their long, black capes draped around them, listening to Chinese hymns on the Carr's little phonograph. In appreciation for the treatment Dan had given to their children, the Nosu brought the Carrs a chicken, and then, within a few days, invited all of us to visit them in their mountain home, sending two armed guards to give a secure escort.

Visiting a Nosu home was an unforgettable experience. The chief personally ushered us into his "strong tower" that had gun slits placed along the top. A fat pig was brought into the room and killed right in front of us, so that we would know that the meat was fresh and prepared specially for us. They threw the sliced-up pieces into the hole-in-the-ground fireplace to be barbecued in the middle of the room. Roasted potatoes, rice, and a very tasty soup filled out the meal. Plates, bowls, or chopsticks were not used; rather a very cleverly-designed long-handled wooden spoon served both as dish and eating utensil. Often a meal like this included *zanba,* oatmeal mixed with water, also a favorite food of the Tibetans. As a present-for-the-road the chief presented us with the pig's head, the Nosu way of honoring guests.

Lucille devoted one day a week to work with the women. Quite a mixture could be found even in a small town: the Muslim lady who, along with an entire Muslim neighborhood, was firmly committed to Allah, but who was willing to learn more about Jesus; the middle-aged woman whose home was an opium den and who implored Lucy for medicine to kick the habit; the women on the bridge, selling dried peppers, peanuts, and thread and who trusted their Buddhist vegetarian vows to give them hope for the future life.

Most needy was an elderly lady who spent her days and nights making sandals. She never got ahead, and the signs of poverty in the home were everywhere. Lucy did not understand why until one day the daughter living with her explained their situation. This daughter had four sons from her fifteen years of marriage to a worthless husband, who, to feed his opium addiction, had sold two of their children into slavery with the Nosu. One son disappeared, but the other was in the mountains about ten miles north of Lugu. The mother and grandmother were working diligently to earn three lumps of silver—about fifteen U.S. dollars—to buy him back. Just when the goal seemed in reach, the husband made one of his rare appearances, hung around for a few days, and then absconded with everything that they had saved. The actual amount of money was so small and the pain so grievous, that Dan and Lucy assured the family that they would cover this "ransom" amount. Within a few days, the son was joyfully returned to his happy family.

What a wonderful triumph of God's grace that our first believer in Lugu would be this grandmother, Mrs. Zhou. She began to attend chapel regularly and, although illiterate in common with most of the women, did her best to learn the truths of the Gospel. Her daughter, faced with the same difficult domestic situation, never seemed to sense any need for the comfort and hope that Christ could give.

Since Ruth had joined me in Lugu, we expanded our activities. We needed a few days to get settled in our new home and to set up housekeeping. This was our first attempt, either singly or as a couple, to train a cook. But in this part of the world, anyone whom we had working in the home was without any previous experience helping foreigners. Our male cook had no problem with our noon Chinese meals, but a foreign-style breakfast came a bit more slowly. Things we took for granted puzzled him. One evening Ruth told him to pour out the coffee grounds by a rose bush in the yard. Later in the evening when she looked for the coffee pot, it was nowhere to be found. After some looking and questioning, we found it sitting out by the rose bush!

Our best contacts for the Gospel came through the medical ministry, simple as it was. Lack of personnel, limitations in the kinds of things we dared to attempt, shortage of medicine, and uncertainty as to how to replenish our supplies restricted our efforts to two afternoons a week from about 12:30 to 5:00. We handled anywhere from twenty-four to forty-five patients in one afternoon, even though many more were clamoring to get in.

Before the treatments began, we held a short fifteen-minute chapel service for the patients. Although they sat patiently while we explained the Gospel, I never felt comfortable with this procedure. We probably were living more by the sacred traditions of missionary medical practice, but I often asked myself whether Jesus would have done it this way. Had this been more a time of prayer rather than a preaching service, I think we could have communicated better that we were depending on God for healing to take place.

We had no continuing pipeline for medicines. Our initial supply had come from Dan's doctor friends at the Philadelphia Naval Hospital, where he had once been a patient. Included were all of the latest "wonder drugs" and twelve modern, medical textbooks. Bill Simons brought in more supplies from Chengdu, but it was not long before these were exhausted.

The Nosu were hesitant to come to the dispensary. They preferred to come directly to our home on the hill, maybe out of curiosity and possibly to avoid contact with the Chinese. This led increasingly to opportunities to visit with a number of them in their mountain villages. Each Monday Dan, Ruth, and I took turns and went alternately to the villages of Tiehchang and Dapinba, both within three hours walk of Lugu, but two or three thousand feet higher. We treated a large number of eye and stomach ailments, many of the latter due to worms. We had as many as fifty people to treat, particularly as they got used to our weekly schedule.

In between regular visits were emergency calls for help. Once Dan and Lucy were called to a mountain village to treat a middle-aged Nosu woman whose hand had been terribly mangled by a gun that exploded while she was holding it. Another time a *bimo* by the name of Lo, who supposedly knew all the tricks of the trade, came on behalf of his wife. Even as he begged Dan to give her some western medicine, he prepared to use some of his powers of exorcism.

First, he cut three little bamboo sticks about eight inches long and a quarter of an inch in diameter. When his preparations were completed, he moved silently across the room with these three sticks and a rice bowl. After placing a little water in the bottom of the bowl and ordering his wife to dip the fingers of her right hand into it, he waved the bowl over her prostrate body. Next he placed the bowl on the floor and tried to balance the three sticks in the center of it, all the time calling out the names of familiar devils.

When he reached the name of "Lin" devil, the sticks immediately stood upright in the bowl. In fact, they seemed to jump into place! Now that Lo Bimo knew the devil's name, he placed some rice in the bowl, mixed it with the three sticks and added a bit of salt for flavor. He then waved the bowl in circles over his wife, politely calling out, "Please, Mr. Lin devil, come out and eat this tasty bowl of rice." As he repeated this invitation, he moved slowly toward the outside of the house, sprinkling a little of the rice along the way. When he reached the edge of the courtyard, he flung the remaining portion of rice as far as he could. Supposedly the devil responsible for his wife's sickness, sent as a curse from the Lin family, had now left his wife's body, and she would soon be well.

This art of divination and exorcism, Lo Bimo claimed, came from the knowledge contained in six scrolls of Nosu script which he carried about carefully in a little brown leather bag. We all tried to repeat the feat while still in the village and failed. Still skeptical, Dan tried it again back at our home in Lugu and found he could get the chopsticks to stand up without any incantations or waving of hands, although he confessed to stacking them like a pyramid. We were not about, however, to add this wizardry to our medical repertoire! While relieved that what we had seen was not necessarily the result of demonic power, we did not lessen in one whit our conviction that "we wrestle not against flesh and blood, but against principalities, against powers, against the rulers of the darkness of this world, against spiritual wickedness in high places." The *bimo's* wife did recover, but Mr. Lo and we disagreed on whether it was due to our medicine or the exorcism.

These trips into the mountains were often wretched. Once we had gotten over the exotic thrill of seeing something new, we were appalled at the living conditions of the Nosu. Their small, single-roomed mud houses were smoke filled and windowless. Trachoma was rampant. Sanitation was unheard of. Mutual distrust, hatred, suspicion, and fear existed even among neighboring villages. Some of those whom we visited were white bones held in slavery by the black chieftains above them. Sexual promiscuity was the norm of life.

Just getting to the villages, perched along the mountains, was a problem. We usually needed guarantors, and they were not always available. This was the rainy season and trails were treacherous. They tried now and again to furnish us with horses for the trips, but these were small, and our feet scraped lightly on the ground. Once in the villages, we had to be very sensitive. Too many visits to one place made the local *bimo* jealous that we were about to preempt his role of diviner and healer. We made it clear that we were guests only once; otherwise we would pauperize them with the need to roast a piglet for us at each visit.

Whether with Nosu or Chinese, the medical work did not bring all the physical results for which we hoped. Too often cases were brought to us as a last resort, and people literally died by our front gate. For people who gave no priority to cleanliness, how could we enforce sanitary measures? The people did not wish to keep dressings in place or to use soap, even when we gave it to them. Tragic also were the cases when people would not follow directions. Dan once treated a case of opium poisoning, and it seemed as if the woman was well on her way to recovery. Returning the next morning, Dan found that she was dead, victim of a vial of adrenalin given to her by a Communist army medical officer, who refused to heed Dan's warning that she be given no more medication. Adrenalin vials could be purchased at any two-by-four pharmacy. The Communists had gotten them from the Nationalists when they surrendered, and the Nationalists had received them in medical supplies from the U.S.

The people were not accustomed to taking medicines properly. When the Nosu came for treatment to our home, we gave them only enough medicine for one day and insisted that they come daily. If Dan or Ruth gave a medicine such as sulfadiazine or sulfasuxadine, they insisted that the people drink several large glasses of water right on the spot. Because of their superstitious beliefs, people attributed serious ailments to the work of demons. This led them to trust their own divination practices more than our treatments.

These beliefs were hardly out of character for the people—their entire lives were religious in orientation. Often a long drought preceded the late spring rainy season. The people used every conceivable method to produce rain. Returning home one day, we came upon a dozen scantily-clad men, with willow branches draped around their bodies and over their heads. They danced madly up one street and down another, stopping long enough at each house for a bucket of water to be poured over their heads. This, they reasoned, would encourage the gods to grant rain.

Failing in this, the people then took the gods from the safety of the temples and paraded them in the scorching rays of the sun. If the gods suffered as much as the people from the heat, they would more readily hear their followers' petition for rain.

We felt the power of the Evil One as we persuaded men and women to come to Christ. Soon after she arrived in Lugu, we met Lin Kaizhen or Lin Sanjie (the Lin family's third daughter). Although formerly a vegetarian who had lived for many years as a Buddhist nun in a local temple, she showed an interest in the Gospel and came to the women's meetings. One night in the Carrs' living room she fell on her knees and begged God's forgiveness. But when Lucy offered her cookies (containing lard), giving her an opportunity to break her vow and show a repentant spirit, she refused and went her way.

For many months she avoided all of us, fearful that believing in Christ meant she must break her vegetarian vow and provoke the scorn and derision of her vegetarian friends. Shortly after this, her body was infected with nasty sores, and she asked Lucy if God could heal her. Lucy replied that her main need was to believe in Christ, but that this step of faith would not guarantee any physical healing. After prolonged discussions, most of them out in a thatched shelter in the fields where she was guarding the corn from thieves, Sanjie affirmed her faith in Christ.

Her illness continued to get worse, and the Carrs ordered a special drug from Xichang. When it arrived, Lucy hurried to Sanjie's home, only to receive the shocking news that she had been murdered. Bit by bit the story came out. The young son and wife of the landlord, Sanjie's uncle, had clubbed her to death, angered that she had broken her vegetarian vow. This rationale apparently was compounded by the fact that they thought her disease was leprosy. A smoldering family feud, unrelated to her vow, probably also contributed to this tragedy.

Could we have dealt with this problem in a culturally more appropriate way? At that time, our solution seemed correct. In retrospect, we might have urged moving more slowly toward the decisive break with her ties to Buddhism. Was there any way for those coming from Buddhism to retain the form of a vegetarian vow and transform its function to serve the Christian faith? These questions troubled us as we tried to relate our Gospel to the local context.

During the summer months, we not only continued all of our services in Lugu but also maintained a regular schedule of rural itineration. We preached from Gospel charts, sold Scripture portions, and talked personally with many interested in the faith. If possible, we steered clear of soldiers. The common people felt no differently about us than before liberation, but it was embarrassing both to them and to us if there were soldiers about. Some friends whom we had met on former trips were surprised that we were still in Lugu and still preaching. A few of the school teachers confessed their early disillusionment with the new state of affairs. What bothered them the most was that their discipline problems had increased several-fold now that their students felt that they were "liberated" from the yoke of their teachers' oppression!

In mid-October, I visited the Nosu village of Dapinba for a three-day period of intensive language study. I did not have enough of a foundation in speaking Nosu for this to be as profitable as it might have been, but it introduced me more intimately to the minority culture. In the village was a small schoolhouse, and I was given a bed in a room with a Chinese teacher who conducted the school. If I had actually been in one of the Nosu homes, I would probably not have had the comfort of a bed. The room soon became like Grand Central Station. The Nosu school boys who ordinarily sleep in their own homes took on the responsibility of entertaining me, and all moved in with me. A Nosu *bimo* who came from a nearby village to teach me also moved in.

Very soon others who did not find room to sleep there gathered about the fire to take up what sitting space remained. I have never had so many "public" days! Every place I went there was a companion, and everything I did—ordinary as it seemed to me—was a cause of great excitement. We ate as is the custom sitting on the floor, and the food was just simple Nosu food—mostly rice, oatmeal kneaded by dirty fingers into a dry roll, a spinach-type vegetable, and an occasional potato, baked in the charcoals of an open fire. I had taken along half a dozen cookies, but I tried to eat them on the sly for fear my hosts would think I despised their food.

One evening I had my first experience in seeing a *suni* at work. In contrast with the better-known *bimo* who exorcises and heals according to the ancient traditions recorded in the Nosu written records and whose position is hereditary, the *suni* is anyone whom the gods seize—he works by divine inspiration.

The ceremony that evening was to heal a sick child. As I sat for over four hours in this smoke-filled room, the sense of demonic power was overwhelming. The performance was divided into two parts. During the first hour the *suni* chanted and exhorted the devils to leave the child. After a short pause, he took his drum and beat it for nearly an hour, imploring his "god" to come. Soon a helper waved a small pig over the kneeling bodies of the whole family, and then killed it. In doing this he was bribing the devil to return the spirit of the child in return for the spirit of the pig.

During the latter part of the service the *suni* not only beat his drum but danced in a frenzied manner. At one point the mother of the child joined in his chanting, almost as if to have ownership in the effort to heal her child.

One day when I wished to visit a village no more than a mile away, the people quickly warned me that this would be dangerous, both for me and the village where I was staying. It was the same old story of the Nosu "triangle." One man had lost his wife by death, and he took her sister for his new wife. Unfortunately, however, this sister was already married, and her husband rushed across the valley between the two villages and killed the man who had taken her. From that day the enmity between the two villages knew no limits.

The people were friendly and showed me every kindness possible, urging me to return often. They repeatedly pressed on me the possibility of teaching their children English in the little school. This would be a valuable way of helping them, and it would also help me to pick up some valuable clues about their language.

One very helpful spin-off from this trip was that I was able to get the *bimo* who had taught me in this village to come to Lugu and give me Nosu lessons. We studied in my old room at the chapel. Ideally, he should have been an excellent teacher. Since he was a priest, he knew the written language far better than others did. Over a period of time I began to build up my vocabulary, got a beginning feel for the way words and phrases fit together to make sentences, and learned how to write some simple pictographs. Unfortunately, he was very undependable. I could never be certain when or if he would show up. Much time was wasted. The room where we studied was cold; so he excused himself repeatedly to go out on the street and get "warmed up," which, being interpreted, meant to get a few drinks of Chinese beer. In no time at all, he was warm, but also unusable to me for the rest of the day.

By the end of the summer, we were writing letters back and forth to the other stations to arrange an earlier date for the next annual conference. We had faced some personal harassment in the summer after the commencement of the Korean war, but we still did not see clearly that the end was near, that there would be no third annual conference, and that within a few months we would be on our way out of China.

Endnotes

1. "Notes on Reports of Conferences with Premier Chou En-lai Regarding the Christian Church in China." Page 1. This report is FD 605 (China Comm.), B. 10 in CBFMS Archives.
2. *Ibid.*, p. 2.
3. New York Times, December 20, 1950.

11

Left With No Choice

The work continued in all of our stations until the end of 1950. This created the illusion that, even with a change of government, things might yet work out. This dream ended with the start of the conflict in Korea. Soon American troops would be fighting soldiers near China's borders—a voluntary action, it was called. That totally changed the picture. Although meetings continued and a small spiritual harvest was reaped, we began to have problems. First, it was personal harassment; then difficulties were created for our ministries. Eventually, we saw that there was only one solution—to leave China, our adopted land, that we had come to love. This was a painful decision to make, but we were left with no choice.

Personal Harassment

One problem started in Lugu the very week of liberation. Dan and I reported to the authorities through Xieh Wendan that we had a gun, a leftover from Dan's days in the Navy, and a radio. The gun was turned over to the authorities, and we registered the radio. The latter caused the difficulty. Earlier in the year, when all of the men were in Mianning for the week of meetings, Zhang Zhongqi, the Carrs' language teacher in Lugu, had asked Lucille if we had a radio. Mistaking the word "radio" for "phonograph," she said "yes." In early March, Zhang asked me the same question, I answered honestly "no." Two weeks later, Dan and I bought a small radio when we were in Xichang and had it shipped to Lugu. Then, after liberation, we reported we had one. When Zhang, who we found out later was a "plant," heard of this, he thought we had been deceiving him all along and that we were using the radio for wrong purposes, to maintain relations with Taibei, whose signal came in clearly.

The authorities wished to confiscate the radio. I objected and asked for some official notice that radios were unlawful. As I discussed the matter with He Chuzhang of the Mianning Public Security Bureau, which had jurisdiction over Lugu, he referred to the radio successively as a generator, telegraph, and sending set. Although he said he knew the difference among all these, I doubted it. Finally, he agreed to my suggestion that he seal up the back of the radio with paper, thus preventing our using it, and allow us to keep it until he received further instructions.

Our next problem came from my big mouth. Two soldiers came to the gate of our compound and asked to come in. When they did not seem willing to state their business, I kept balking and did not take our dog away from the entrance. As the discussion heated up and touched many subjects that did not seem to concern them, I made the mistake of accusing them of "speaking recklessly." This remark enraged them, and they chewed me out in no uncertain terms. Didn't I know this was a new China, that all people were equal, that the people's liberators could not be accused in this fashion? And so out came their little book, and they registered all of us foreigners in the compound, including the Madges who were visiting us from Xichang.

The upshot of the affair was that I had to go with the soldiers to see their superior at the police station. He patiently explained that the soldiers' mission was to find out if our cook, recently moved with us to Lugu, had a travel permit. If so, where was it? I ruefully remembered at that point that I had carelessly thrown it away. He then lectured me in detail on the importance of this and graciously allowed me to return home. Three lessons learned: let soldiers in when they come to the gate; control your tongue; don't throw away valuable pieces of paper.

The next dispute arose over differing views of private property. The new government had propaganda teams which went about from village to village, putting on plays depicting the struggle of the masses against those who exploit them. Often they needed some of the things we had—kerosene, kerosene lamps, and portable organs. When possible, we tried to work out a loan, trade, or sale.

One evening some soldiers wished to borrow our chapel organ, implying as they asked that we could cancel our evening evangelistic meeting. After a lot of bickering, we said there was no way we could let them have it that evening. Imagine our surprise then when later in the day, Pastor Yang came to our home and said that some soldiers had come and taken the organ. Apparently, the three soldiers to whom we had talked returned to their headquarters, had a slip written out guaranteeing the safe return of the organ, taken it to Yang, and given him the impression that we had agreed to their using it.

I figured there was nothing we could do and wanted to drop the matter. Not Daniel, though and so, with me in tow, off he went to the headquarters of the propaganda group. No one stopped him as he walked in, picked up the organ, put it on his back, and walked out. Since I did not appear to be as determined, a couple of men stopped me and demanded an explanation. I replied that their taking our organ from our property was an "improper" action. Furiously, the head of the team said my answer made no sense. A slip had been made out, taken to Yang, and the organ was taken. Now we had come and taken *their* property. If the sparks had not been flying so furiously, I could have laughed. But they were very serious! In fact, they said that if Dan did not return the organ to them immediately, they would take me to Xichang. Fortunately, Dan did return, but the organ was now in our hill home, and they finally relented in their demand that we return it to them. As we reflected on this type of circular reasoning, we saw how they might convince themselves that South Korea had attacked North Korea.

Dan had a way of getting into trouble. After Lucy had given birth to Marilyn in early September, he went to Xichang to be with her, leaving their small boys, Danny and Jimmy, to stay with Ruth and me. While Dan was there, he went up on the wall of our compound, something we often did, to watch some soldiers beyond the rear of our property doing target practice. Only this day was not target practice, but soldiers repulsing a Nosu attack. Immediately the soldiers suspected Dan of being an accomplice of the attackers, and they rushed him off with bayonets drawn to the military headquarters.

After several hours, during which time Dan was passed back and forth from one office to another, the garrison commander appeared and took over the questioning. Eventually, they believed Dan, and after giving him a fifteen-minute reprimand, they sent him back to the compound with the warning never again to get on the wall.

When Dan and Lucy were ready to return to Lugu, they faced another hassle. In fact, during their first attempt, the soldiers halted them with the verdict that they could not make the trip. Then it became a chess match. The local authorities told them to bring Danny and Jimmy to Xichang to join them. Dan and Lucy said they must return to Lugu. Finally, after five days of negotiation, the Carrs were allowed to rejoin us in Lugu.

Anti-American propaganda both escalated and became more specific after the outbreak of the Korean conflict. We sensed this for the first time on August 1, 1950, the *bayi* (8/1) holiday, celebrating the founding of the Communist party in China. Troops were brought in from Yuexi, Mianning, and Qilong to swell the number ordinarily stationed at Lugu. Authorities organized a huge parade, consisting of armed soldiers, government propaganda troops, school children, farmers, and workmen with their tools of production, and even the Nosu. The big slogan was "oppose American imperialism for invading Korea and Formosa." Soldiers painted this big propaganda sign on our chapel wall. They drew a large map of China next to it. Pictured standing on the map and leaning toward Formosa with a fixed bayonet was a Chinese soldier, preparing to plant on the island the five-pronged star of Communism.

While the town was caught up in such demonstrations, we did well to keep off the streets and observe from a distance. Local people were slow to believe the propaganda, because they viewed us as their friends and not "evil imperialists." Our Chinese co-laborers, who had to take the brunt of associating with us, found these propaganda days very difficult. Soldiers berated the Yangs in every way possible, calling them "running dogs of the imperialists," telling them they should have nothing to do with us, and making sarcastic remarks about their children, such as "oh, this is what American children look like!"

Searches were made at any time of day or night. We had to steel ourselves not to become alarmed easily—never an easy task unless we laid hold of the reality of God's grace and presence. The first serious search—as contrasted with wandering soldiers who wanted to come in casually and "look around"—came early in the morning, when both Dan and Lucy were in Xichang at the time of Marilyn's birth.

Two soldiers came into the compound with no warning and asked me immediately to show them our sending set. When I denied we had any, they asked to be shown the telegraph. When I again denied that we had these types of things, they got down to their main concern. "Where," they asked, "is the 'thing'"? I immediately knew that the "thing" was the radio they had sealed up. I told them that this belonged to Dan, and he was in Xichang.

This answer sparked them to make a thorough search of the Carrs' side of the home. Neither upstairs nor downstairs did they find any trace of the radio. Finally, one of the men asked me to open Dan's locked study, but I said, honestly, that I did not *have* the key, which just a few moments before I had placed in a metal water pitcher, filled with water, on the side board. Thoroughly frustrated in not finding the radio, they came over to our side of the home, interested apparently only in determining for sure that our typewriter was just that and nothing more.

Looking through our clothes closet, one soldier asked what need I had of two suits. "After all," he said, "you can't wear more than one suit at a time!"

We were glad that the radio, hidden away in Dan's studio, had not been found. We usually listened to the Voice of America broadcast every evening, while Lucy loudly played the piano or organ. This was our only source of news in these hectic days. While we listened to the radio, we took care that the cook was out of the kitchen and in his own little house. We made sure also that Danny was asleep, for had he known that we were using the radio, he surely would have told the cook.

If the radio had been discovered, we would have had to do some tall explaining. We had taken off the paper with its seal, so that we could use the radio, afterwards replacing it with some similar paper ordered from Xichang. This resulted in a partially-torn seal. Even more serious, some house rats, attracted by the paste we had used, ate off most of the paper and the seal. Eventually, when we did have to turn the radio in, the authorities found it difficult to believe that rats could cause this much damage!

Three months later when things were tightening even more, Dan and I were called down to the police station and told we must find twelve people—three for each foreign adult—to guarantee that we had no radio sending station. The official who had come from Xichang to care for our affairs, plus a local soldier, spent the rest of the afternoon trying to intimidate our guarantors. Although they were all scared, no one backed down.

Intimidation of this type occurred regularly. One time some soldiers told Chen Dajie, the servant who worked faithfully in our chapel and who had cooked many meals for me when I was single, that all of the foreigners were very "rotten." She stubbornly protested that when she worked for us, she was well treated, but her husband was a "rotten" man. The soldiers left without a word. The Chinese proverb said it well, "the eyes of the common people are clear as snow."

Dan's language teacher, who taught in the local high school, revealed himself as a Communist official after the take-over. Later, Dan realized that the teacher had often pawed through papers on his desk when he had left him alone in the study for a few moments. He also took down the names of local officials and others who paid friendly visits to our home.

Our colleagues in Xichang and Huili were experiencing the same kind of harassment. While this created a great deal of stress and personal inconvenience, we all could live with these types of things, as long as we were in health and our witness for Christ continued. In mid-summer, when the Cole children were having some health problems, possibly not as serious as first thought, and when signs of trouble were beginning to appear, the Huili personnel as a group applied for exit permits, only to be turned down by the government. While a disappointment, it gave to them a certain security in knowing that it must be God's will for them to stay—all other options were gone.

A Changing Context

If life in Lugu was changing for us, the transformation was much more radical for the Chinese people. We tried not to talk to our friends about the changed situation—that was not why we were in China. We tried to preserve our neutrality. But they seemed to need someone "safe" to share their burdens with, and talk they did. In general, they were not that happy about "liberation." Initially, they hoped that this was the panacea to solve all of China's century-long problems. And many very good things did happen. What bothered them most was the rigid control and discipline that the Communists had imposed on every facet of life.

Propaganda teams held endless meetings and "group therapy" sessions every evening—and often throughout the day—in every town, village and hamlet. This discussion and sharing usually led to times of confession, duly reported on bulletin boards and in daily newspapers. Every effort was made to *zhui qiu*, reach far back into the past and find the evil influences in your background. If the past were badly compromised by your own or your family's activities, authorities imposed severe penalties, even death.

The dwellings in our town were divided into cells of ten homes. At least one member from each family had to attend these indoctrination sessions. At the end of each session, an examination was given. Anyone who flunked was punished in one way or another, even to the extent of being jailed. How important it was for these family representatives to learn their lessons well, for they had the responsibility of teaching the other family members.

No need continued for the ubiquitous "secret police," so common under the Nationalist regime, to monitor the "brain washing" that went on in the community. Each political cadre spent most of the time watching over his assigned cell, free to enter homes without knocking at any time of the day or night. Added to this was the "watch care" offered by the neighbors, and even other members of the family.

With all of these learning activities going on and the constant confessions, anyone who opposed the new party line was immediately exposed and reported. This often came from members of one's own family, especially the children who were kept in school from morning to night, seven days a week. They were taught that to be good little Communists they would have to report even the faults of their own mothers and fathers. How shocked we were one day when leaving our chapel to notice a crowd of people standing in front of the shop-home on the other side of the street. The soldiers were leading the parents off to jail because of the testimony of their own children.

At the same time, the people were glad for many things. The government had curbed inflation, for one thing. Right after liberation, it was possible to continue using silver and copper coins, and even the silver ingots. After a short while, all of these were made unlawful, it was said, "because of the righteous demand of the people." This meant using the paper currency for everything: all payments to the government, government-issued bonds, stamps, and payment of taxes. Gradually, as the value of the paper currency increased, people's confidence was restored. How different from the Nationalists who had brought in planeloads of paper currency each week.

Prices also were stabilized, largely through setting up a government-run cooperative. If the price of rice boomed, the government took rice from the tax storehouses and sold it directly to the people at a pegged price. This quickly brought the price of the market rice into line. These cooperatives sold most things, including staple products such as oil, cloth, and salt.

Less popular was the new policy on opium. Now it was unlawful to plant, sell, and buy opium as well as to conduct an opium den. This law had been on the books before, but too many people were dipping into the pot for it to be enforced. The new Communist program was not all force. Propaganda teams went throughout the countryside and into the tea shops denouncing the evils of opium. The full effect of this policy was not felt for two or three years. The final opium crop in the late spring of 1950 was so abundant that there was enough on hand in the Ningsu area for three years of smoking.

The people were ambivalent about the program against the landowners. These men had fleeced them unmercifully, and they welcomed the thought of having their own land. But all the niceties of Confucian thought and the idea of "face" made it difficult to bring accusations directly against those who had exploited them. Oppression had become a way of life; they had learned to "eat bitterness" and to "bend with the wind." Only when urged on by the new liberators, did the common people muster enough hatred for this initially distasteful task. Which is precisely why these liberators, intent on creating a new China, labelled Confucianism as "feudalism," an attitude that made people docile in accepting past and present injustice.

When the Communists first came to power, only the most obvious prisoners were put in jail, and they were usually released later. In due course of time, after much indoctrination, the Peasants' Society was formed, and, in our area, this group implemented all facets of the government policy. It organized local parades, gave permits for people to move from one area to another, took the initiative in the program of "reduce the rent, return the rental deposit" and helped to organize land reform.

From their ranks the government formed the armed guard who alone was allowed to carry guns. When the military authorities imprisoned some political prisoners, they called on the Peasants' Society to make the actual accusations. When there was a public trial or execution, it was usually the leader of the Peasants' Society who presided over the occasion.

For farmers who had had no more status than animals to be kicked around, this was a heady experience. The process was a distant cousin to democracy, although highly centralized. No one doubted that the real power continued to be with the higher-level authorities who very quickly could negate anything they did not approve.

The government knew that land must be taken from the landlords, but only very recently have they reached a more satisfactory decision on who is to get it. Initially, the land belonged to the state, and the people worked about as hard and with even fewer rewards from the state as their master. Everyone had to find land to work. People came to us and begged to be allowed to till our unused land, since it was now very obvious that we were not going to erect a hospital there. We were very happy to permit this; otherwise we would have needed to farm it ourselves. All land, even in the most impossible places, had to be cultivated to help meet the needs of China's multitudes, as well as to produce more taxable crops.

When there was increased production in agriculture and in business, authorities imposed higher taxes. These ostensibly were to meet many needs: more airplanes and guns for use in Korea, better schools for the children, construction of roads, bridges, and new government buildings. The state was highly exalted and people were urged to have a spirit of self-sacrifice. On the surface, people were happy to identify themselves with the state—we watched many parades in which the people danced in the streets with joy at the privilege of paying taxes. The people were rightly proud that China "had stood up" among the nations of the world, but dancing for joy at tax time was hard to believe.

During these first few months when the ship of state was getting settled, people were fearful, particularly of saying something wrong. One innkeeper advised me that when I talked to soldiers or authorities, I should "include a large area in what I said." By this he meant I should never be so specific that anyone could "pin me down."

At night time, the soldiers wandered around the street looking into windows, seeing what the people were doing and engaging them in apparent casual conversation. Seldom was it just this. Each soldier was a self-constituted investigator. Had a guest arrived in the home? Where had he come from? Does he have a permit?

At this stage, the government had cause to fear. Whenever the soldiers were not around for a time, a few counter-revolutionary wall signs appeared. The most common urged people not to use the new paper currency, because it would surely depreciate. That could have been true, for whenever rumors were about that guerilla bands were in the nearby mountains, the bills depreciated substantially.

We have no way of knowing how many people were killed in Lugu. This was a revolution, probably a very needed one, and it was not, to use Chairman Mao's wording, a "dinner party." Serious crimes had been committed in the past, and severe punishments were meted out to repay the violators. An execution ground was not far from our home, and it was used daily. Some of those killed probably deserved death for the murders they had committed. Others had been guilty of very bad crimes, but probably would not have been killed in a different kind of society. Many of those who had befriended us were put to death, not because of their relationship with us, but because they were classified as the exploiters and oppressors. Their friendship with us, however, helped neither them nor us.

Clampdowns in Our Work

The problems which we faced in our ministry were different from those which the churches and missionaries were experiencing in other areas of China. Our work was too new, and the few believers in our two churches in Xichang and Huili were not aware of the bigger picture elsewhere. After leading church leaders had held their noted conversations with Premier Chou En-lai, they returned to Shanghai, determined to take steps to rid the Chinese church of all elements of imperialism. They drew up a Christian Manifesto for all Christians everywhere to sign. At first, few wished to sign it, and many dissented. However, as the international situation heated up and as some church leaders made more accusations against missionaries for alleged "reactionary" activities, the movement started to "snowball." Even many evangelical leaders—Marcus Cheng, head of the Chungking Bible Seminary—signed this Manifesto. Many felt that the only course for the church was to agree with this document which recognized the role of American imperialism in using and exploiting the church in China.

This movement was given further impetus when, in late December 1950, the government begin to regulate all organizations receiving American funds. A group of church leaders in Shanghai praised the government for its action, declaring that this would enable them to reach self-support immediately, rather than in three years as initially planned.

The following April, representative leaders of the nation's Christian churches met in Beijing and urged local churches to initiate "accusation" meetings. These were designed to bring to light and denounce all those reactionary activities which missionaries had been allegedly carrying on under the cloak of religion. This same resolution deplored the action of the World Council of Churches for declaring that the Korean war had been started by North Korea.

A speech given in close conjunction with this resolution urged that the churches participate in all of the programs which the government was promoting at that time. These included: 1) Resist America, Aid Korea, Defend the Fatherland, Protect the Home; 2) Eliminate bandits; 3) Sign the Public Covenant. The latter referred to the six-month covenant which each factory, business, and home business unit was to use, declaring production aims and patriotic attitudes. Workers were to sign this with great solemnity and seriousness.

Some leaders suggested that Christians be urged to participate actively in the program to buy airplanes, tanks, and bombs to aid in the Korean War. Even though they may have already given as members of business, industrial, or workers' groups, they now should give more because they were Christians. Some proposed that perhaps a plane could be bought and named "The Church of Christ in China." Church leaders reminded Christians that as they previously had supported the "bandit" Chiang Kai-shek, now they must publicly display their patriotism in resisting imperialistic aggression the world over and in aiding the free peoples of the world.

Difficult Days in Lugu

In this isolated area of China, we never faced these kinds of demands. We did have many difficulties unique to our situation. If many soldiers were passing through town, places to quarter them were at a premium. Often they wished to use the chapel premises, and we welcomed them. But with every space occupied, even the preaching hall, we could hardly have services. This did not happen regularly, but enough to be disruptive.

More common were soldiers wandering in an out as an evening service was in progress. Most likely they had never heard a Gospel message before, and, not surprisingly, they either did not understand or misunderstood. Our preaching was very simple, geared for unlettered country folk. Posters helped vividly to get the message across. I think of one I used frequently when explaining Romans 6:23. A man with Chinese features and dress was stretched out on the ground. Two huge dice were on his thigh. A person at his side poured hot water on his head. Another person poked an opium pipe into his ribs. It was a picture of the oppression, bondage, and wages of sin. Newly indoctrinated Communist soldiers, possibly ex-Nationalists who were now fighting for a new cause, wondered why, if China had been "liberated," could there be the "oppression of sin?"

One night when Dan was preaching on Jesus as Lord, a soldier at the back whispered his question out loud to me, "If Mao Tse-tung is chairman of our country, how can he say, 'Jesus is Lord'?" If I had explained fully, it would have created confusion and made it difficult to continue the meeting.

Once someone tried to spy on us. A girl approached us with a fabricated story that she was a member of the Huili church. Somehow she and her boy friend , although probably spies, had gotten into the Huili church. When things became too hot for them, they left. She said that Esther Nelson in Huili had written a letter of introduction to me, asking that I help her to find work in Lugu. But, her story went, as she went through Mosoyuin, authorities inspected her and took the letter from her. The story did not have a true ring to it, and we avoided her like the plague. She returned to the chapel several times, but we continued to keep her at a distance.

Our first real difficulty commenced with the visit to Lugu of a Nosu preacher named Zhang. He had formerly worked with Dr. Broomhall in Zhaojue, but, as a southern Nosu, found the situation there too difficult and was returning to the Salawu area where he had been trained in the tribal Bible institute. When he went through Xichang, the missionaries there persuaded him to come and see our work.

He preached several times, and the Nosu, who often crowded the chapel, hung on his every word. Here was one of them who had believed in this foreign Jesus. Formerly, he had been a bandit, and this impressed them even more. Unfortunately, some soldiers, lounging about the chapel, found that he did not have a valid travel permit for Lugu and hauled him off to headquarters for questioning. Later I was asked to vouch for him, to no avail. He was sent back to Xichang, and, very shortly, was released. But in Lugu soldiers began spreading the tale that in our chapel we had been harboring a bandit.

Shortly after this, on Monday evening, November 26, we had our first direct run-in with the military. We were holding a special inquirers' class for children, and we tried to keep out passers-by and even uninterested adults. Ordinarily none others tried to get in, which made us feel that those who made the attempt this evening were planted by the authorities. One irritated man protested that we would not let him in because we were "preaching our American imperialism."

We ignored this, and the four of us teaching that night—Mrs. Yang, Ruth, Lucille, and I—taught as we ordinarily did. Once or twice a few soldiers came in and looked around, examining our teaching materials and listening for awhile. When the children were dismissed to go home, we found that the street around the doorway was filled with soldiers. They effectively blocked the children, taking their names and addresses, as well as their parents' names. They also took the small lesson notebooks which the children were carrying. The night was clear and moonlit, and spectators overflowed the street. The children were afraid and crying, and we had no idea what to do. The soldiers ordered us to go on home and mind our own business. We replied that this was our business and stayed on until all of the children had been allowed to return to their homes. At one point, Lucy pointed to a policy statement tacked up on the outside wall of our chapel and called attention to the "freedom of religion" clause. A soldier tartly retorted, "Yes, we have such a policy, but it doesn't apply to the likes of you."

The next trouble came the following Sunday morning when we held our Sunday school meeting. As might be expected, only the very boldest of the children showed up—about fifteen out of the normal thirty-five or forty. It was a replay of Monday night. Soldiers again detained the children, took their names, and examined all materials carefully. They asked one boy what we had taught him, and, very fearfully, he replied, "I don't remember." He was so afraid that he did not return home until much later in the day, causing his parents to be very worried.

Again, the obvious leader of the soldiers ordered us to go on home. Rather unwisely I replied, "The street is public and we intend to stay here." At this remark, he became quite nasty and retorted, "You Americans are all alike, you think you own everything. For now you can take care of your own matters . . ." The obvious implication was that a day was coming when they would take care of them for us.

That afternoon the Carrs delegated me to go down and talk over the state of affairs with the Yangs. They agreed that we had better be careful for a time—none of us foreigners would do any of the preaching in public meetings, and if we had children's meetings, we would not divide the classes. The path of confrontation was not wise, and these were not the days, if there ever had been any, when we should pretend we had any rights or insist on them. This was not the weak China of the past 150 years when the foreigners could do as they pleased!

How gratifying that, with us out of the way, we had some of the best meetings we had had in a long time. And the soldiers, realizing that they were alienating the children by their tactics, seemed to be more friendly to them on the streets, often playing simple games with them. Often two or three of the soldiers sat at the back in the evening evangelistic meetings and played with some of the children who showed up.

The next move in this ongoing chess game came when all foreigners were required to register on December 9. Both Pastor Yang and our teacher, Xie Cenyuan helped us fill out the many forms. Included in the registration process was a short oral inquisition. Among the questions they asked us were the following: 1) Have you read any of the bulletins and posters which we have put up? 2) What do you think of the PRC policy toward the minority races? 3) What is your impression of life since liberation? 4) What do you think about the American invasion of Korea? 5) Did you read in the Chinese newspaper the material concerning the Sino-Soviet treaty of friendship and mutual help? 6) Since liberation have you gone into Nosu territory? If so, for how long a period, to which places, and for what purposes?

These questions were read to us by Mr. He, and another man sitting at a desk recorded our answers. Where possible we gave positive answers. We were impressed by many improvements. Where discretion seemed to be the best course, we tried to be honest, while not giving a direct reply. The upshot of the whole process was that they told us that our church activities must be restricted to the streets of Lugu. No longer would they permit us to do rural or mountain itineration for any purposes.

This restriction only buried what had been dying over a period of time. People in the country markets were not as friendly as they once had been and bought very few materials. Not as many sick people showed up when we visited Nosu villages. Even the *bimo* who had been serving as my language teacher was more hesitant about welcoming me to his village. Not only was he afraid of the worsening political climate; he was concerned for his own status in the village, for he saw clearly that our kind of ministry, both teaching and healing, would undercut the need for his magic and sorcery.

Technically, we were still free to conduct meetings in the chapel, but the handwriting was on the wall. The amount of good that could be done by a few more meetings or a few more sermons was distinctly limited. Despite this, we did what we could. We kept the dispensary open, and people continued to come, even from two or three days' distance. We went ahead with planning for a Christmas program. Ruth, Lucy, and Mrs. Yang made up little packages for the Sunday school children. Very simple, they contained pieces of local candy, peanuts, rice candy, and a picture of the Christmas narrative. We were gratified when sixty-five children defied the odds and came to our short program. The military apparently were taken off guard and made no attempt to disrupt us. The next day some soldiers visited one of the homes on the street and asked the parents to show what their children had received. With some relief the man replied, "The children have already eaten them!"

We celebrated Christmas in a leisurely fashion and sensed God's grace sustaining us in our stressful situation. We had prepared several small presents for the Yang children, and they had some candies for us. Ruth and Lucy had sewn several bits of clothing for the children in Xichang, and we sent these off by ricksha, but only after an extensive search of each article had been made. The presents they had prepared for us did not arrive until several weeks later. On Christmas day itself we had a tasty geese dinner and whiled our time away singing carols, telling stories to the Carr children, and playing games on our crude, home-made Parcheesi and croquenol boards.

Even though we could not go into Nosu territory, the people came to us from their mountain villages. We had paid them to prepare sets of Nosu clothes for all of us, and they completed these just about Christmas time. The Nosu were anxious to receive little household items from us, and although, technically, we were not to give people any of our things, we managed to do it with them. Underneath their long-flowing robes they found it easy to take all kinds of things out of the compound.

From our contact with the Nosu leaders, He Zitin and Lo Ziqin, we knew that the new regime had not impressed them. He's brother once told me that the liberation army was like the mountain tiger that ate Chinese but not Nosu flesh. This saying expressed the fact that the new government's policy toward the Nosu was much more lenient than toward the Chinese. The Nosu, however, could not carry guns on the streets, and in some areas they had been required to turn in all their weapons.

When Nosu leaders visited our homes, they assured us that we did not need to leave China. "Come and live with us," they stated, "and we will protect you." Mere politeness or a sincere invitation? We could not tell. We were never tempted to take them up on this offer.

The authorities took some encouraging steps to treat the Nosu and other minority groups in a respectful fashion. Much of the taxes received from them was being used to promote Nosu schools in the principal cities of the Jianchang Valley—Mianning, Lugu, Lizhou, and Xichang. The government established a school in Xichang to train Nosu students for government service. The assistant magistrates in many areas were Nosu. A special investigating team came from Beijing to find out the true needs of the Nosu. On this team was a Communist Nosu. This team made it clear that Chinese policy deplored what they called Chinese nationalistic chauvinism. They wished the Nosu to have equal rights with the dominant Chinese, to cease their inter-clan warfare, to unite, and to establish a self-governing, autonomous area.

Many years earlier, when fleeing Communist leaders had retreated on their "long march" through this area on their way to Yanan in north China, they had taken a few Nosu young men with them. Over the next few years they assigned some of their linguists to analyze the Nosu language, reduce it to a Latin orthography, and prepare study materials. Now with liberation they put out their propaganda in the new script and began to teach it to the Nosu. We could have wished to have had the power to do this kind of thing when we were faced with trying to use this hopeless, priestly pictograph system for Bible translation.

The war in Korea was escalating, and our position as expatriates in China was becoming more untenable each day. On December 28, 1950 the Executive Yuan announced that 1) all property of the American government and American business enterprises (including mission organizations) should immediately be controlled by the local government and be investigated clearly; 2) American public and private bank deposits within the PRC should immediately be frozen. The following day the Executive Yuan promulgated detailed regulations which spelled out the fine print of registering all cultural, educational, and charitable organizations receiving foreign aid or dependent upon foreign funds.

The government immediately implemented these provisions. On January 16, 1951 each of our mission stations was thoroughly searched by the Public Security Bureau. In Lugu the soldiers started first with the Covell side of the compound. They did a thorough job, but, fortunately for me, they missed one of Dan's stray bullets that I had placed among some tools. They also overlooked two army air maps of the Ningsu area that Lee Lovegren had given to me.

Our hearts were literally in our mouths as they started combing the Carrs' side of the compound. Although Dan had turned in his gun and one box of bullets, he somehow had forgotten about one more box of some four hundred bullets. What would he do with this damning evidence now? Quickly he dumped them into the bottom of what we called a Nanking heater, a small ten gallon drum cemented into a large fifty gallon drum around which heat could circulate. He inverted a small wash basin and put this on top of the pile of bullets, so that if the soldiers poked a stick into the drum of water, they would hit a flat surface. Indeed they did poke around, but the hot water kept them from sticking their hands into the heater.

Unfortunately, a couple of cartridge pouches were found, and up to the time that Dan left Lugu, the authorities were convinced that he had another gun. When Dan had served as a Navy Chaplain in the Philippines, military authorities had issued weapons to him, since the Japanese did not respect chaplains and did not treat them as non-military personnel. After the war, Dan had asked a missionary friend to remove the weapons from a foot locker stored in Manila, and send it with the non-military articles to him. The friend removed the carbine, but overlooked the belt of cartridge pouches.

When the search was completed, they sealed up all cameras and photographic materials, and put a new seal on the radio. They made two lists of everything they had taken, with both sides signing one copy. They also asked us to sign a statement saying that they had treated us courteously throughout the search. We did not wait long to find a more permanent resting place for those bullets! One evening Lucy played the organ as loudly as she could, while Dan and I dug a deep hole in the courtyard and buried them.

Danger in Xichang

The same types of problems were being faced by our colleagues in Xichang—personal harassment and obstacles in the work of the church. Since they were in a larger city with officials of higher standing, they did not have some of the little nuisance "run-ins" with the authorities that we had.

Far more dangerous, though, was that one of their members and the leader of our China party, Lee Lovegren, was imprisoned on spying charges. This had happened on January 16, the same day when all of our mission stations had been given a thorough search. In the Lovegren home the investigators found what they deemed to be incriminating evidence against Lee. Immediately they sealed up his home, and marched Lee off to the Xichang jail. Only after several jails, much interrogation, and four years of imprisonment did they release him.

Why did the authorities suspect Lee more than others of the Xichang group? Possibly it was because the wife of Lovegren's cook had been offended by Ida, who accused her of taking a "squeeze" from the daily food money. From that time on, Ida did not give the cook any money and did her own shopping. The wife may have reported to the authorities that Lee was apprehensive and burning important documents.

Shortly before his release, the Conservative Baptist Foreign Mission Society paper claimed that he had been "arrested by the Communists on trumped-up spy charges."[1] We must put this statement in perspective. First, Lee Lovegren was not a spy. He was a dedicated missionary seeking to preach the Gospel in China. Second, the charges were not "trumped-up." The Communists had every reason to believe he was a spy. During World War II, he had been working in China with the U.S. Army in the Office of Strategic Services, an intelligence agency. In searching the Lovegren home, officials found his old Army uniform packed away in a foot locker. In Chinese thinking, once a military officer, always a military officer. The presence of this old uniform only confirmed their suspicions. They also found several detailed U.S. Army maps of the area. Equally as damaging were detailed types of meteorological data which Lovegren collected as a hobby: daily temperature and barometric pressure readings, cloud movements, humidity charts, etc. Lee submitted these regularly to the American Geographical Society.

Americans find it difficult to believe that missionaries could be spies. The Communists have no such problem. Past missionary history and their own worldview which sees religion as a possible center of danger to the state, made this very natural. All of this incriminating evidence, although subject to other interpretations, only confirmed their deepest suspicions.

Had Lee not been aware of the danger he faced? This is difficult to know. He was a very open, honest man, always willing to put the best possible light on a difficult situation. He may have thought that others could never view him in this negative way. He had not told any of us that he possessed these things or that he was engaged in these activities. Had he done so, we might have been able to warn him. But even this is uncertain. We found it difficult to analyze the dynamics of Chinese culture—to see why the Chinese acted as they did. We certainly had not advanced far enough to think through clearly what our actions communicated to them. And, coming from a country where there were such cordial church-state relations, we hardly were prepared to think and act correctly in this type of hostile environment. We had not done our homework sufficiently well to know the depth of non-Christian Chinese feeling toward the ways in which the Christian movement had literally forced its way into China along with opium at the time of the unequal treaties. We were babes in these political woods.

When word of Lee's arrest reached us in Lugu, we feared that we would all be under suspicion. We took immediate steps to destroy any maps that we had around and to burn mission records and other letters that had the potential of being incriminating.

During the years that he was in prison, Lee's captors subjected him to intense interrogation. This included indoctrination in Marxist philosophy and attempts to get him to "see his mistakes" and confess his espionage activities. Lee had a tightly disciplined mind, giving as well as he received. He did not admit to the charges for which he was accused, and he continued to insist that his only purpose for being in China was to preach the Christian faith. Many of us younger missionaries reflected on the fact that Lee undoubtedly did better under these difficult circumstances than any of us would have done. He had a way of resisting adverse opinion without antagonizing his opponents.

Government authorities allowed Mrs. Lovegren to remain in the same city with Lee while he was detained in Yaan and Chungking. Eventually it was necessary for her to leave China and to go to Hong Kong where she carried on a ministry among refugees from mainland China. Here also she could be near to her daughter, Mildred, a missionary with the Southern Baptist Foreign Mission Board.

Toward the end of his imprisonment, largely as a result of the Geneva Agreements of 1954, Lee was able to receive weekly food and clothing packages channelled through the Red Cross. He also wrote and received letters regularly from mid-1954. His captors did not mistreat him physically, and his health was relatively good at the time of his release.

Lee's arrest created difficulties for the Xichang church. In the view of the officials, all that Lee and Ida had taught was fatally poisoned with American imperialism. "You have freedom of religion," they insisted, "but you must not use it as a cloak to hide these kinds of sinister activities which oppose the new government."

Very quickly the chapel was closed down, and the baptized members of the church were encouraged to join with the Christians worshipping at the Border Service Department of the Church of Christ in China. This step which unified the Christians in Xichang was the only path for their survival.

When the compound was searched on January 16, authorities sealed all of the mission money. This meant that the Simpsons and Simons could no longer hire domestic help, and that they did not have any money for their personal use. The officials, however, were reasonable, and, when they could prove their need, they were able to get funds—their own funds that had been frozen. In Lugu our money was not frozen, and, for the time, we had enough to get by if we were careful.

Financial Woes in Huili

Things went well in Huili until the end of November. At that point mission members were harassed even as they tried to go back and forth between the old and new sections of the city. Officials ordered them not to leave the city of Huili, but overanxious underlings, always on the make, made issues of travelling back and forth from the missionaries' homes in the north "suburb" to the old city where the chapel was located.

Although the first one-month session of the Bible school had gone well, no students were bold enough to come for the second session. The authorities used misdirection, never directly forbidding anyone to come, but their attitude was clear. You could get into trouble as a "running dog of the imperialists." Shortly after this, all meetings in the chapel came to a halt, again not because there were any formal prohibitions, but because people did not wish to jeopardize their lives.

The search on January 16th began before the missionaries were out of bed. Many possessions, including all their money, typewriters, binoculars, photographic equipment, canned foodstuffs, bicycles, and rice were sealed up. Only about five American dollars was left for everyone together. To the authorities, accustomed to a much lower standard of living, this ought to have been enough. Ever so politely they said, "Whenever you need any money, just ask us." Except it did not work out that way. The next day George Cole got some milk powder released, but no money.

The financial situation was compounded by the fact that in early December George had loaned the Post Office a million dollars in local currency. Although this represented only thirty-five U.S. dollars, it would have gone a long way in relieving the immediate pinch. This money got mixed up in the procedures of the financial freeze, making it almost impossible to get back.

Much earlier George had also loaned some thread to the bank and could not get it back. Another portion of the thread had been stored in a private warehouse, and the warehouse watchman "borrowed it." George and Jim had taken both of these steps to protect their thread from being stolen from their own warehouse. They concluded that there was no way to win.

January 16 was the day when stark reality hit us. Our time in China was up. We had tried in good faith to stay, but to continue any longer would be foolhardy for us and dangerous for the believers. Our money was frozen, and even survival was now in question. Our decision to return home was confirmed when we learned that the CIM had just told the Broomhall party in Zhaojue to evacuate China as quickly as possible. Now that the message was clear that we should leave, it was increasingly difficult to do so.

Endnotes

1. Conservative Baptist Foreign Mission Society Monthly Newsletter, January, 1955, p. 1, columns 2-3.

12

A Painful Exit:
Death, Detention and Deportation

Elusive Exit Permits

The new government used every indirect stratagem possible to force our exit from China. But when we applied to leave, it delighted in making us cool our heels. We had no idea when we might leave—tomorrow or after three months! If we were uncertain and confused, the board and our families at home were in a state of near panic. Letters were not getting through, and, with no news for several months, even the most placid of our fathers and mothers were imagining every possible tragedy.

The board called several urgent, national days of prayer specifically to seek God's protection. Dr. Brushwyler, General Director of CBFMS, wrote in March 1951 to each of our families expressing the board's deep concern. He assured them, that, despite the freezing of America's funds in China, the board had received a special permit from the Federal Reserve Bank to send in to us through the China Inland Mission such funds as we needed. Family members wrote the board every few days, seeking any tidbit of information to assure them that we were safe. One mother suggested that the board should charter a helicopter to fly in from the Burma border and rescue us. Another mother retained a law firm to gain satisfaction that the board was acting responsibly in the crisis. Ray Buker replied in great detail to the lawyer's legally-framed letter, pointing out that 1) we had stayed of our own choice; 2) the board had made money available to us; 3) the board was in touch with the U.S. State Department through the National Association of Evangelicals; and 4) all concerned could do nothing now but trust God.

When word reached Chicago in February 1951 of Lee's imprisonment and in June 1951 of the death of one of our group, fear turned to despair. This period, undoubtedly, was the worst crisis the board had yet faced and forced its leaders and us to a new level of trust in God.

Soon after the big January 16th search, John Simpson sent to us in Lugu exit application forms, and we began the complex procedures that required us to get photographs and guarantors from the community.

The ball was now in the government's court, and we kept ourselves busy with almost anything while we waited for the next move. Although difficult, we had some limited contact with Mrs. Zhou, possibly the only fruit from our Lugu labors. She continued to face great sorrow from her opium-smoking daughter with whom she lived. They argued constantly, particularly over her daughter's plan to sell her three children to an uncle. Although this was far better than selling one of them as a slave to the Nosu, as her husband had done with two of the children previously, it caused her mother much grief. She finally decided to move in with another daughter, who lived outside of Lugu, and to go into business selling corn cakes. A pitifully small amount of capital would have given this business a big boost, but for us to give any type of financial aid at this time would be both misunderstood and dangerous. We rejoiced that her faith weathered all types of adverse circumstances, even as we regretted that we had no more time to nurture her growth in Christ.

With all of our work stopped, we terminated our rental contract at the chapel and turned it back to the owner. Since this left Pastor Yang and his family without a home, we arranged for them to return to Xichang. Our concern and his was how he might be productive, a Marxist euphemism for working with your hands. The new authorities were convinced that it was unjust for pastors and religious workers to be supported by the free-will offerings of productive church members. They must get out and work for themselves, to be tentmakers like Paul. We did not object to this; we believed, in fact, that this was the path for the church to survive with foreign funds cut off, to become a truly independent Chinese church, free from the epithet of "foreign."

We tried to teach Pastor Yang how to make soap, but both times our method failed. Blind leaders of the blind! He made some inquiries about purchasing a stocking machine from Chengdu. We understood that the Border Service Mission had installed weaving machines, and we hoped that he might be able to learn this skill when he reached Xichang. With heavy hearts we bade this dear brother and his family farewell in mid-January, knowing full well that we should not ever see him again. We had had a wonderful partnership in the Gospel over a two-year period and could only wish we had more to show for it.

We did nothing specific with the property on the hill where we were living. Since we could not find the landowner, it was impossible to receive back the rental deposit; any sum would have helped us in our money shortage. On the other hand, there was no way for us to pay the monthly rent.

My daily schedule was monotonous. Up early to start the fire in our wood-burning kitchen stove, a period of worship, breakfast, an hour trying to learn to play the Carrs' small Estey pump organ, study on the Nosu language for two hours, lunch, to the street to buy things to eat, another hour at the organ, reading until about four, an hour on the organ, to the postoffice for mail, and then supper. Two evenings a week we had prayer times with the Carrs, and the other evenings we spent reading or playing games. Ruth occupied her time cooking, sewing, ironing, or reading. The stress was considerable. We did not know what was going to happen from day to day. A predictable schedule, even if it really accomplished nothing, and a sense of God's upholding grace enabled us to rejoice in our trials.

Without the help of servants, we had to do everything on our own. As a city boy, I had not learned much about farm chores, like killing chickens. I had seen our domestic help whirl chickens several times about their heads and then throw them violently to the ground. All that was left to do was to bleed the chicken. It looked simple, and I gave it a try. I followed their example to the "t," but the chicken bounced off the ground, let out a squawk, ruffled its feathers, shook itself, and walked away!

We had many interruptions. Some were not welcome. During these days of waiting, robbers made us their target several times. Our home was built of mud, and it was tempting for people to try to burrow through the back walls directly into one of our rooms. Fortunately, on each occasion, they ran into a bookshelf or closet, and this stymied them. We lost nothing and needed only to fill in the holes with a fresh supply of mud.

The Nosu continued to visit us, particularly at their New Year time, which, this year, was in early January. Their celebration lasted for three days and consisted largely of racing horses and drinking wine, along with a few traditional religious observances. My teacher visited me during one of these days and brought a pig's head as present in honor of the New Year. We appreciated this token of respect and gratitude, particularly at this time when we sensed that our friends were becoming fewer and fewer.

We had little idea of what was happening in the world. Now that we could no longer use the radio to listen to the Voice of America, we lived in a little world to ourselves. If our colleagues in Xichang sent up anything to us by ricksha, Bill Simons included a cryptic note that "uncle was having a hard time" or "uncle is taking a trip north." These were just long enough to be exciting, but brief enough to be tantalizing. We had to guess most of the time. Even these notes were censored, and officials accused Bill of "political activity" before they gave him his exit permit.

On February 12, an officer of the Public Security Bureau came to Lugu to handle some of our business. He called me down to his office at 7 a.m. and curtly informed me that we must make an inventory of all of our property for registration. All that day, with the help of Xie Cenyuan and Lo Xianlin, the chapel owner, we made an inventory of all personal and mission property. All forms must be filled in with a *maobi*, a Chinese writing brush, which we could not handle that well. We finally turned in the finished list to the officer that evening at 7 p.m., having not even stopped to eat lunch or supper. He reprimanded me for not completing the task on time and admonished me to be more careful the next time. Finally, he gave me a receipt for all the property they were taking, with a brief written statement that, at the appropriate time, I could reclaim it.

The next morning I was called down to see the same officer again. He informed me in a grave tone that I was to be expelled from China because of the picture of opium I had taken three years previous: "Although you did this under the bandit Nationalist regime, you took a picture of a contraband article and thus dishonored the law of China." Seeking further clarification, he asked me to relate the story of this incident. I did so, denying, however, that I had taken any picture, since the day was cloudy, and I did not wish to waste my color film. He did not accept my version, but, in the course of our talking, asked me to turn over carbons of the letters Ray Buker and Milt Baker had written to me. When I said that I had destroyed these, he was furious and sealed up the few remaining letters that I had.

He concluded our conversation by stating: "You must be ready to leave Lugu on the 16th with Lovegren." This caused a momentary scare as I had visions of occupying a jail cell. He assured me, almost as if it were good news, that I was only being expelled; there would be no jail. The next few days were filled with furious packing. Then, with all ready and a down payment of $100,000 Chinese currency paid on the horses which we had engaged to carry our luggage, he said there was yet another step in my exit procedure. "You must write a repentance paper and put it in the newspaper for seven days. Only if no one accuses you of anything more will you be allowed to leave." This was not the time to quibble over whether I had or had not actually taken that picture. In their eyes I was already guilty, with no hope of being proved innocent. So I wrote it and sent it with the local mason to Xichang to be published in the newspaper there.

At this juncture, it seemed best for the Carrs to go to Xichang and join the Simons and Simpsons. In fact, this is what the authorities desired—it gave them only two groups of foreigners (those in Xichang and Huili) to supervise rather than three. Lovegren had already been taken on his way north to Yaan, the capital city of Xikang Province, and Ruth and I would be travelling alone. We had applied later than any of the others for an exit permit, and now, much to the envy of our colleagues, we were leaving first. Of course, we did not have an exit permit; I was being expelled.

We hired a small pack train of five horses to carry our luggage. We could have taken more things with us, but it would have cost more, and we were not sure where our next money would come from. I left most of my library and many other valuables. The Nosu had brought our suits of Nosu clothes in the last day or two, and we filled up our last bit of available space with these bulky items. We did not travel alone. In addition to the horsemen, there were three soldiers, bayonets fixed on their fine American-made rifles, who were escorting us. We had a sense of being criminals as we went on our way. As best they could, many of our friends in Lugu found ways to bid us a tearful farewell. We were grateful for their concern, care, and friendship. We regretted only that we had done so poorly in communicating the Gospel message to them.

Eleven Days of Walking

Only so many options were open for us to leave the Jianchang Valley area on our way to the outside world. Planes were not flying regularly, the roads were hopeless, and the present rail system was only a distant vision. Ray Buker wrote suggesting that we might go south through Yunnan to Burma. "Johnny (Simpson) will know where the old ABFMS stations are. You would be welcome there." China was too tightly controlled, even in the border areas, for such a plan to be feasible. The only direction open to us was north toward Yaan and Chengdu.

We could have ridden horses, but this was expensive and boring. Ruth might have used a *huagan*, a type of sedan chair carried by one man in front and another in the back. Most foreign women liked this method for long trips. But not Ruth! She insisted on walking, even when her feet were covered with sores and blisters. And so we walked over hill and dale, averaging about twenty to twenty-five miles a day and staying in horse inns in the evenings.

This was the way to see China. The scenery was breathtakingly beautiful—green valleys, cultivated fields stretching to near the top of most of the high mountains, and, on several mornings, a veritable

A Painful Exit: Death, Detention and Deportation

winter wonderland. Our second night out from Lugu we stayed at the small village of Denxiangyuin. The weather was bitterly cold, and Ruth and I were unable to get warm in our two separate sleeping bags placed on straw mats. Finally, in desperation, we tried to cuddle up in one bag. This was before two sleeping bags could be zippered together. We stood this for about half an hour, and Ruth told me to leave!

We were a bit drowsy the next day as we continued climbing up what the Chinese called a "small mountain." Higher and higher we went up this precipitous peak—a beautiful river winding its way in the valley far below, long icicles dangling from the tree branches, snow along the path, and hoarfrost about two inches deep pressing down the bushes along the narrow path. The climbing was hard, and it did not help that the day's schedule never called for us to eat before 10 a.m.

Going down the other side was even worse. Ice-covered stones, a steep path, patches of mud, and leather shoes on our feet made for a lot of slipping and falling. Once we got lost and ended up at the rear of a Nosu village on the side of the mountain. The villagers were far more friendly than many Chinese whom we had met along the way and directed us back to the main path.

Our first two sets of escorts, from Lugu to Yuexi and from Yuexi to Fulin, were very friendly, and we had good conversations as they "guarded" me. Like most Chinese, they wished to learn more about America, and were very anxious that we teach them a few phrases of English. They hardly paid any attention to what we were doing, seemingly more concerned to go ahead and guard our luggage, although it had been sealed up and was immune to any petty thievery.

We had no problem getting enough to eat. We seldom had more than a bowl or two of rice during the day, and we usually found some bean curd soup to go with it. We made up for this in the evening when we joined with the horsemen in eating a big meal. The Chinese have an expression which says that "foreigners eat many vegetables but little rice; Chinese eat much rice but few vegetables." In these eleven days along the road and for three months in Yaan on a completely local diet, Ruth and I became more like the

Chinese. Even though the vegetables were sparse, we had no problems subsisting on rice.

We stayed largely in no-name sites—Denxiangyuin, Baoan, Hanyuan, Qinjin, Huang Liupu, Yuin Jin—but two major cities were Yuexi and Fulin. We got used to the long walking, to our sore feet and aching legs, even to our escorts, some of whom paid more attention to us while our luggage became lost temporarily. The steep mountain trails—and they got worse the farther we walked—we took in stride and tried to view them as a challenge.

Some things irritated constantly. One was that officials never tired of searching our belongings. As we went over passes, entered villages, left them—everyone from the Public Security Bureau to the Peasants' Association wanted to be in on the action. Once when some members of the latter group stopped us to see our identification and road permits, I asked them if they could even read the documents they were looking at. Sheepishly, they replied, "we do not recognize the characters." People who had been "nobodies" in the previous society had now been given top posts in the new government. They felt good about this, and it added to their self image, but they often took on jobs beyond their ability to perform.

Everywhere we were pestered by unruly crowds, often made up largely of children, who followed us when we entered city streets, shouting out loud anti-American slogans. If they could get close enough to where we were sleeping at night, they threw pebbles and even larger stones through windows from which the oil paper had been torn. At Hanyuan we had one particularly bad experience. Our luggage had become separated from us, and while I went to run it down, Ruth remained behind at the inn where we were staying. As the children, men, women, and even soldiers gawked at her—maybe the first foreign woman, at least with this kind of light blond hair and blue eyes, that any of them had seen—a man stepped forward and asked her to come out farther into the street where they could see her better. When she politely refused, he grabbed her wrist, apparently egged on by some of the local soldiers, and tried to drag her out. She shook loose and went back into the room, slamming the door.

When I learned about this upon my return, I forgot my resolve to be patient and berated our two escorts, whose task, allegedly, was to "protect" us. I think I made my point. They immediately took action to disperse the crowd, and from that time they were more considerate, not only about our peace of mind, but about our safety.

One day out from Yaan, our destination city, we stayed overnight at Yuinjin. The children here were well versed in all of the latest propaganda slogans and songs. We had become used to the "Resist America, Defend Korea" slogan, but we now heard some choice epithets directed against President Truman for his various actions in Korea. For once, however, we had a nice inn on the second floor, about as private as anywhere we had slept since leaving our home in Lugu. The innkeeper's wife was kind and graciously agreed to go out on the street and buy us some moon cakes to supplement our evening meal.

None too soon, the last day of our long walk came to an end, and we were within reach of our long-anticipated destination. Only on this portion of the trip did we have long, flat roads on which we could have ridden our bikes easily. Outside of Yaan we and all other travellers were stopped at a health inspection station to have throat specimens taken. Only now did we realize that we had been passing through a meningitis epidemic zone for the past several days. We filed this away in our minds, almost without thinking, not realizing what portent it would have for us in a few weeks.

Life in a Yaan Tea Shop

When we arrived in Yaan, a pleasant city surrounded by mountains, we were taken to the Public Security Department, where we had our first meeting with Li Dezhang, the officer in charge of public security for the entire province. He had me rehearse once more the picture-taking incident. He accused me of having a man carrying opium pose for my photography on the streets of Mianning. I hotly denied this, but his demeanor never revealed whether or not he believed me. He was much better than most of the officials whom we had met, polite, reasonable, and firm. He would take no nonsense. As I was talking with him, I absent-mindedly crossed my legs. He shouted something at me, and as I leaned forward to hear him more clearly, I naturally uncrossed my legs. He seemed satisfied, and I sat back and crossed my legs again. He repeated his command, even more forcefully; only then did I realize he was telling me to uncross my legs. He viewed sitting with crossed legs as too informal a posture to assume before an official. I did not repeat this mistake.

After repeated conversations with Comrade Li, I felt that I knew him better. One day he told me why he had become a Communist. In the early days after the war of resistance with Japan, he had a responsible position with UNNRA. When he saw all the corruption connected with foreign aid, he realized that a more adequate philosophy was necessary to save China. Gradually, he was convinced that only Communism had the answer to China's ills. Among the many officers and party members whom we met, Li best represented a man of integrity and ideals.

Yaan authorities placed us in the second story of an inn across from the bus station. We were allotted two rooms, one that we could use for sleeping and the other as a small living room. The major inconvenience was that we had to go out into an often-busy hallway to pass from one room to the other. The toilets were unisex, and Ruth had to choose carefully the time of her trips there. In common with most public lavatories in China, they were smelly, dirty, and located over the top of a very messy pig pen.

Food was no problem. A little "greasy spoon" restaurant was located near the tea shop, and we daily ate two adequate Chinese meals, fitting well into the two-meal-a-day custom of that part of China. Gradually we found ways to supplement our diets. We bought luscious, baked sweet potatoes outside of the tea shop; we found a bread shop not too far away; and we got Chinese-type cakes and cookies whenever we wanted them. During cherry season Ruth used one burner on the kitchen stove in the tea shop just as the shop was closing, and made jam to go with the other goodies we were buying. She had a wonderful "let's make do" attitude which helped us keep our stomachs happy! Later, when Dr. and Mrs. Crook, ABFMS missionaries, left their Yaan home, they willed us some staples, and a few cooking utensils. Ruth found a neighbor in the inn who let us have a small charcoal burner, and with these she began to turn out some super meals to substitute now and again for our Chinese evening fare.

We arrived on March 10 and were assured that we could leave by March 22. Once again it was the problem of the elusive exit permit. Authorities rethought my "crime" and concluded that we must have these permits. This required us to repeat the weary procedure of application forms with photographs. Even then, we would not have believed our stay could drag on for three months.

How do you keep sane for three months when you have been told that you are under house arrest and that you can go only a short distance from the inn? By keeping busy! We held religiously to a tight schedule. We were lazy in the early morning, often not arising until about 8:00 a.m., even though by this time the tea shop was bustling with early-morning activity and noise. By the time we had cleaned up and had a time of prayer, it was time for breakfast, about ten o'clock on the local schedule.

Following breakfast, I usually strolled across the street to the outside wall of the bus station where I read one of the newspapers pasted up there. The best time to do this was when no soldiers were around; otherwise they engaged me in a political conversation. Most of what I read was political, at times almost exclusively news about Korea. Reading the one-sided accounts day by day caused me, over a period of time, almost to adopt the Chinese viewpoint. I saw clearly how Chinese people could not be blamed for the way they felt about Korea, Americans, or any other item of international significance.

By noon we were ready to settle down for some reading. Many of our best books we had already posted to Hong Kong from Lugu. I had two volumes of Latourette's seven-volume *History of the Expansion of Christianity*, and these I consumed quickly. Even before leaving Lugu, I had kept for the trip the two-volume commentary on Revelation by R.H. Charles and the two-volume work by G.A. Cooke on Ezekiel. Times were tough, we were in a mess, and I wanted to understand prophecy better. Both of these books were from the International Critical Commentary set and much more critical than devotional in nature. Each day for six weeks, I immersed myself for several hours daily in Revelation, and when this study was concluded, I went on to Ezekiel.

Giving concentrated attention to this apocalyptic literature in the Old and New Testaments changed my understanding of what prophecy was all about. This was hardly my first study of this subject. As a sixteen-year old, I read prophetic books by the pound; noted Bible scholars and radio expositors assured me and my friends where Mussolini and Hitler fit in the prophetic scheme; and all loose prophetic nuts and bolts were put in proper order. When events did not pan out as they predicted, and these men never had the courage to say they were wrong, it eroded my confidence in the Bible and in the integrity of so-called prophetic spokesmen. Evangelicals, I concluded, were not very serious about Bible interpretation, only their own views.

I settled nothing in these weeks of study. But in the midst of the small, troubled world in which Ruth and I were living, when we frequently despaired of ever leaving China or even of life itself, I gained a new glimpse of the risen Lord of Lords and King of Kings who had revealed Himself to John on Patmos. He was Lord in Yaan, in China, and in the world. He was in control, and His kingdom would continue to spread, no matter what happened to us. Such a vision was assuring and exhilarating. Life was worth living. We need not be afraid. Now I saw the purpose of prophetic literature—not to tickle the speculative fancy of well-off Western Christians who wanted to avoid all conflict and danger in the Kingdom of God, but rather to give hope, courage, faith, and love to Christians going through the fires of persecution and calamity.

Despite the freeze on American funds in China, we had no serious money problems. We carried enough money when we left Lugu to pay for expenses to Yaan. Once in Yaan, we used American dollar bills that we had stashed away to exchange at $20,612 local currency for $1 US at the People's Bank. Living expenses in Yaan were not high—we got by comfortably for the equivalent of $1 U.S. a day. Once we got to Chengdu, Sam Jeffrey of the CIM had enough of our money on hand to pay for all costs in getting from there to Hong Kong. We were grateful that along with the stresses of house arrest and relative confinement, we did not need to worry about where tomorrow's money was coming from.

We spent our evenings in a number of ways. We surely set a Guinness world record for playing Parcheesi on consecutive evenings. We used a make-shift board that we put together after arriving in

Yaan and local dice that we bought in a nearby store. A big bother in our room was that rats came in through the many holes and nibbled happily on our soiled clothing. We became experts in running them down. We closed up every hole but one, armed ourselves with sturdy boards, and patiently waited. Once the varmint was in the room, we quickly covered up the remaining hole and started the chase. Over several weeks, we eliminated dozens of rats. Ruth never enjoyed this game as much as I did.

After several weeks, we were moved to one larger room that gave us a view over the street. We saw clearly when other foreigners departed from the bus station. We were not allowed to talk extensively with them, but occasionally we bade them farewell. The Broomhall family, Ernest and Edna Madge, and Ruth Dix, all from the Xichang area, came through in late March. We learned while watching them what not to do when being inspected. The Broomhalls' stuff had already been cleared for loading on the bus, when Jim remarked jokingly to the inspection officer that the mosquito repellent canister he was examining was not an "atomic bomb." The man blew up almost like a powder keg, and Jim tried to no avail to make amends. The Madges and Ruth Dix were allowed to go on their way, but the Broomhall luggage was taken off the bus, and they had to remain in Yaan. Two days and a detailed "repentance paper" later, they were permitted to go on their way. Their oldest daughter, Pauline, confided to her Dad on the morning of their departure, "Daddy, if you have any jokes to crack this morning, please crack them on us!"

To bid farewell to so many at the bus station, while we continued to go nowhere, was disappointing. Life became a day-by-day proposition. Ruth became ill with a respiratory infection once, and, with the help of Comrade Li, we were allowed to have the services of Dr. Crook, who long had carried on a medical practice in Yaan. He was even permitted to loan us a few books. Comrade Li watched carefully that we had no opportunity to exchange any small talk with Dr. Crook.

Ruth spent some of her time learning to type better on the old typewriter we had with us. When it looked as if I might run out of reading material and the supply of rats was running low, I began to use her as a teacher to learn German. She had grown up bi-lingual, but now her German was mixed up badly with Chinese. Lacking any good bathing facilities, we waited until ten or eleven o'clock at night and walked fifteen minutes to the large river where we skinny dipped. We celebrated Ruth's birthday on May 5th with two cans of tomatoes that I was able to buy on the street. We postponed an elaborate celebration of our first wedding anniversary, until that uncertain future when we would be out of the country, although we did get a local bakery to do a sponge cake with some tasteless frosting. It made our day to get a telegram from our colleagues in Xichang, wishing us well on this important day in our lives.

From our second-story street window, we had a good view of May 1 celebrations, when about twenty thousand people celebrated international labor day. We tried to keep away from conversations that might take a political turn. Once, however, when I wandered into the tea shop, a frequent site for propaganda teams to put on a performance, I was confronted with a group getting signatures on the Stockholm Peace Appeal. Not to sign would be to affirm you were for war, so I did not hesitate in affixing my signature. In fact, I was caught once again with people shoving it in front of me; only this time I signed it for Ruth!

We did not know it at the time, but Lee Lovegren's place of detainment was not too far from us, across the river and more toward the center of the town. He was being held in a small room on the second story of what had been one of the principal banks of Yaan. The surroundings were austere, with only a cot and mosquito net, but he was not mistreated. Ida could not see him or send in mail, food or clothing, but she could relay verbal messages to him through an intermediary.

Finally, on June 6, Comrade Li came with good news and bad news: Ruth's exit permit had been granted, but mine was denied; I would be deported from China under armed escort. At this point, we did not care how we got out—we just wanted to get going! George and Pearl Kraft and their daughter Lois, CIM missionaries to the Tibetans and stationed farther west in Kangding, had reached Yaan just a day earlier. Our two families were allowed to charter a bus to Chengdu and Chungking, and we were on our way.

The Final Lap

Several months earlier, before we had any idea how we might leave China, Dan had written to some friends that we would walk to Leshan, a city farther east than Yaan, and then go by raft or boat down the Yangtze River to Shanghai! That would have been quite a trip and very dangerous. Now that we were on our way in this relatively comfortable bus and with good friends, we could only marvel at God's grace.

Our first stop was Chengdu. Ruth and I were put in a hotel under armed guard, but she had freedom to go where she wished. I was the guilty one whose freedom was limited. Two guards trailed me absolutely everywhere. She took most of her meals at the CIM home, and Signe Jeffrey, whom we had known well during our language-study days in Chengdu, sent over salads and cookies to supplement my meals. We were grateful for the many at the home who were praying for us as we continued our journey. Ruth cared for all items of business, including the regular inspections we encountered.

The Krafts were joined in Chengdu by their two older sons, whom they had not seen in three years, and we continued to share a chartered bus as we headed on to Chungking. This two-day trip had an overnight stay at a mid-way point that was not too pleasant. Beds in these inns were lousy with bedbugs, and so we slept on the top of tables. This was not too comfortable, but it was a choice between two evils.

Once we arrived in Chungking, it was the same story all over again. I was holed up under guard in a hotel, and Ruth ran busily about the city visiting friends, caring for our business, and getting some dental work done. Although prepared for a two-week wait, we got away on June 20, after a delay of only seven days. Our guards, who had now been with us steadily for two weeks, were very friendly. They were country bumpkins and did not know urban China very well, and, rather than helping, they hindered us. We needed to get our luggage from the hotel down to the boat dock, and they just casually told the hotel service boys to help in this. Immediately, we were in trouble with the local transport union workers who insisted that in "new China" it was only they who could do this job.

We had second-class cabin accommodations on the *Guimen*, the nicest boat sailing on the Yangtze. We shared our bunkbed cabin with two Chinese men, and the two escorts, still fully armed, slept right outside our door on the deck. Such a bed was not that comfortable, and the next two nights they used extra space in the dining room. Fifteen CIM missionaries, including the Kraft family, were sailing with us. This made for some great times of fellowship and prayer. The scenery from Wanxian to Yichang was breathtaking, particularly the famous Yangtze gorges. Our minds, however, were on other things, and we could only wish the trip to be over soon.

When we arrived in Hankow, our disembarkation point, we were put first in a sleazy hotel. I tore the bed apart and scalded the joints with boiling water, effectively ridding it of about forty bedbugs. Imagine our despair then to be moved to a better hotel where the beds had not been debugged. We might as well have relaxed, for we would not need to spend the night in Hankow. Our friendly escorts learned another lesson about China travel when we boarded our train that evening, June 23, for the thirty-six hour ride to Guangzhou (Canton). They had sat with us on the same bus and stayed near us on the boat, even when the tickets they purchased for us were different from their own. But that would not work on the train. They got first-class, or soft-seat, tickets for us and third-class, or hard-seat, tickets for themselves. What a surprise for them on getting to the gate to see us go in one direction, while the ticket puncher shunted them off in another direction! They quickly returned to buy first-class tickets for themselves, barely getting back before the train left without them.

Our CIM colleagues were in the same coach with us, and we continued the good fellowship begun on the boat. We arrived in Guangzhou early on the morning of June 25th. We learned in a hurry that our short stay here was going to be a bad experience. The local officials at the Public Security Bureau were appalled that our guards were so friendly with us, these evil American imperialists! Peremptorily, they dismissed them and replaced them with two who were mean. They put us both in a hotel room and told us not to "run recklessly about." Meals were brought to us in the room. We even needed permission and a chaperon to go to the toilet!

A Painful Exit: Death, Detention and Deportation

We stayed holed up in this room all day. In the evening it looked hopeful, for our escorts brought in two agents of the China Travel Service who got the money and needed keys to process our luggage from Guangzhou across the border to Hong Kong. Still no sure word, however, as to whether or not we would be leaving the next day. It was a short night, as we fought mosquitoes, bed bugs, and the humid heat. At 5:30 we were awakened and told to come immediately to board the train for the border.

We had a new set of escorts, one from the foreign affairs department and the other a soldier. They helped us get aboard and sat across the aisle from us for the entire trip. When two Chinese sat in the seat across from us, the escorts ordered them not to talk with us. This five-hour train trip through green rice fields with mountains in the distance was pleasant, for it did seem we might make it! We did not find much to eat but munched on some cookies and washed them down with orange pop, a drink that we had even forgotten about.

What an unimaginable relief to get to the small village bordering on the New Territories of greater Hong Kong. After another inspection of ourselves and our luggage, a currency exchange, and a glad farewell to our escorts, we crossed over a narrow bridge leading into British Hong Kong. No sight has ever been so beautiful as the Union Jack fluttering gently in the breeze! Along with the many other passengers, foreign and Chinese, we were met by a British official who ran us briefly through entry procedures and let us go on our way. We gulped down two chicken sandwiches and two cokes and boarded the train to take us on the forty-five-minute ride into Kowloon City, across the harbor from Victoria Island.

What a relaxing train trip—no soldiers to harass us, no need to look around nervously to see if someone were eavesdropping on our conversation, no dread of what would happen next. As Ruth mentioned in a letter to her mother, "Give me the imperialists any day!"

We met a friendly British policeman upon our arrival at the downtown train station. He hurried us on to a taxi and took us to the CIM home on Nathan road, where we stayed until we found hotel accommodations. Only when we arrived here did we receive some shocking news that totally dampened the exhilaration that we had felt in standing again on free ground. The missionaries at the home somberly informed us that Hannah Cole had died in Fulin on her way out of China.

Tragedy in Fulin

The money squeeze in Huili had continued to tighten, and from January 16 to March 29, the group of missionaries had no money. How did they live? Garrison stated it simply, "The ravens fed us." The local Christians knew what the missionaries were going through and managed to get them wood for heat and cooking and see to it that they had meat, vegetables, and oil.

For Pastor Wang, Pastor Lo, and all of the Christians, this was a calculated risk. In most of China, including Xichang, pastors and Christians felt the need to sever completely their relationships with the missionaries. Wang and Lo had already told the missionaries that they should leave, but they specifically refused to break with them and helped as much as possible until they left Huili.

As they tried to get action on their frozen money as well as to get more, Jim and George had serious run-ins with the local police. At one point the police chief was about to put them in jail, but the conflict never quite reached that extreme. The frustrating thing was that neither would the local officials furnish them with exit permits. That was the dilemma in a nut shell: no money to stay and no permits to go!

This dilemma provoked George and Jim to take a new tack. They wrote several letters to high provincial and national leaders, including one each to Premier Chou En-lai and Chairman Mao Tse-tung asking why it was impossible either to get money or permits. Since these were double-registered to assure delivery, all of the workers in the Huili postoffice knew from the return receipts from these various people that the letters had been received. That lit a few fires, and within a short time the frozen money was returned to them, and they were able to have funds wired from both Kunming and Chengdu.

Local authorities had impounded all incoming mail; nothing was delivered to the missionaries for a two-month period, and they were refused permission to send or receive telegrams. When the dike burst on the money, this was the signal to release the mail. Within a period of about ten days, they received over 350 letters. They suspected that the post office kept many more.

Toward the end of May, George returned from a routine visit to the police station, excitedly shouting that he had been given exit forms for everyone. That set in motion a string of hectic activities that wore everyone to a frazzle. First, they filled out all the exit forms in Chinese, a hard task with so many children involved. Second, they had to post printed notices of their departure all over town. Indeed, a few people did come to them and say the missionaries had forgotten to pay them this or that. Even though they doubted they had this many debtors, this was no time to quibble and risk long delays. Third, they had to make several lists of all their possessions. Local officials were not about to be accused of taking things wrongfully from them.

After they had listed various things, one sharp-eyed official noticed that they had not mentioned a radio. In the ensuing discussion, George admitted he had given it to Pastor Lo. This upset the officials, and George had to write a confession and hand the radio over to the police. Later, after they had arrived in Yaan, they learned that the radio had been returned to Pastor Lo.

Travel for such a large group in this part of China was not easy. For six adults and six children, they needed thirty-seven carriers and ten horses, eight to carry luggage and two for Jim and George to ride. Most of the carriers were assigned to the sedan chairs, three for adults and two for the children. On most days they did not cover more than twelve to fifteen miles. With this many people, they crowded out local inns in the villages where they stayed at night.

If Ruth and I had a problem with children pressing in on us to see the strange "foreign devils," how much worse was it for a party with six little devils! Often they could not get away from the inn to go out on the street to eat or do anything until eight or nine o'clock in the evening when the crowds had dispersed. After that the mothers washed diapers, cleaned nursing bottles, and prepared formula for the next day's travel.

They seldom turned in much before midnight, and then, on several occasions, local officials on-the-make woke them up at 1 or 2 a.m. to examine their road permits. Day in and day out, such experiences were tiring and exasperating. The first five days were relatively easy, as were the several days in Xichang where they caught up on sleep and energy.

The evening before the Huili missionaries left Xichang, they gathered with the Xichang group to have a worship service. No one knew what the future held or when they would see each other again. Their ultimate hope was symbolized by the hymn "Beulah Land," which Hannah asked everyone to sing as the evening came to a close.

Beyond Lugu, the going became almost unbearable. "Indescribably beautiful scenery over equally indescribably tortuous trails" was the way Jim Garrison stated it. Two days beyond Lugu, the party had a particularly bad day and night, pressed even more than usual by large crowds. Here began the meningitis area that had taken a large toll of Chinese lives.

The missionaries arrived in Fulin on the eighth day out of Xichang. Early in the morning there had been another investigation of their belongings, and just before they reached Fulin, officials conducted two very thorough inspections. They must have thought we were very clever. How we could have managed to give away anything or to have added something to our possessions between these several examinations in one day was incomprehensible. But it was their time in the sun, and they wanted to make the most of it.

Fortunately, when they arrived in Fulin, they found fine quarters in the Catholic Mission, located in a quiet place away from the noise and clamor of the street. Since everyone was desperately tired, they decided to delay a day here and rest. Hannah did not feel well, but at that stage of the trip no one was doing that well. The next morning she had what she thought was one of her oft-recurring migraine headaches. Shortly after breakfast, she went to bed and soon had chills and a high fever.

The Catholic priest and Esther Nelson, a nurse, thought she had malaria and gave her some quinine at first, and then some Atabrine later. These appeared to help, and she slept soundly. The next morning, George was not able to awaken her, and she remained in this comatose condition throughout the day. By now everyone feared Hannah had something worse than malaria, and the priest and Esther began a series of penicillin shots. Nothing had any effect, and at about 4 a.m., June 19th, she quietly slipped into the presence of her Lord.

Everyone was stunned, but there was no time for grief. The police were summoned, took pictures, had George and Jim fill out endless forms, and then gave permission for the burial. Jim purchased a crude, unfinished coffin from a farmer, and the priest made available a burial plot alongside the Catholic cemetery. He was not permitted to allow non-Catholics to be interred in the cemetery itself. The carriers dug the grave and carried the coffin. Jim led in a brief burial service, reading some Scripture and praying. The priest also offered a prayer. By this time it was 7 p.m. of the day on which Hannah had died. George left money with the priest to have a stone prepared as a marker over the grave.

Even in the midst of their grief, all were concerned as to who next would get sick. Judy Garrison had a bout with sickness shortly after this, but it turned out to be nothing more than a bad skin irritation. Another immediate concern was to care for Ruthie who had been nursing at the time of her mother's death. Esther took over this responsibility and got the baby switched to a suitable milk formula.

They arrived in Yaan on June 24, after five more days of walking from Fulin. They were held up there by the usual delays—forwarding their passports from Huili, permits to carry U.S. currency out of the country, and endless searches of baggage. On July 3 they departed for Chengdu by a chartered bus, and when they arrived unannounced, even at the awful hour of 11 p.m., they found a royal welcome awaiting them at the CIM home.

Mr. Jeffrey got them all on a plane for Chungking on the 5th, saving the rough two-day trip by bus. The Coles and Esther flew on July 10 to Hankow, took the night train on to Guangzhou the same night, and exited July 13 to Hong Kong. The Garrisons and Flora Mae took a river steamer to Hankow and followed them by four days, arriving in Hong Kong on July 17.

Transit Through Hong Kong

Hong Kong then was nothing like Hong Kong now, but the difference from China was profound. We had nothing more than the clothes on our backs. Not only were they dirty and road-worn; they made us feel like tramps in Hong Kong's glittering society. The hotel rooms and beds were so nice, that we wondered if we could sleep in them. And we stuffed on food, as if we would never have another meal. We lived as in a dream world for days—everything was too good to be true. We were alive and wondered how it had happened!

Ruth and I had the sad task of meeting George, the children, and Esther at the border on July 13. To return to the border was scary—we didn't get too close. To see George and his four motherless children was almost more than we could bear. George took the two boys, Georgie and Gary, under his care, Esther watched over Bethie, and Ruth and I took baby Ruth. George wanted to get on to the States as fast as possible to be with his and Hannah's families. Hong Kong was beginning to feel like home after my three weeks there, and I helped him with many matters of business—procuring needed tickets, arranging for the transfer of money from the States, and caring for various procedural matters. Within a week they were on their way, flying to Tokyo and then on to Minneapolis.

During these days, I was in charge of CBFMS business matters in Hong Kong, but depended largely on people living in Hong Kong who would still be around after Ruth and I left. The biggest issue was to be sure we had enough money on hand for all needs. Ray Buker and I exchanged many letters, sent telegrams back and forth, and even talked by phone. Everyone at home was very supportive and wished to help in any way possible. Ray often raised to me the possibility of stopping by Formosa on our way home to assess possible opening for CBFMS work among the Chinese and the mountain peoples. After the trauma of China, we did not feel emotionally ready for any new ventures, even if exploratory in nature.

Never before or since have we had more discretionary money—the several months' worth of saved-up salaries awaited us. We needed clothes, luggage, a camera, and many other things to replace what we had lost. Everything was a bargain, and we spent freely. We never tired of filling up on the things we had missed in China, particularly all flavors of pop and ice cream. Hong Kong is a delightful place to sightsee, and we couldn't miss out on all the enticing souvenirs. We rejoiced that our freight, turned over to the China Travel Service in Guangzhou, came out in about a week's time with everything intact, even the Nosu clothes which we felt custom inspectors might take from us.

We soon realized that it was hopeless to wait for the Xichang group to leave China. The Garrisons agreed to wait for a while longer, and Ruth and I began our voyage to the U.S.A. on July 29 on a freighter, the *SS Edward Luckenbach*. On board were two other missionary families and a single male missionary from Pakistan. The return home was pleasant with several stops in Japan. We were disturbed that at one of the Japanese ports, a member of the American Central Intelligence Agency came aboard and urged us to give him some detailed information on the Ningsu area of China. This had happened once in Hong Kong, and would happen again after we returned home. Each time we politely declined to give any information. We were loyal American citizens, but we believed that the work of the church and government must be clearly separated. I have no reason to believe that other missionaries felt any differently.

As we arrived home and had a joyful reunion with our families, we were very conscious that the Carr, Simons, and Simpson families were still in Xichang. We told our story in bits and pieces, but we were very careful that nothing we said would endanger them. We were appalled at the way in which the strong China lobby in the States was perpetuating the myth of how America had lost China, but again we held our tongues. It had to be low-key constantly until our brothers and sisters in China were out of danger.

Safe At Last

The situation in Xichang had remained unusually tense for the missionaries because of the difficulties Lee Lovegren was having. He had been arrested in January, but the case against him was built up over a period of about a month. After his arrest, there was an accusation meeting, at which time people made accusations against Lee. The authorities played a trick on him, in that he was not allowed to be in any of the meeting except for the time he was asked to make a statement. When they asked him to speak, they merely asked him to make a talk on the work of the Office of Strategic Services, without any reference to its being an accusation meeting. Inasmuch as Lee did not know what had gone on in the meeting, he made the talk as requested. Only when it was completed, did the Communists represent what he had said as being a confession.

During the time of his early detention, authorities permitted Lee to return home once or twice a week to get papers. About the middle of February, he was brought home, and he and Ida were ordered to pack up their things. Shortly after, they were taken first to Yaan, and then to Chungking and Guangzhou.

These developments with Lee meant that greater suspicion fell on the other missionaries than on those of us in Huili or Lugu. For one thing, everyone was placed under house arrest and, if there were particular needs, such as for money, they had no way of appealing for this. No money remained to pay servants, and all the work about the compound was done by the missionaries. Not that any of them were unused to hard work; it was only that in the China context it was viewed by all the Chinese as very demeaning. The much longer-than-usual delay for exit permits was probably to enable authorities to determine whether or not the other families were involved in Lovegren's alleged spy activities.

The days were weary with waiting. You can do only so much reading, working at little tasks, gardening, sewing, puttering around, caring for children, and resting. The chapel was closed, and no gatherings for prayer were allowed. All who wished could go to the one Sunday morning service held at the Border Service mission of the Church of Christ in China. Pastor Yang and his family were still in Xichang trying to make a living by selling soap and stockings. He refused to recognize any of the missionaries on the few times when they had occasion to pass him on the streets. Nor was he willing, probably wisely, to receive money which the Carrs tried to leave with him through a middleman. Along with the local pastor at the Border Service church, he had taken a firm stand against the foreign missionaries. They were hardly to be blamed for this, and yet it was a very painful experience.

During these months of waiting, the missionaries were placed in difficult situations. One day Dan and Bill were required to pick up horse manure in front of the compound gate. They did not view this as demeaning, except when the soldiers, who stood around laughing, steered several horse trains past the area they had just swept clean, messing it up again. This continued for several hours.

One day soldiers stationed in front of the compound gate turned back coolies carrying wood for cooking. Lucy followed them back down the road, but, rebuffed once, they refused to return. She noticed a ranking Communist official standing by the side of the road and asked him to intercede. "How," she asked, "can we live? You won't permit us to leave, and yet you won't let us buy what we need to live." He saw her point and allowed her to go after the carriers and bring them back.

Some officers were more friendly than they dared to show. Shouting out obscenities when their fellows were nearby, they were very cordial and offered to help as they could when they were alone for a few minutes with the missionaries. Before the Xichang group left, officials ordered one of the leading local Christians to come to the compound and settle local matters. He received the property papers as well as large amounts of literature which were stored there. Once again we saw the "legal" side of the new government—everything must be done decently and in order.

Finally, the long-awaited day arrived, and on September 16 all of the remaining foreigners left Xichang. The Carrs, Simons, and Simpsons, with their families, were joined by the Upchurches and their children. Altogether there were eight adults and eleven children. Their route out, the same as that for Ruth and me, included no flying, and yet they were able to make it the whole way to Hong Kong in thirty-one days. With a group this large, not everyone could get good rooms at the inns, and tensions were inescapable.

Dan continued his love-hate relationship with the local beasts of burden. In the early part of the trip he rode on a small mule. On one particularly dangerous mountain pass where the road was both narrow and slippery, the mule stumbled and started to slide over a steep cliff. Dan just managed to grab an overhanging branch of a tree, as the mule kept right on going into a waterfall at the bottom of the incline. The poor animal survived, but Dan had had enough—he walked the rest of the way despite the pain he had in his bad knee.

As the group went through Fulin, Dan, and Bill were allowed to visit Hannah's grave. They had great difficulty in getting a local photographer to go with them to take a picture of the grave site with the engraved marker in place. All along the way crowds of children, lining both sides of the route, jeered the photographer for associating even briefly with the despised foreigners. The two men waited around only long enough to get the negative, since the photographer had no paper at his shop to make any prints. The epitaph on the simple stone marker was "Hannah H. Cole 1919-1951 John 15:13."

Within a few weeks after arrival in Hong Kong, all of the Xichang group were on their way back to their respective homes and the ministries which God would give them in the days ahead. The mission to China's Nosuland was over. The people whom we had gone to reach with the Gospel message were still there, still unreached.

Post-China Reflections

In the days immediately after our departure from China, a gamut of emotions swirled over and about us. We could have been bitter, but we were not. Our hopes had been dashed, our dreams unrealized, and God's work *seemed* to be at an end. We had been battered emotionally, with our reputations and character maligned. One of our members was dead, another detained in prison, I had been deported, and one of the children had been damaged psychologically.

Yet we realized the need for perspective. What other than a revolution of this dimension could have begun to solve China's overwhelming problems? We had often said, rather simply, that "Jesus is the answer for China," but we raised only spiritual questions. And these were inextricably tied to the political, economic, and social problems which had been mounting over the centuries. A mini-revolution had occurred in 1911; 1949 was its final step.

Revolutions solve many injustices; inevitably, they create others. A long shake-down of the political state is necessary before any kind of equilibrium is reached. Nineteen fifty-one was too early to see this; we only saw friends killed, people terrorized, and many injustices committed. This is the nature of a revolution.

Our misfortune was to be in the wrong place at the wrong time. We were people of good will, committed to doing the work of God's kingdom. We made bad mistakes, often not walking as worthy envoys of the Gospel. This was true of all boards and all missionaries. But even had we been perfect in all we said and did, the end result would have been little different. The weight of history and the emotion of the moment left the Communists with no alternative except to see us as "spies," as agents of imperialism seeking to get our noses inside of China's tent on behalf of our government.

Despite our distaste for Marxism as an ideological system, we knew that God could use it even as he had used enemies of his people in Old Testament days. If the Communists did only half of what they promised to do, the people would be better off economically and socially than under the previous government. Personal freedom and human rights, at least as we know them within our society, were lacking. But how much freedom was there under the Nationalist regime, when millions were oppressed by landlords and sold their children to escape starvation? Freedom surely must include more than the right of belief, of assembly, and of free speech.

To recognize that we were caught up in forces beyond our control, for which we could not immediately bear responsibility, is not the same as saying we were faultless. We were culpably ignorant of the past history of the missionary movement's complicity in evil, of the current culture, and of the perspective of the Biblical message on the national needs of China. We did not work hard enough at developing empathy, at seeing China from an inside perspective. We were insensitive to others and to the burden our life-style and methods placed upon them. We lived within our own secure perspective, and found it difficult to get beyond our own parochial worldviews. Our only proper response to these mistakes is to repent, a common practice for God's people through the ages as they engaged in his work. Only after such a repentance, may we honestly reaffirm our ongoing love for the Chinese people. This is not a guilt trip, a *mea culpa*, or a condemnation of the Western missionary enterprise. It is only an attempt to give an honest appraisal, an exercise in which evangelical missions rarely engage. Hopefully, such an attitude will enable us all to share again in some way, if only by prayer, in God's ongoing kingdom in the Middle Kingdom.

13

A New China
God's People Alive in a Bitter Sea

What Hit Us?

As we left China and returned to our homes, we were not certain what had hit us. Missionaries and mission boards alike wrung their hands and gnashed their teeth. What had gone wrong? How could we have lost the biggest of all American mission fields? Might we have done something differently? How could we avoid the same things happening in other mission fields? A whole spate of books, far too numerous to even mention here, were written to explore these and other questions.

For the most part, these books dissected methods, life-style matters, strategy—what we did not do and what we had done that was wrong. Hopefully, if we really got to the bottom of these mistakes, we would not be doomed to repeat them endlessly in other mission situations. The effort was well-intentioned, but the past rarely gives us an agenda for the future—at least not in American evangelical missions. Many years later, in 1970, as I travelled together with Peter Wagner in south Vietnam to hold workshops on Theological Education by Extension, I was amazed, as was Pete, to see missionaries, in apparent ignorance, repeating the China syndrome.

What most of us failed to see, and continue to miss, was that the roots of "missionary failure," if we indeed wish to give it such a bad label, went back much farther than the years when we were in China. This strangling rope of history had many strands. First, was a very weak Qing dynasty that was forced to submit to the shame and disgrace of the unequal treaties from 1842-1860. At this time, strong western nations imported opium and Christianity into China. Second, these treaties and the consequent mass invasion of foreigners into China produced hundreds of anti-missionary riots between 1860 and 1900 which culminated in the tragic Boxer rebellion of 1900. This extreme anti-foreign reaction resulted in the loss of lives for hundreds of missionaries and converts, both Protestant and Roman Catholic.

Following the overthrow of the Qing dynasty in 1911, China went through a long period of ideological, political, social, and economic turmoil. During this time she was looking for national models. The liberal Western model, with its pragmatic and utilitarian views well advocated by John Dewey, who lectured extensively in China over a two-year period, was championed by Hu Shi and Cai Yongpei, chancellor of the National Beijing University. For many students and the more radical leaders, this model lost much of its authenticity when the Versailles treaty failed to rectify the great injustice China had suffered in Western acquiescence to the twenty-one demands of Japan for control over German holdings in Shantung province.

The widespread discontent sparked by this injustice erupted in the May 4th movement, which ushered in a new era of cultural upheaval marked by nationalism and anti-imperialism. Lu Xun's novelette *AQ* became the symbol of a new China seeking to escape from its chrysalis of control by feudalism, imperialism, and bureaucratic capitalism. In this moment of high resentment, many Chinese leaders turned toward Marxist thought. Russia was an attractive new model, particularly as its government, newly in power following the 1917 revolution, revoked its series of unequal treaties with China. The United States could not bring itself to do this until 1943. Attracted to Russia and its new revolutionary thought, radical Chinese leaders formed the Chinese Communist Party in 1921.

In the early and middle 1920s both Marxist thought and liberal Western ideologies produced a New Culture movement, as well as an anti-Christian reaction. The chief sin of Christianity, it was alleged, was that it was an ally of both imperialism and capitalism, and thus, in essence, an enemy of the Chinese people. To Chinese students, enamored of Dewey and other anti-Christian Western philosophers, the Christian faith lacked the scientific rigor capable of carrying China into the new age of progress and modernization.

This agenda for the future was laid aside during the long "war of resistance" against the ruthless Japanese invaders, when both the Nationalist government and its Communist antagonists had to expend their united energies against a common enemy. Once Japan was defeated, the Kuomintang and Communists turned on each other in a vicious internal struggle. Widespread corruption, political and economic incompetence, questionable military strategy, and weakened morale led to the Nationalist debacle and victory for the once greatly undermanned Communist forces. Unfortunately, American and Chinese Nationalist leaders understood only the military dimensions of this momentous struggle, and they were never able to address realistically the deeper economic, social, and ideological factors.

When the revolutionary dam burst, bringing a new government to power, the missionaries were caught in a no-win situation. Their predecessors in the mid-1850s were a part of the original problem. Over the years they had done nothing directly to bring about a solution to the charges of imperialism. Now with the situation totally out of their control, they were caught in the maelstrom of a strong anti-foreign sentiment which forced them to leave China. Nothing they had done or not done in the immediate past was to blame. It may have added fuel to the fire, but it was impossible at this late date to put out the fire.

The Christian Faith Under Mao

Because of its past history, notably its very apparent "foreign connection," Christian leaders needed to take drastic action to prove that the church was not, as alleged, a continuing imperialistic presence, a kind of trojan-horse, in China. A few pious denials and business as usual would not suffice. The only adequate response, as Chou En-lai put it cryptically, was to "put your house in order." If this had not been done, it is only too probable that Christianity would have been banned outright, much as it had been in 1724, at the time of the Rites Controversy between the Vatican and the

Kangxi Emperor. Churches would not have disappeared, even as they did not in this earlier period, but waves of persecution would have overwhelmed them and ultimately prevented an effective witness relevant to the life of the nation.

The radical action that some prominent leaders took included drawing up the Christian Manifesto which put the church on the side of the government in its fight against any imperialistic encroachment by the western nations. Many rank-and-file Christians signed this statement, including not a few leading evangelicals. Others, such as Wang Mingdao, resolutely refused, claiming that to do so compromised the Gospel and "betrayed the Son of Man into the hands of sinners." Their failure to sign was interpreted by government officials and the cooperating church leaders as an anti-government political stance. This resulted in numerous accusation meetings and, in many cases, imprisonment for long periods. In these early struggles between those who explicitly supported government policies and those who seemed to be opposing them are to be found some of the roots of the current antagonism between the Three-Self movement and the so-called house churches. Some put in prison at that time, because of the accusations of other church leaders, do not find it easy to forgive and join forces with the churches related to the Three-Self.

Even in the pre-cultural revolution years from 1949-66, many Christians in China began to meet in smaller home worship services that were not related to churches in the Three-Self movement. Some wished to avoid the epithet of "foreign" which non-Christians put upon the churches; others did not wish to associate with churches that they felt were compromising the Gospel.

Although there was the constitutional right of "religious liberty," and the government affirmed its desire for church members to be a part of its "united front" in fighting imperialism, many pressures were brought to bear. Church buildings were often closed, particularly when land reform was being carried out, endless meetings were held for political indoctrination, and churches in most cities were reduced in number. The Gospel was being preached, but the whole tenor of society did not encourage Chinese people to believe in any religion. In 1956 the principal Protestant ministerial training school, Nanking Union Theological Seminary, was closed down.

When church leaders, like others, accepted too eagerly Mao Tsetung's offer to "let one hundred flowers bloom" (i.e., speak your mind freely) in 1958, they were put in prison for as long as twenty years. Churches tried hard to relate themselves to the Chinese political reality, but many leftist government leaders obstructed them.

Even the ebbing degree of "religious freedom" disappeared in 1966 with the advent of the misnamed "cultural revolution." These years of chaos from 1966-1976, later referred to by the Chinese as "years of disaster," saw the disappearance of all forms of institutional religion. During this period, a leftist clique within the government, encouraged by Mao himself, sought to create a new Chinese society by destroying all vestiges of imperialism, feudalism, and bourgeois ideology. Rather than wait for religion to wilt away in a coming utopian age, classic Marxist ideology, these elements sought to destroy it as a hotbed of superstition. Christianity, along with traditional Chinese religions, came under vicious attack. Church buildings were taken over for use as factories, storehouses, offices, and public meeting places. The Red Guards burned Bibles, hymnals, and church furniture. Pastors were sent to factories and farms to do "productive work" which would force them to depend on their physical labor, rather than upon offerings given to them by their parishioners.

The Red Guards were determined to create a new Chinese society and a new Chinese person. This meant that they must destroy all those values, customs, attitudes, and habits of traditional China. No one was safe from their ranting rhetoric or their senseless destruction. From the lowest to the highest in society, everyone suffered. Seldom, even in China's long history, has there been such a tragic period.[1]

During this period of time, all Christians were in house churches, dispersed throughout society as small worshipping communities. If anything, the Christians who had been associated with the Three Self movement suffered more than others, since they had not gone into hiding earlier and were more exposed to the Red Guards and their rampages. Looking back on this period, church leaders say that it was God's way of strengthening his church. Christians were incarnated in society, experiencing the same struggles and suffering as other Chinese. No longer were they the elite who could escape suffering and problems because of their connection with foreign missionaries. When churches were later reopened, church members saw the church as "their church." One pastor explained that before the cultural revolution, potential members asked what the church could do for them; now they queried what they might do for the church and the pastor.

Following the death of Mao in 1976, China began to reveal a willingness to rejoin the family of world nations and started on the "long march" of the Four Modernizations (agriculture, industry, science-technology, and defense) under the leadership of Deng Xiaoping. In order to encourage religious groups in China to join forces with all Chinese citizens in promoting the progress of the country, Deng reestablished the "united front" policy which restored to institutional religious groups the religious toleration wrenched so violently from them during the Cultural Revolution.

In 1979, the government restored the Religious Affairs Bureau, dismantled during the Cultural Revolution, and very shortly Protestant Christian leaders were encouraged to revive the Three-Self structure and Catholics the Patriotic Association of Chinese Catholics. Daoists, Buddhists, and Muslims reestablished comparable organizations.

With this type of official encouragement, members of all the major religions of China, as well as those committed to myriad superstitions, came out of the woodwork. They were the vanguard of a tremendous religious revival that swept over the country, surprising the many observers who had concluded that Communism had inaugurated a post-religious era. In this general resurgence of the Chinese religious spirit, the Christian faith in both its Protestant and Catholic forms expanded rapidly. With government encouragement and help, over four thousand Protestant churches were reopened and a thousand new buildings were constructed where previously there had been none. Some twenty thousand meeting points, serving the needs of those who could not easily attend the larger worship services, were established through the country. Beyond this number are those referred to as "house churches," which may or may not be related to the Three-Self churches.

With religious revival came the restoration of many institutional forms of the church. In addition to the Three-Self Patriotic

Association, which oversees relations between Protestant churches and government organs, the Protestants organized the China Christian Council, responsible for matters of ministry, leadership training, and church life. Church leaders have taken the lead in publishing hymnals, devotional materials, limited editions of the Bible, and the monthly magazine *Tian Feng* ("Heavenly Wind"). The YMCA and YWCA have been reestablished in many Chinese cities.

In February 1981, church leaders reopened the Nanking Union Theological Seminary, a school with both a three-year graduate and four-year undergraduate training program. Since that time, thirteen schools with two-year programs have been opened. Initially, only skeletal activities were conducted in the newly-opened church facilities, but now a full range of services is offered in addition to public worship: Bible classes, prayer meetings, short- and long-period lay training programs, baptisms, weddings, funerals, memorial and thanksgiving services, choir practice, observance of the sacraments, and regular visitation of the sick and elderly. Most of the leaders, both clerical and lay, are elderly and some have only recently been restored to pastoral duty after long inactivity in factories, labor camps, and prison cells.

Christian leaders, along with a few other Chinese, took the lead in 1985 in forming the Amity Foundation, a humanitarian organization which receives charitable contributions from abroad to fund useful projects in China. One of the most notable of these endeavors has been the cooperation between the United Bible Societies and the Amity Foundation to fund a modern printing press near Nanking that devotes itself primarily to printing Bibles and Christian literature for Chinese Christian churches.

Missionaries do not have the right to live and work in China as religious workers today. They probably are not needed, if the church is going to continue to be viewed as a truly Chinese church. However, many Christian people, affiliated both with secular groups and religious agencies, are using their talents and gifts to aid in China's modernization. These students, foreign teachers, and foreign experts are doing a responsible job in their chosen vocations. Undoubtedly, God often gives them opportunity to share their life in Christ with many whom the churches of China cannot reach with the Gospel.

Old Wine in Old Wineskins

As God was doing his work of grace and power in the new China, many concerned evangelical Christians, some "old China hands" from the pre-1949 years, were concerned for the needs of unevangelized areas in the country. Through the radio facilities of Transworld Radio and the Far East Broadcasting Corporation, they broadcast many Gospel programs into China. While many of these were culturally relevant, some popular made-in-America broadcasts were beamed toward China under the assumption that they had universal appeal. Many strategists were clinging to time-worn attitudes and approaches. The time had come for "new wine in new wineskins," but the prime concern of many was to restore the old relationships and old methods. Some mission leaders set up elaborate schemes to reestablish relationships with churches that had formerly been under their jurisdiction in pre-liberation days. Professional couriers smuggled Bibles into Guangzhou, where they were then passed into the interior by a kind of "underground railroad." One rather bizarre effort was made in late December 1978 to use balloons launched from an offshore island near Taiwan to airlift Christian literature into China. The well-publicized "Operation Pearl" sought, unsuccessfully it would appear, to float a million Bibles ashore near Swatow, a city along the southern coast of China.

Some para-church groups have systematic discipleship programs to train Chinese from China to be leaders in the house church movement. With the greater openness now prevailing in China, some American Chinese leaders have arranged for American pastors to spend one or two weeks discipling house churches here and there. To help pastors, intellectuals, and children, literature agencies have prepared special materials which they seek to bring into China by a variety of means.

Leaders of the China Christian Council have not welcomed these activities. They claim that the responsibility for evangelizing the unreached in China and discipling believers is theirs, and that all such outside efforts are attempts to control the church from the outside. Bishop Ding Guangxun has asked for a temporary "protective tariff" on outside religious help, until Chinese churches can develop a stronger sense of their own self-identity and fully escape the label of "foreign." They resent the way in which mission agencies and missionaries controlled and dominated them in the past and do not tolerate anything that seems to smack of these old attitudes and strategies. They claim that God has done a great work in China apart from any outside help, and that a continuation of what they view as unwise interference from abroad can only endanger Chinese churches, possibly even to the extent of provoking renewed government crackdowns.

Faced with these attitudes by the CCC leaders, many American evangelicals are pessimistic about the "open" churches of China and claim that the only true churches are the house churches. They judge the Christian situation in Marxist China by the same standards they apply to the American scene. They wonder, for example, why the shape of religious freedom is different, and they seem to want nothing less than the types of liberty we have in the United States.

This kind of freedom did exist, for the most part, during all of Protestant Christianity's first 150 years (1807-1949) in China, a period when the government was pitifully weak. Authorities made many anti-religious proclamations and sought to impose controls, most notably in education and medicine, but chaotic conditions meant they were unable to enforce them. The government, in effect, was struggling to control China; and, in the confusion, mission agencies and Christians did what they pleased. In fact, the Christian church believed it could exist with less control than in Western countries.

No wonder, then, that some Christians within and outside China want to see this as the norm now. Such total religious freedom, however, was an historical aberration. Indeed, whenever there has been a strong central government, with firm sovereignty over all of China, a kind of state orthodoxy (be it Confucianism or Marxism) has produced tight control and supervision over all religious groups. These groups, in turn, learned to live within these limits and to grow and prosper, even as they might have wished for something more ideal. The government viewed those not willing to submit to this type of surveillance with suspicion—as possible centers of dissidence and a threat to the government-sponsored orthodoxy.

Many American evangelicals are puzzled by the post-denominational status of churches. They wonder whatever happened to Baptists, Presbyterians, Methodists, and Episcopalians. Denominational labels disappeared soon after liberation. Initially, this probably occurred because of government pressure. A Marxist government may grant "religious liberty" to Christian churches, but can we expect it to deal with all the complex differences of hundreds of agencies or denominations? Whatever the origin of the churches' unified worship services, the pastors of these churches are high in praise for the quality of their present experience. They would not go back to the pre-liberation days, when there might be ten agencies working in one city, none knowing about the others. Although church staffs and worshippers come from many different denominational backgrounds, they work on the principle of "mutual respect" for one another's opinions and practice.

All churches in China, whether affiliated with the CCC or the independent house churches, face problems from the Marxist government. Several factors produce these conflicts. First, local Christians, zealous to witness in ways traditionally accepted (but not specifically mandated by Scripture), may engage in activities that the government has proscribed. That is, they may read Matthew 28:16-20 and say that this demands that they travel to the next county to preach. If they violate a specific law, they can expect to receive punishment for what they have done. We may or may not agree with the government attitude. But the political reality is still there, and Chinese Christians must determine whether or not they will adjust to it. Given the wide latitude of freedom they enjoy, they need to choose their battlefields with care.

Second, most of these conflicts are purely local—the overzealous activities of pockets of leftist-leaning cadres who have never been able to understand or accept their government's attitude granting freedom of religion. Most of the apostle Paul's problems were with local officials on-the-make. Many lower level officials are opposing Deng Xiaoping's economic policies in an adamant fashion. Is it unreasonable to expect that this would happen in the religious realm as well? Local conflicts may be due also to matters of *guanxi*, personal relationships that have gone sour. This is particularly true where local Three-Self leaders are a part of the conflict. Within the Three-Self movement, some leaders are more politically active, even leftist, and this reality creates more difficulties in some areas.

Third, the official distinction between permitted religious activities and proscribed "superstition" is a very narrow one. Zealous cadres and officials, not familiar with these technicalities, easily confuse the two and make mistakes. Those most familiar with the independent house churches agree that they have sometimes been confused with the Witness Li "yeller" groups and with many varieties of cults and heresies.

Where the potential for these deviations is present, local churches related to the Three-Self have assisted the Religious Affairs Bureau in restoring order or orthodox belief and action. Independent house churches in some areas have also been more directly opposed by more politically-minded leaders in the Three-Self movement.

Fourth, restrictions on religious freedom may occur in connection with the meeting of a National Congress or as a part of a campaign to deal with a national problem, such as bourgeois liberalism. We need to be aware that the situation is extremely complex, whether within the government bureaus, such as the Religious Affairs Bureau, or within the Three-Self churches or within the house churches. We must not make easy generalizations or draw either-or, black-and-white conclusions.

We often read, for example, that evangelism cannot take place in the open churches—that it only happens away from these "government-controlled" bodies. This reflects an outside viewpoint which says, in effect, that if you cannot evangelize as you do in America, no evangelism is taking place. Church members cannot hold public meetings in parks nor rent public facilities for a Billy Graham-type mass evangelism campaign. Would we really expect this in a Marxist society? But they can do personal evangelism outside the church, and they invite friends and relatives to church services where fine evangelistic sermons are regularly preached. The result is that multitudes are finding Christ and being baptized openly in these churches.

Cannot we conclude that God is at work in China with all those who call upon his name, whether within or without the churches of the China Christian Council? Ought we not give thanks for this and praise his name, rather than trying to snoop out all the problems and magnify them? When I was visiting in a south China city, the pastor asked me how I felt about an area in Sichuan through which I had passed two weeks previous. I expressed to him some disappointment over what I had seen—small building, relatively few worshippers, a rather old congregation, and an infirm pastor. He quickly asked me, "But isn't it wonderful that they even survived, that they are still there?" I had to agree with him. My attitude was not right—praise was far more fitting than complaint!

We who live in America have never developed a good understanding of the church-state relationship. We have never had to do this, for our government is benign and grants many privileges to churches. Therefore, when we view the church in a Marxist society, we have a knee-jerk reaction which says that the church must keep its distance from the state. We may even see the state, particularly if it is Marxist, as the creation of Satan. Can our options include the possibility that God, the Lord of history and the Sovereign over nations, raises up governments that do not believe in him to accomplish his purposes, even to do many good things of benefit to the people.

We cannot make decisions for believers in China. If some have chosen to follow one route and others a different one, we must give praise to God and ask him to continue to give wisdom to both. Hopefully, at some future time there may be an even greater degree of unity that will increase the impact of the Christian witness in China.

I regret that missiologists have failed to pinpoint the unique reasons for the growth of the churches in China. No one knows the exact number of Christians, and, in comparison with the tremendous number of non-believers, is it really important? But even if we take the very lowest figures of five or six million Christians, this represents a five or six-fold growth in a forty-year period. How has this happened? We have been given many superficial answers—prayer, suffering, high use of lay people, "signs and wonders," and true commitment to Christ. This is an impressive list. Unfortunately, all of these things happen in other areas of the world with minimal growth.

What is unique to China that makes the spiritual climate there different from that in other places? At the heart of the answer is the fact that the churches no longer have any "foreign connection." Throughout its 150-year history, the Protestant church has labored under the burden of being foreign. No longer is this the case; neither is the church divided, at least by explicit denominational labels. The "Chinese-ness" of the church, not so much its message as its connection, and its unity create the climate under which some of the factors commonly mentioned as producing growth can be effective. Hopefully, slow-growing and struggling mission-connected churches in other areas of the world will take note. As church leaders in China devote more attention to the development of the church and its ministry and are less preoccupied with continuing the structure of the Three-Self movement, the potential for growth is unlimited. However, the massacre in Beijing and the subsequent repression of popular dissent could thwart evangelism and Christian nurture, both for the Chinese and for unreached minority peoples.

Why have evangelical missiologists been slow to recognize the lack of foreign connection and unity of the church in China as the necessary climate for church growth? First, to do so would be to admit the serious damage done by the previous foreignness and disunity. Second, to affirm these two factors would badly harm evangelical agencies in promoting their work in other mission fields. Our denominational distinctives and our ties to churches in the third world are too strong and have too much promotional value.

Travel Back to the New China

The number of foreign tourists in China began as a trickle in the mid-1970s, broadened to a stream by 1980, and has now become a torrent. Unfortunately, not too many try to see the Christian dimensions of China's past. You can visit newly reopened churches in nearly every tourist site, and Christian brothers and sisters extend a hearty welcome, often giving visitors their own seats and offering to interpret every part of the service. Even beyond seeing the churches, one can appreciate much of historic Christian interest. It may be the statue of Xu Guangqi—an important official of the early Ming dynasty and one of the first of Matteo Ricci's converts—located in a Shanghai park, it is one part of what used to be Xujiawei, the center of Roman Catholic work in China.

In Nanking we may see the museum of the Taiping Heavenly Kingdom, a huge Christian peasant rebellion that made Nanking its capital. Visitors are amazed to learn of the indigenous Christian elements of this movement, which came within a hair of overthrowing the Qing dynasty and installing a Christian one. Sun Yat-sen, the father of modern China and an earnest Christian, is buried in an elegant mausoleum outside the city. Few tourist guides will tell visitors that many of Sun's ideals were Christian in origin.

The list of things to see in Beijing is long. When you go to the Summer Palace, northwest of the city, recall that it was the principal occupant of the palace, the Empress Dowager Ci Xi, who was ruling over China at the time of the tragic Boxer Rebellion that made martyrs of hundreds of Catholic and Protestant missionaries and converts. Most tourists visit the Ding Ling, tomb of the Wan Li emperor, but they may not know it was he who was ruling China when Matteo Ricci, the great Jesuit, and his colleagues came to Beijing. Within the tightly closed walls of the *Gu Gong*, the Imperial Palace, Jesuit missionaries had the unparalleled opportunity to serve as school masters to the Shan Zhi emperor when he was still very young.

Even as the first Protestant missionaries noted rather ruefully, signs of the Jesuit presence abound in Beijing. It may be the burial site of Matteo Ricci, the one foreigner whose tomb is still found in Beijing, the two famous Catholic Cathedrals, the Beitang and Nantang, and the old Jesuit observatory where these Catholic missionaries outwitted the Muslim astronomers.

Some visitors are anxious to see the site of the old Union Medical College, the campus of Qinghua University, once Yenjing University where John Leighton Stuart, last pre-liberation U.S. Ambassador to China, served as president, or the site of the old foreign legations where nationals of at least eight foreign countries hid from the Boxers in 1900.

At the provincial museum in Xian you can view the Nestorian Monument, probably the single most important Christian record ever to come from China. As you examine this huge black stele in the "forest of steles," you are filled with awe as you reflect on these first hardy missionaries who came into China from Persia over the silk route about 645 A.D.

In Guangzhou you can visit Shamian, the little island in the Pearl River, and the nearby area on the shore where the foreign commercial factories, representing the first modern contact of the West with China, were located. Here Robert Morrison and many of his missionary colleagues, from both America and Great Britain, commenced their study of the Chinese language and planned their forays into the closed Middle Kingdom. If you have the courage, visit the Zhenhai Lou in Yu Xiu park and be chilled by the many displays in this museum which document how China's current government views the imperialism of China's past missionary enterprise. This is a sobering experience, but with too much evidence to be ignored.

In four trips to China in 1984, 1986, and 1987, we visited these and many other sites of interest to Christians. Wherever we went, we saw a China struggling to emerge from its traditional past. Paved and widened roads, improved methods of transportation, building cranes, new factories, modern hotels, free-wheeling entrepreneurs, operating over eleven million private enterprises, all testified to this fact.

Modernity is a key word to the change. You can eat a cheeseburger in the Great Wall Hotel, a Beijing branch in the worldwide Sheraton chain, lunch on Dutch Gouda cheese, salami, and French bread at the large deli in the Holiday Inn-managed Lido Hotel, get a snack at Maxim's de Paris, or play a round of golf on the new international course built incongruously along the "spirit way" leading to the famous Ming tombs outside of Beijing. Colonel Sanders' fried chicken is now competing with Beijing duck.

Back to the Great Cool Mountains

When Ruth and I visited Kunming with Bill and Flossie Simons in June 1984, we made one fruitless effort to get permission to travel by train from there to Xichang. The reason, undoubtedly true, was that this area was not open because the facilities for sleeping and eating were inadequate for foreigners.

As we planned our next trip for 1986, we learned through Jim Garrison, now living in San Jose, that China Sightseeing, Inc., a San Francisco-based travel agency, managed by American Chinese, had connections through travel-agency friends in China to get us permission to travel to Xichang. We asked its manager, Rowland Xu, to work on this for us. How surprised and gratified we were to learn in March 1986 that the government would issue us a special permit to travel into this still-closed area.

When word was out that we had been cleared for this two week trip, we had an "instant tour." Quickly, sixteen of us signed up for this nostalgic travel venture back down memory lane. All of our original China team, except the Coles, were represented: John and Irene Simpson with their three girls, Linn Ann, Marjorie, and Jean; Lucille Carr and her oldest son Dan; Bill and Flossie Simons with their daughter, Martha, and son Russell and his wife Ramona; Mildred Lovegren and her sister, Edith; Ruth and I. Three of these children, now in their early forties, had been very small when their parents brought them to China, and the other three had been born in Chengdu or Xichang. Jim and Virginia Garrison, their Huili-born son, Jimmy, and several family relatives took the same trip as we did about a month earlier.

Our first stop was Chengdu where we spent too much time trying to find old #51 Huaxiba. More important was our visit to the Sichuan Theological Seminary, a two-year theological college located on the grounds of the old Pifangjie church, where we were able to see Hu Kaixiang, the woman evangelist with whom we had worked so many years previously. I do not know whether she or we were the most thrilled. She had fun trying to determine which of the young people, only babies when she knew them, went with whom. She had suffered much during the Cultural Revolution, imprisoned for several years, but now had a radiant smile of joy. She explained the difference of the present from the past in a nutshell. Before liberation, she noted, she and others visited extensively on Saturdays, urging folk to attend church, but only a handful showed up. Now the pastors and leaders prepare and pray on Saturday, and the worshippers on Sunday are so many that the church building can hardly hold them all.

We cannot comment on the extent of changes in most parts of China, because we never lived there. But the changes in what used to be called the Ningsu area were so profound as to be almost beyond belief. Frequently we had to shake ourselves to believe that this was indeed the same place where we had once lived. The unbelief started with our trip by train from Chengdu to Xichang.

When Lee Lovegren and John Simpson made their first trek to Xichang in the spring of 1947, they took a bus to Leshan, but from then on it was a dangerous trip by truck, often with long delays or long stretches of walking because of high rivers and mountain slides. The trip required at least a week from Leshan to Xichang, and often much longer. Now we had a comfortable train ride of twelve hours to cover the same distance of about 350 miles.

Trains for long trips are equipped with hard seats, soft seats, and soft sleepers. We had the latter, which meant that we had sleeping compartments that would seat or sleep four people. An aisle along one side of the train enabled us to walk from car to car. A nice diner provided food for all the passengers. Once we reached the more mountainous section of the trip, we were almost constantly going either through tunnels, some as long as two or three miles, or over bridges. In the entire distance from Chengdu to Kunming there are a total of 450 tunnels and 650 bridges.

Commenced in 1958, the year of China's ill-conceived "great leap forward," and halted for two years due to political turmoil from 1962-64, this remarkable project was finally completed in July 1970. Many lives were lost in the construction of the Cheng-Kun line, and at several points along the roadbed are neatly-kept little cemetery plots with memorials to those who died.

The scenery was spectacularly beautiful. A Chinese publication describes it well:

> All along the route are lofty peaks, precipitous ravines, swift rivers, complicated geological formations and extremely changeable weather. A third of the line is situated in an area where earthquakes are frequent and reach a magnitude of seven or above. Displacements of rock mass have been known to occur over large areas in some places. Deep gullies retain heat, building up to temperatures of from 40 to 50 degrees C., while in some valleys force-ten winds often rage. Like a geological museum, these areas exhibit karst caves, underground rivers, faults, drifting sands, gas-filled layers, magmatic explosions, mud-rock flows, silt and Glauber's salt

deposits. The building of a railway in such conditions is an unprecedented engineering feat in the history of China's railway construction.[2]

The train was an express, but we tried to get station names as we sped by the markers. We remembered only a few—Pu Xiong where the Nosu had inflicted a serious loss on Kuomintang troops in 1946 and Xide, only forty-five minutes east of Lugu. By this time, we had reached Nosu territory, and we saw them everywhere—in stations, sitting on freight cars, waiting in slow trains for ours to pass, walking along the road and on high mountain paths. The Dadu River, along which we travelled for long periods of time, was muddy, but still beautiful, as it wound majestically among the high mountains which are terraced almost to the top with crops of rice, vegetables, and fruit.

The countryside, once very isolated and backward, is now totally electrified, and we saw many factories, petroleum plants and dams along the way. Equally amazing was that the roads we saw paralleling the tracks are well-paved, and even have sturdy stone bridges.

Lucille, Danny, Ruth, and I were most interested to view Lugu when the train stopped there for five minutes. The track and station are to the east of south street where we had our chapel. This area, once just barren fields, is built up with many homes, brick kilns, and petroleum containers. The town on the other side of the river is not that different from what it was when we left. Our old residence on the hill is still standing, no longer surrounded by the wall, and now occupied by two or three families who have filled several rooms with Buddha images. We saw that there is a new bridge south of town for traffic going on to Mianning and Yaan.

As we continued on toward Xichang, we were amazed at how cross-road hamlets have now grown into thriving little cities. Particularly is this true of Manshuiwan, now busy with lumber and coal activities. We knew that one of China's big satellite launching sites is in a valley off to the west behind the first range of mountains. The presence of this base midway between Lugu and Xichang is undoubtedly the reason that we have twice failed to receive permission to travel back to Lugu. It is considered to be a national security area.

Even before we left Lugu in 1951, the countryside had been rid of the curse of opium, but the debilitating effects of the "black poison" had not disappeared. Now it is different. Fields all through the Anning River valley and right up the mountain sides are lushly green with crops that take care of the basic needs of the people and produce excess capital for them to invest in rural industries or other money-making schemes.

This entire area was designated as the *Liang Shan Yizu Zizhi Zhou* (The Cool Mountain Yi Nationality Autonomous Prefecture) in October, 1952. The prefecture, comprising seventeen *xian* or counties, has a total population of 3,300,000, including 1,400,000 Nosu (*Yi*), and 1,900,000 Han Chinese and minority nationalities such as Zhuang, Mongol, Naxi, Hui, Miao, Tibetan, Buyi, Lisu, Bai, and Dai. Xichang, the prefecture capital city, has 70,000 people in the city proper and 80,000 in the near environs. The distinction between an autonomous prefecture and a regular prefecture is that a majority of the government officials are minorities, the spoken and written language of the dominant nationality is in common use in the area, and local government officials may independently run certain educational and cultural affairs in their own area.

Our group was housed at the Qionghai Guest House right by the lake and across from the city. From there, we had easy access to the Guangfu Temple, built during the Tang dynasty and now being thoroughly reconstructed. Very near the hostel on the side of the mountain overlooking Qionghai Lake is the beautifully-designed Museum of the Yi Slave Society. This museum was opened in 1985 and, previous to the coming of our large group, had been visited only by a few dignitaries of foreign governments who had business in Xichang. The director of the museum, Chen Wenzhuan, himself a black Nosu and a lord in the former oppressive society, graciously showed us around and answered our questions as we sipped tea in the reception room.

The museum has an extensive display of pictures and Nosu artifacts. A great deal is made of the ancient origins of their slave society, of ways in which the blacks mistreated the whites, of how the Yi warriors welcomed the tattered Red army during its long march through this area in 1935, and of the ways in which they helped the liberation army overcome the Kuomintang in the Liangshan area.

Many exhibits display facets of the religious life of the Yi, particularly at birth, sickness, and death. In common with Marxist theory, the origin of religious belief is explained to be the irrational response of the people to the mysterious forces of nature. No explanation is given of the *Tian Pusa* (the heavenly god) of the Yi. I asked Director Chen about this. He dismissed this concept rather lightly, expressing his belief that it had come from the Chinese sense of the emperor as the "son of heaven." When I asked him the state of Nosu beliefs, he admitted that the old superstitions and sacrifices remain and that there continues to be a sense of black prestige in their mountain society. The social distinctions and the economic inequalities have been removed, but it is not so easy to erase old prejudices and traditions.

During June of 1987 when Ruth and I visited Xichang again, leading a group of twenty-one tourists, an assistant director of the museum gave an extensive lecture dealing with most facets of traditional Nosu life. Far from being an oral history, these traditions are inscribed in written materials which can be traced back for thirty-seven generations.

During our stay in Xichang in both 1986 and 1987, we saw evidences of better attitudes between the Chinese and the Nosu, as well as toward the other minority nationalities in the area. While the Chinese themselves confess that Chinese chauvinism is far from dead, there can be little doubt that progress is being made. The museum itself is a noted symbol of this fact, as is the large statue, erected in the center of the city's new section, that shows a famous Chinese general, Liu Bocheng, and a Nosu warrior leader posing together as friends. As is common in autonomous regions, provinces, and prefectures, many of the officials, including the mayor of Xichang, are Nosu.

Another evidence of the current Chinese-Nosu rapport is the prominence now given both to the written and spoken Nosu language. I noted in a previous chapter that the new government had linguists working on the Nosu language from the time of the long march in 1935. Shortly after liberation, it introduced a new romanized orthography which was intended to replace the hodgepodge script controlled by the *bimos*. The Nosu refused to accept the new script as a substitute, and over a period of time a plan was developed to use both romanization and the script.

In public places I seldom saw the romanized script. Most commonly it is used in beginning textbooks to help children learn their language. Even here, it is usually found in charts of vowels, consonants, and syllables. Linguists have unified the vast number of script symbols, that had been multiplied many times over by innovative *bimos*, and reduced them in number to about nine hundred. Unlike the Chinese character, these do not carry any meaning, but they may be used either to help the Nosu pronounce Chinese characters or to give written form to their own language.

The improved Chinese attitude to the Yi and their language is not unique. In Beijing there is a Committee for Research in Minority Languages. Also in Beijing is the Central Academy for National Minorities where many minority languages are studied and taught. The Institute of Linguistics of the Chinese Academy of Sciences works out the scripts for minority languages.

Unlike the past when it was difficult to find books about the Nosu, we found any number of these in Xichang bookstores. Some focus on the language, culture, customs, traditions, and economic life of the people. Most notable is the fact that some of these are written by Nosu scholars and represent original "hands-on" research into the life of their own people. As we read over this material, we got the feeling that the writers feel very good that the present regime is belatedly recognizing the culture and achievements of the Nosu people.[3]

If in the future, the Chinese church is able to translate the Bible and other Christian literature for the *Liang Shan Yi*, there is now the foundation for this to occur. Previous to this time, it would have been a hopeless mess. The Yi churches of Yunnan on the other side of the *Jinsha Jiang* (River of Golden Sand) have Bibles and hymnals. These will not work well in the Xichang area because of serious language differences.

During our visit in 1987 to Xichang, we had extensive contact with the Nosu in local country markets, in the village of Tuan Jieh near Xichang, in the prefectural cadre school, and in a primary school. Local officials gave us great freedom in visiting these areas, in taking video pictures, and in mixing with the people. The Nosu are still a poor people, but compared with the past, they are dressing, eating, and living better. Progress is not to be measured in large steps. Their energies are not now being sapped by opium, large-scale sacrifices of animals, or interclan warfare.

When we visited the cadre school which prepares Nosu young people and those of two or three other nationalities for government jobs in their villages, teachers and students gave us a cordial welcome. The Nosu teachers at this school do some of their teaching in their own language. Directors of the school have taken the lead in preparing useful language books that are area-specific. Many students have gained a good grasp of Chinese. The school has a small library with both Chinese and minority-language books.

I was disappointed to learn that no specific efforts are being made to use Yi culture—traditions, the distinctive Yi calendar, and other cultural elements—in the training process. While the Yi language continues to be used, future generations of Nosu young people will be absorbed into Chinese life and culture. This may be necessary for a country with this number of nationalities, but it would be tragic if, in the future, the only vestige of minority nationality life will be preserved in museums.

When we visited the village of Tuan Jie, about five miles to the west of Xichang proper, we were told that it was a "model village." From my perspective, it was like the many villages that we had visited in pre-liberation days. Some differences were apparent. Tile had replaced shale or grass for some house roofs; the courtyards were cleaner; guns were not apparent; there were fewer dogs; some of the houses had windows or transparent ceiling tiles. The dress of the men and women had not changed, with the exception of a new tasseled type of straw hat.

I talked to one man with the prominent forelock of hair representing the *Tian Pusa* (the heavenly god). I asked him if people still believed this. He nodded a vigorous affirmative, but noted that only those over forty-five years of age held to this tradition. We had not gone very far, however, before we saw some young people, even children, who had the same symbol on their heads. We conclude that this ancient belief, whatever its origin, continues to afford a fine preparation for preaching the good news of the one true God.

The primary school was impressive for several reasons. How unusual to see first-hand that the Nosu language itself was used in these schools to train youngsters. This I never saw in Taiwan, where the educational agenda completely rules out anything but Mandarin Chinese. The young Nosu woman doing the teaching knew Chinese, and while we were there led the children through a noisy sing-song exercise of shouting out and stroking the Chinese characters written on the board. Primary books written entirely in the Nosu script, with no Chinese characters at all, are basic in the curriculum.

On both of our trips to Xichang, a high-priority item was to visit the Christian church. We knew that there was an "open church" in both Xichang and Huili, because of letters written to Mildred Lovegren by Hu Kaixiang and because Christian leaders from Kunming had made periodic training missions to Huili. The church building in Xichang was the old one used by the Border Service Department of the Church of Christ in China. What a thrill as we walked into the premises to be greeted by old friends whom we had not seen since the day of our wedding, now nearly forty years ago. The pastor we had not known previously, but some of both the men and women leaders were won to Christ as teenagers by our Xichang missionaries. Now they serve faithfully in the Xichang Christian community. One elder reminded me that the last time I had seen him was when, as a fifteen-year old boy, he had "drunk our wine," a colloquial expression meaning to attend our wedding feast.

Only thirty or forty believers attend the various weekly services in Xichang. The Huili church is also very small and consists largely of rural people. Wang Daoran continues to serve as its pastor and is also involved in local civic activities. Despite their lack of numerical strength, Christians do what they can to let their light shine for the Lord. Since the fall of 1986, a young woman graduate of the two-year Sichuan Theological Seminary has been helping the Xichang church.

In participating in China's long march of four modernizations, the church seeks to be productive. It operates a hostel in the courtyard for travellers through Xichang, and it runs a noodle factory. A portion of its property is shared with the Revolutionary Kuomintang Committee. Leaders of the church were happy to receive some of the study literature that the local officials permitted us to give to them. We could have wished for more time and opportunity to learn of the difficulties of the past years. Mildred Lovegren reminded me, however, that they and we should try to live in the future, rather than rehearsing the horrors of the past.

As we left the Xichang area, our hearts were filled with praise that God had allowed us once again to visit "our home" and to see old friends. We continue to pray for them as they seek to be God's witnesses, salt and light, in a Marxist society. We also pray that through the churches of China and neighboring minority nationality Christians, God will yet give the Nosu of the Liangshan Autonomous Prefecture the opportunity to hear the Gospel. In a conversation with Bishop Ding Guangxun in Nanking, I asked if the China Christian Council had made any plans yet for the spiritual needs of the unreached minority nationalities. Very deliberately and thoughtfully, he answered, "As yet we have not even had time to think of this." The churches of China have rightly claimed responsibility for evangelizing all of China, and, in God's time, I am confident they will take up this significant task. We pray that for them it will be "mission accomplished."

Endnotes

1. For a detailed and chilling narrative of this tragic epoch see *Life and Death in Shanghai* by Nien Cheng. New York: Grove Press, 1986.
2. *Mountains and Rivers Make Way: The Chengtu-Kunming Railroad in Photographs*. Peking: Foreign Language Press, 1976. Foreword.
3. One book dealing specifically with the Yi of the Daliangshan is *Liangshan Yizu Zizhizhou Kaikuang* (A Description of the Autonomous Prefecture of the Yi Nationality). Chengdu: Sichuan Nationality Publishing House, 1985. Language books dealing with the specific language of this area have been published by the Sichuan Provincial Yi Language School and the Cool Mountain Prefectural People's Cadre School. These were published in 1986 in Xichang and given to me in 1987 by the director of the schools.

Pinyin Alphabet Pronunciation Guide

a   Vowel as in *far*
b   Consonant as in *be*
c   Consonant as in *its*
ch Consonant as in *chip*; strongly aspirated
d   Consonant as in *do*
e   Vowel as in *her*
f   Consonant as in *foot*
g   Consonant as in *go*
h   Consonant as in *her*; strongly aspirated
i   Vowel as in *eat* or as in *sir* (when in syllables beginning with *c, ch, r, s, sh, z,* and *zh*.)
j   Consonant as in *jeep*
k   Consonant as in *kind*; strongly aspirated
l   Consonant as in *lard*
m   Consonant as in *me*
o   Vowel as in *law*
p   Consonant as in *par*; strongly aspirated
q   Consonant as in *cheek*
r   Consonant as in *right* (not rolled) or pronounced *z* as in *azure*
s   Consonant as in *sister*
sh Consonant as in *shore*
t   Consonant as in *top*; strongly aspirated
u   Vowel as in *too*; also as in French *tu* or the German Munchen
v   Consonant used only to produce foreign words, national minority words, and local dialects
w   Semi-vowel in syllables beginning with u when not preceded by consonants, as in *want*
x   Consonant as in *she*
y   Semi-vowel in syllables beginning with i or u when not preceded by consonants, as in *yet*
z   Consonant as in *zero*
zh Consonant as in *jump*

Additional copies of this book may be obtained
from your local bookstore or by sending
$10.95 for each copy, postpaid, to:

Hope Publishing House
P.O.Box 60008
Pasadena, CA 91116
FAX (818)792-2121; Orders Only (800)326-2671